The Ambiguous Image
Roy Armes

Last Year at Marienbad

THE AMBIGUOUS IMAGE

Narrative Style in Modern European Cinema
Roy Armes

Art, in a sense, is a revolt against everything fleeting and unfinished in the world. Consequently its only aim is to give another form to a reality that it is nevertheless forced to preserve as the source of its emotion ... The artist lives in such a state of ambiguity, incapable of denying reality and yet eternally bound to question it in its eternally unfinished aspects.

Albert Camus, 1957

INDIANA UNIVERSITY PRESS
Bloomington & London

Copyright © 1976 by Roy Armes
First published in the United States by Indiana University Press

Manufactured in the United States of America

Library of Congress Cataloging in Publication Data
Armes, Roy.
The ambiguous image.
Bibliography.
Includes index.
1. Moving-pictures--Europe--History. I. Title.
PN1993.5.E8A7   791.43'094   75-37266
ISBN 0-253-30560-8   1 2 3 4 5 80 79 78 77 76

Contents

Anna Karina in Godard's *Bande à Part*

Part One: Introduction

1. The Context of Modern Cinema

'The time of the image has come,' wrote Abel Gance in 1926,[1] and his sentiment is amply borne out by the great achievements of the last years of the silent cinema: Murnau's *Sunrise*, Eisenstein's *October* or Gance's own *Napoléon*. This powerful and excitingly extravagant cinema seemed to have vanished for ever with the coming of sound, as the expressionist style of Murnau and his fellows was tamed by Hollywood in the classical lighting style of the tightly wrought thriller or *film noir* of the 1930s and 1940s, in much the same way that the audacities of Eisensteinian *montage* were scaled down to form the basis of the cosily conformist pattern of British documentary. Whereas the theorists of the 1920s saw their art, for all its silence, as the apogee and synthesis of all the arts – a music of images and an architecture of light – the dominant theme of European theorizing in the 1930s and 1940s was the need for realism.

From *La Chienne* in 1931 through *La terra trema* in 1947 to *Umberto D* in 1951, the director's potential stylistic extravagances – Renoir's theatricality, Visconti's operatic vision, De Sica's Neapolitan exuberance – were confined within the bounds of an art which, for all its contradictions, was essentially realistic in intention. The argument of this book is that in the late 1950s and the 1960s the time of the image returned, but with a new ambiguity, as artists as diverse as Bergman, Resnais and Antonioni brought

7

The ambiguous image: Antonioni's *Blow-Up*

about a fresh fusion of the realist tradition (in which they had all made their beginnings) and the heritage of the silent era. The imagery of *Persona, Je t'aime, je t'aime* or *Blow-Up* is as complex and expressive as that of any silent masterpiece, and the growing visual sophistication of the new cinema audience allows the problems of narrative to be solved in ways inconceivable in the classic days of Hollywood dominance. At the same time the links between the cinema and the other arts have grown closer, as films increasingly reflect the artistic climate of the age.

The present study deals specifically with that sector of cinema which, for want of a better term, we may call 'modern' or 'modernist'. It does not set out to cover the whole range of current film-making but considers simply those films which cut themselves off from the past by a rejection of both the traditional recipes of the Hollywood movie (as exemplified by the Western or gangster film) and the demands of a neo-realist aesthetic (socially defined characters, a coherent story-line, an avoidance of fantasy, etc.). Quite clearly, 'modern' in this sense is not synonymous with 'recent', for many of the preoccupations of these films have been common currency in other art forms for fifty years or more. Nor does 'modern' take in all that is best in the work being produced at the present moment, for much excellent contemporary art pursues traditional paths. For film-makers like Yashujiro Ozu and Luchino Visconti, and for those younger film artists who follow their example, the movement we associate with Joyce and Picasso need never have happened, and their best films show the continued strength of an approach that sees the ultimate purpose of cinematic images and sounds as the articulation of a narrative. By contrast, the work of, say, Alain Resnais is conceivable only in a strictly mid-twentieth century artistic context.

The distinction between these two kinds of cinema – the modern and the traditional – is best defined in terms of impact on audiences and critics. If this 'grid' is applied, the definition of modern art that emerges is that of an art which the general public and those critics who reflect its standards find baffling, obscure and pointless. It is indeed, as José Ortega y Gasset pointed out as early as 1925, an art which is 'essentially unpopular', even 'anti-popular'.[2] We can test the validity of this statement and begin to build up a list of 'modern' works of the last two decades by turning to an outspoken, but rigidly middlebrow reviewer like Pauline Kael. Her four volumes of collected magazine journalism contain many accounts of films she does not like, not because they are bad, but because she fails to understand them.

There is Alain Resnais' *Last Year at Marienbad*, which she dubs 'Sleeping Beauty of the International Set, the high-fashion experimental film, the snow job in the ice palace';[3] and Pier Paolo Pasolini's *The Gospel According to Saint Matthew*, which she found 'so static' that she 'could hardly wait for that loathsome prissy young man to get crucified'.[4] Ingmar Bergman's development from *Wild Strawberries* to *Hour of the Wolf* earns him the title of 'the Billy Graham of the post-analytic set',[5] while Michelangelo Antonioni's *La notte* provokes the comment: 'What kind of movie making, what kind of drama is this? Is the delicate movement of the *derrière* supposed to reveal her *Angst*, or merely her *ennui*?'[6] This catalogue of non-comprehension could be extended to cover most of the films and film-makers dealt with in this book, but what is important here is not just the rejection but the tone the reviewer adopts. Like the modernist art of sixty years ago these films have the ability to arouse intense antagonism. They cannot simply be passed over in silence, but have to be scorned and abused because they create unease by the challenge they offer to the unquestioned assumptions about art on which the reviewer bases his or her approach.

Within the range of film-making that breaks in this way with nineteenth-century ideas of what a story or a character is and what constitutes reality, there is a further distinction to be made. Much of what we think of as modern art is, at one and the same time, a culmination and a superseding of traditional art. This is as true of James Joyce's *Ulysses* as of the Cubist paintings of Braque or the sculpture of Henry Moore. These works do not fit the pre-existing, traditional categories of art, but they belong recognizably to the same order of things. It is not absurd to consider *Ulysses* in relation to the history of the English novel or to compare Moore's *Locking-piece* of 1963–4 to the work of the Italian sixteenth-century sculptors. But there is a great deal of modern artistic activity of which this is no longer true: those manifestations of art as an *idea* rather than art as an *object*, such as happenings, environments, light shows and so on. While Schoenberg and Stravinsky used the traditional materials of music (players, instruments, a written score, etc.) in totally new ways, a composer of electronic music such as Stockhausen is dealing with a different order of sound from what has traditionally been considered 'music'.

If we follow this line of argument there emerges a clear distinction between the music of Boulez and that of Stockhausen, between a sculpture by Barbara Hepworth and a Jim Dine happening. The cinematic equivalent of this latter brand of extreme modernism is the underground film. In his admirable critical history of the movement, Parker Tyler points out how distinct the ethos of the underground is from that of the commercial cinema and demolishes the idea that the independent film-maker is in any way a Hollywood director *manqué*. The underground's rejection of the Hollywood style is accompanied by an equally strong revulsion against the whole commercial system within which the cinema as a whole has traditionally flourished. As a result, film-makers like Stan Brakhage or Kenneth Anger adopt very different standpoints from those of the directors working in the European art cinema, and their approach does little to illuminate the attitudes of men like Resnais or Antonioni.

The modernist film-making in Europe, which parallels the underground's rejection of Hollywood by its own highly ambivalent attitude to the realist tradition, is in many ways even more difficult to categorize, but it does have its own distinctive character. The modern cinema with which we are concerned here may be a minority cinema, but it is as much a part of the conventional producer–distributor–exhibitor system as the Hollywood movie. It finds its justification when the films produced are shown to audiences in a normal cinema, and has its counterparts in the painting and sculpture produced for the dealer–critic set-up and the music designed to be played and performed by live musicians in a concert hall. It is still, in a way that much experimental *avant-garde* work is not, an art of communication. While we must be wary of distorting it by an approach based on rigid categories, it is not absurd to consider it, partially at least, in traditional terms. To pass from Howard Hawks to Michelangelo Antonioni may, as Robin Wood points out, require 'an act of adjustment',[7] but it is clearly reasonable to use the same word, 'film', to describe both *Rio Bravo* and *Red*

Last Year at Marienbad (Delphine Seyrig)

Desert. This is surely no longer the case if we turn to an underground character like Nam June Paik, who 'uses a film projector, but the film he runs through it is absolutely clear. He then stands in front of the projector light, meditating or performing some simple act, declaring in this way that he is, in that moment, a living movie.'[8] He may call this Zen for Film, but we have here a new order of cinematic phenomena, as remote from Antonioni as from Hawks.

Modern cinema in Europe turns away from some of the limitations of the neo-realist approach, but it retains an interest in human beings, their roles and relationships (it has none of the dehumanization of contemporary 'minimal' art). This humanism is typified by the maintenance, in some form, however embryonic or rudimentary, of a narrative line. Often, however, this is not the kind of story that can be reduced to a synopsis. In this connection it is instructive to compare two synopses of *Last Year at Marienbad.* The British Film Institute's *Monthly Film Bulletin* tells us that

In a vast, gloomy baroque hotel a man, X, meets A, a beautiful woman staying there with M, who may or may not be her husband. X tells A that they met the previous year at Fredericksbad, or perhaps Marienbad, and had some sort of affair, but she eventually refused to go away with him, and arranged instead that they should meet again in a year's time, when she would give him her decision. She apparently does not recognise him and denies all knowledge of their supposed previous encounter, but little by little X brings her round to acceptance of what he says, and finally they leave together.[9]

By contrast, John Ward explains what happens in these words: 'A year ago a man X met a woman A at Marienbad in a château where they were both guests. Under the nose of her husband M, he began an affair with her. After trying several times to persuade A to leave with him, X is warned off by M. Finally M kills A and X is left alone to mourn.'[10] Both critics agree that a narrative line of some sort exists in the film, but their totally different conceptions of what this line is show clearly that with *Last Year at Marienbad*, as with so many other modern films, it is impossible to decide what the narrative says until the film has been interpreted.

In addition to this possibility of using the narrative heritage of nineteenth-century realism (story, characters, etc.) in a new way, film has potentialities which bring it closer to modernism than to traditional art forms. Its power to range to and fro in time and space and to treat reality and fiction in the same terms make it a potent medium for modernist ideas. The interaction of these modernist possibilities with the humanist tradition offers the chance of a highly creative synthesis, as the films dealt with in this book show. But before we turn to these works it is worth looking very briefly at the earlier relationship of film and modernism. The cultural life of the pre-1914 period, which saw the emergence of the cinema as a new form of expression, was dominated by the revolution in sensibility deriving from the modernist movement which began to flourish in virtually all the traditional art forms. The rejection of nineteenth-century values united figures as diverse as Eliot and Klee, Schoenberg and Kafka and gave rise to a proliferation of fragmentary and conflicting movements: cubism, constructivism, futurism, expressionism, dadaism, surrealism, etc. One might have expected this modernity to be reflected in the new medium of film, but in fact there was comparatively little interaction between the cinema and the new tendencies of art at this time. Genuinely modernist film works are rare: *The Cabinet of Dr Caligari* and a few German films in the 1910s, *La Coquille et le Clergyman* and the first films of Buñuel and Cocteau in the 1920s – the list is soon exhausted. The reasons for this need to be considered in some detail, since they tell us much about the nature of film.

First and foremost among the barriers to modernism was the newness of the cinema as an art form. In the years during which Joyce was writing *Ulysses* with its conscious manipulation of the linguistic resources of several centuries of English prose, D. W. Griffith was engaged in hammering out a basic grammar of film. An art which was still taking its first faltering steps as a narrative form could hardly compete with the complex virtuosities of Joyce's novels. It must be remembered that the first generation of modernists turned to this form of expression only after they felt they had exhausted the traditional possibilities of their art. By contrast, the cinema had no tradition to react against. Certainly there were a number of ideas inherited from other arts, but these did not amount to a tradition, for the latter, as Herbert Read has pointed out, is not a body of beliefs but a knowledge of techniques.[11] Griffith's great achievement before 1917 was to master the basic range of techniques that enabled the cinema to capture some equivalent of the narrative power of Dickens and the dramatic vigour of nineteenth-century melodrama. When these first steps had been taken, the rest followed quickly and, by drawing on the accumulated experience of other arts, the cinema was able to solve, within a single generation, those problems of representation which had occupied painting and the novel for centuries.

By taking over, in this way, the content of its nearest predecessors, the cinema was following a line of development observed elsewhere in the arts by Marshall McLuhan.[12] The first products of the printing presses, for example, were the pastorals of an earlier age, and television built part of its appeal on movie techniques and a liberal showing of old films. In similar fashion the cinema took over the styles and techniques of the theatre or, in the case of silent comedy, of the music hall. It has been well stated that one of the distinctions between artists like Titian or Rubens and modernists like Picasso or Klee is that, in the case of the latter, the age-old intermediary between the artist and what he produces – the artist's model – has disappeared. It was hardly to be expected that the cinema, invented as a way of reproducing the real world in motion, should separate itself from this world before it had even evolved the techniques necessary to render it accurately.

Instead the cinema developed initially as a representational art, following the pattern set by painting and the novel. It is important to separate this notion of representation from the idea of art as such. It is the former alone which gives us our sense of progress in art. From Giotto to Rubens there is no progress in the art of painting, only a development in the techniques used to reproduce or represent reality. Similarly it is the representational element which makes a critic like Bernard Bergonzi find it 'remarkably difficult to see the eighteenth-century novelists entirely on their own terms, without considering them as in some way foreshadowing the achievements of the next century'.[13] When critics confuse art and representation in forms which use such basically artificial media as paint or words, it is hardly surprising that the same confusion should arise with the cinema, which, as Alberto Moravia has pointed out, 'robbed the novel of the objective representation of reality'[14] and which employs direct photographic images of reality as its raw material.

The traditional film historians of the Paul Rotha–Lewis Jacobs generation saw the evolution of new realistic techniques as the crucial thread of film development, so that the British documentary, say, was shown to absorb the lessons of Eisenstein, who learned from Griffith, who followed Porter, and so on. Clearly there is some truth in this line of argument, but in practice it has led to a totally inadequate view of what constitutes realism in the cinema. Securely placed as the culmination of an unimpeachable tradition, the documentary movement and those critics who drew their standards from its work could despise the products of the Hollywood studio system, whose formalized language and economy of expression offered an important lesson in the art of communicating through cinematic images and sounds. As a result of this insular approach such potentially realistic technical innovations as colour, stereophonic sound or wide-screen format were often dismissed as fit only for 'mere' spectacle, and realism was exclusively associated with the cinematic slice of life, chosen to reveal the film-maker's social or political commitment and preferably reproduced in technically inadequate black and white images. The great films of the realist tradition rise above these limitations, but they have been habitually misinterpreted in the light of such assumptions.

The striving for representation in art may be a snare and delusion, but until it has been satisfied artists will continue to pursue it. Even when it has been finally achieved and the artistic redundancy of the effort is apparent to a rising generation of younger artists, the general public will still look for it in art. In the representation of the human figure a Henry Moore sculpture tells us infinitely more than the most realistic wax dummy from Madame Tussaud's, yet it is to the latter that the public flocks. As Ortega y Gasset proclaimed in 1925, the majority is not interested in art as a pattern of forms: 'By art they understand a means through which they are brought into contact with interesting human affairs. Artistic forms proper – figments, fantasy – are tolerated only if they do not interfere with the perception of human forms and fates.'[15] Certainly it was the realistic aspect of the film, not its potential artistic novelty, which first attracted public attention. The cinema found its audience thanks to its very transparency to life: it was an art form which could be confused with life itself, not only by ordinary spectators but even by film critics and aestheticians. Forging the new language of film, Griffith enabled the cinema to take its place as a great popular art which provided the mass audience with a continued supply of entertainment tailored to the nineteenth-century romantic-realist pattern. In fact the cinema established itself as a refutation of modernism, becoming the new refuge of story, character and spectacle, and it is to this that it owed its vast popularity.

Roots: surrealism (Buñuel's *Un Chien Andalou*)

In general, modernism tends to come after a period of realism in the arts –
after Flaubert and Turgenev in the novel, after Ibsen in the theatre or Courbet
in painting. The realistic potential of the film medium had to be fully exploited
– in the documentary movement of the 1930s and in neo-realism and allied
endeavours in the 1940s – before any real steps towards modernism could be
taken. It is true that there were signs towards the end of the silent era, after
the realism of Von Stroheim, that the cinema might begin to dissociate itself
from representation, but the advent of sound after a mere thirty-odd years of
silence introduced a new potentially realistic element and threw the cinema
back to the simple representation of reality (even if this was only the reality of
the stage play). It was not until the 1950s that conditions were ripe for a true,
independent form of cinematic modernism.

In this connection the progress of two film-makers is symptomatic. In the
early 1930s Luis Buñuel followed his two surrealist masterpieces, *Un Chien
Andalou* and *L'Age d'Or*, with a move back into the central realist tradition
with his documentary, *Land Without Bread*, and when he re-emerged as a
film-maker of world importance in 1950, it was with a basically realistic
study of slum life, *Los Olvidados*. Only much later, in the 1960s, was he able
to create a modern synthesis of surrealism and narrative. By contrast,

15

Roots: neo-realism (Visconti's *La terra trema*)

Michelangelo Antonioni, who had been intimately involved with Italian neo-realism from its inception, could move steadily away from this reality-bound aesthetic in the middle 1950s to adopt modern notions of narrative structure. But to state that modernism grows out of a reaction to the limitations of purely realistic methods is not to imply that it is in any way intrinsically superior. If representation is, in some senses, the antithesis of art, it is still possible for a great artist to unite the two. Tolstoy's novels are supreme masterpieces both as formal works of art and as apparent slices of life. Similarly the major films of the great realist directors – *Living* or *La terra trema* or *Umberto D* – have a purely formal richness which few if any modernist films surpass. Modernism is in any case not an enemy of reality. It merely rejects certain conventions used to portray it (perspective, verisimilitude, etc.) in favour of other methods which allow a new relationship with reality to be formed.

The handful of early examples of the connection between modernism and the cinema are, despite their striking audacity, clearly irrelevant to the development of the cinema as a commercial industry and quite marginal to the artistic evolution of the cinema as a whole. In the 1950s and 1960s, however, the situation is very different and the interconnection exists on a totally different footing. For one thing both film-makers and modernists could now look back on fifty years of development in their art. As Edward Lucie-Smith points out, the art of the post-war period forms a genuine new stage of modernism, being ' "late modern" almost in the sense that Giovanni Battista Tiepolo is "late baroque" '. No longer is it a question of reacting against nineteenth-century romantic or naturalistic viewpoints, for contemporary developments are invariably a reworking of themes already explored in earlier modernist movements. Thus, to quote Lucie-Smith again, 'abstract expressionism is rooted in surrealism; assemblage and pop art reached back beyond surrealism to dada; op art and kinetic art are founded on experiments made at the Bauhaus; minimal art interestingly combines both dada and Bauhaus influences'. [17]

The artist's major problem is to find his own place amid what Harold Rosenberg has aptly named 'the tradition of the new'. At times – as in the case of a man like Barnett Newman – the painting may be seen, perhaps must be seen, as an act of art historical judgment. The self-consciousness of modern art – excellently characterized by Ad Reinhardt as 'art preoccupied with its own processes and means, with its own identity and distinction' [18] – is strikingly paralleled in the cinema from the mid-1950s onwards. Film-makers show themselves increasingly aware of the history of the cinema, and directors with a background in criticism (like those who had worked on the magazine *Cahiers du Cinéma*) played a key part in the renewal of interest in film. Cases of looking back to earlier film styles have become commonplace in the work of directors as dissimilar as Franju and Godard, Melville and Bertolucci. Of course film-makers have made allusions to the past before – what is new is the extent to which the references now give the film as a whole its stylistic texture.

Aside from these similarities in their relationship with the past, there are other important links between artists and film-makers in the 1950s. The most significant of these is perhaps the new social role attributed to the artist and to the film-maker. A painter such as David Hockney or Andy Warhol is treated as the artistic equivalent of a television personality, and as a result more attention is paid to the colour of his hair than to the quality of his work (for television personalities are not expected to produce anything). In recent years the same treatment has been given to film-makers – an attitude made explicit by the title of a book of interviews published in 1971: *The Film Director as Superstar*. [19] Hollywood directors of the younger generation are public figures in a way that Sirk, Siegel or Fuller never were. Similarly it is Federico Fellini, not the stars he directs, who is the subject of the newspaper columnists' interest, and when director and star are linked in the public attention, as were Antonioni and Monica Vitti at the time of *L'avventura*, it is the director who receives most concern (a total reversal of the 1930s' situation of Sternberg and Marlene Dietrich).

Linked to this personal interest in the film director is the new public role assigned to him as to the artist or writer. Far from being a man in revolt against society and the embodiment of an alternative set of values, the artist is now a part of a cultural establishment, promoted by privately or publicly owned galleries and fêted at officially sponsored international exhibitions. Art is now a matter of national prestige and, as Harold Rosenberg acidly remarks, 'to fall behind in the "process of technique" in painting would be equivalent to falling behind in electronics. A nation that did so would be making a public confession of backwardness'.[20] Something of the same change is to be found in the film-maker's relationship to the production system, which now approximates more to the European than to the American model. Once the Hollywood director had two choices: either to make peace with the system, as John Ford did, by making three films for the producers and then one for himself, or to refuse all compromise and run the risk of finding himself rejected, as Stroheim and Welles were. Now the director is expected to demand complete freedom, to be his own producer, to follow a personal line of development, to want to work on location away from front office pressures, etc. Often the effects of this new freedom, combined with the need to work in the full glare of publicity, have been anything but advantageous artistically.

In short, what has been described here as the modernist attitude has become in the last two decades a normal part of the cinema, in the United States as in Eastern and Western Europe. To the film-makers of the period one can apply the words of Christopher Finch, who noted that in the 1950s young painters were able to look back over fifty years of modernism and not limit their interest to any one movement or tendency, finding their inspiration partly in the work of the past and combining elements which had once seemed to derive from mutually contradictory, even mutually destructive viewpoints. Now the great surrealist Buñuel and the anti-surrealist Cocteau, the Rossellini of *Paisà* and the Eisenstein of *Ivan the Terrible*, can become part of a common fund of artistic experience, and the task of film-makers, like that of painters, is to 'construct for themselves a new language – creating a synthesis from the dozens of different idioms which had evolved during the crusading period of modernism'. In the cinema as in art, the aim is a mode of expression in which many viewpoints are given an equal footing and in which 'ambiguity had become the *status quo*'.[21]

The analysis that follows draws its examples almost exclusively from the European feature film of the past two decades, but the attitudes and aspirations involved are to be found elsewhere, in contemporary, post-Disney animation for example. In the feature film until the late 1950s the straight narrative, either in the Hollywood or the neo-realist convention, exercised a grip on the imagination of film-makers akin to that of Disney in the animated film. Since that grip has been broken film-makers have gone their separate ways, for, as Herbert Kohl says in a survey of contemporary philosophy, to be modern is 'to give up simple explanations of man and the world, to embrace complexity once and for all, and to try, somehow, to manage it'.[22] As a result, the successive chapters of this book explore a series of seeming contradictions. There is a search to express simultaneity and a desire to fragment the story-line, to record the surface of life as well as the complexities of the imagination. We find a struggle for a more autobiographical kind of film-making existing alongside a desire to create impersonal, autonomous works, an interest in spontaneity and improvisation and, at the same time, a self-conscious manipulation of images and sounds. But these contradictions are more apparent than real, and at the conclusion of this study an attempt is made to define the underlying unity of modern cinema beneath these surface differences and to relate its achievements to a wider cultural context.

Though we are too close in time to the cinema of the 1960s for a genuine history of it to be possible, the division of the main body of this book into three sections is determined largely by age and chronology. In the first grouping we have the older directors – from Buñuel (b. 1900) to Bergman (b. 1918) – all of whom had a long experience in other forms of cinema before they went on to make their modernist masterpieces in the mid-1960s. Their work invites us to look at the roots of modernism and the way in which it arises out of a dissatisfaction with conventional forms. The second group is more homogeneous, comprising the remarkable generation born between 1921 and 1923 and including men like Pasolini, Resnais and Jancsó. They offer some strikingly original films in which they fuse their preoccupations quite unselfconsciously into personal and highly novel forms. The third and youngest group is dominated by Jean-Luc Godard and made up of film-makers born, like him, in the 1930s. The films they have made are much more concerned with fragmentation, discontinuity and, ultimately, a refusal of the primacy of narrative. While these groupings can only be provisional and wide divergences are to be found within all three of them, they do offer us a perspective in which we can begin to see modern cinema as a historical entity.

It is through an investigation of patterns of style that the originality of modern cinema is best defined. Feature films designed for a normal audience are almost inevitably about people, the situations in which they live, the relationships they form with one another. Since of all the arts the cinema has the most direct link with reality (unless trickery of some sort is used, the camera can only record what happens in front of it), it is always possible to see it in terms of content. But to talk about the modern cinema simply in terms of a new analysis of the human predicament, a heightened awareness of the alienation inevitably entailed in urban industrial society, or an examination of the problems of commitment in an affluent society which has failed to follow the predictions of Marx, is to falsify it completely. In this age of instant interpretation film-makers like Antonioni and Bergman are interviewed incessantly and tell us at length about their films in terms of such problems. But our actual experience of *L'avventura* or *The Silence*, of *Blow-Up* or *Persona*, is very different. The formal richness of these films – the complexity of their aural and visual organisation, the ambiguity of image and sound – is such that to reduce them to mere statements of this kind is an extreme impoverishment. It is much better, when confronted with the works of modern cinema, to begin at the other extreme and to consider them in the light of Alain Robbe-Grillet's dictum that 'a work of art contains nothing in the strictest sense of the word'.[23] From a descriptive analysis of structures it quickly becomes apparent that, in so far as modern cinema has an identity, this lies in the meaningfulness of its forms, in a style which moves away from mimesis and towards a greater stylization and self-awareness.

Part Two: Roots

2. The Link with the Past

Though it was not until the 1960s that modernism could be described, even loosely, as a movement, all its characteristic complexity and ambiguity can be found in isolated works of the 1940s and 1950s. The film with which modern cinema may be said to begin – *Citizen Kane* – was indeed made as early as 1941. In it the twenty-five-year-old Orson Welles showed for the first time the way in which the flashback could be used creatively to present a mere hypothesis, a viewpoint, a facet of truth. As in William Faulkner's *The Sound and the Fury*, the adoption of a number of points of view of the same event has the effect of denying a single, all-embracing, godlike certainty. Ortega y Gasset wrote in the 1920s that

one and the same reality may be split up into many diverse realities when it is beheld from different points of view. And we cannot help asking ourselves: which of all these realities must then be regarded as the real and authentic one? The answer, no matter how we decide, cannot but be arbitrary. Any preference can be founded on caprice only. All these realities are equivalent, each being authentic for its corresponding point of view.[1]

The full implications of this for the cinema were demonstrated in masterly fashion in *Citizen Kane* and the most summary comparison between it and the 1930s' work of John Ford (to whom Welles owed so much) shows the

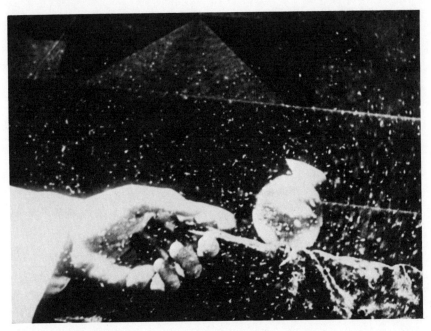

Citizen Kane: 'Rosebud'

enormous stride forward towards modernism which this film represents. *Citizen Kane* still has the studio sets typical of the 1930s – the whole faked-up Xanadu – but the tyranny of the verbal is shattered by the splendid expressiveness of the visuals, devised by Welles and his photographer Gregg Toland (who had previously worked with Ford on *The Grapes of Wrath*). The systematic use of deep-focus – anticipated by Jean Renoir in France in the 1930s – has become part of the basic grammar of contemporary film-making, but Welles's equally striking revolution in plot structure still seems modern today, such is the conservatism of the cinema as a narrative form. Breaking the dominance of the linear plot, Orson Welles could have used in 1941 the words uttered by Jean-Luc Godard some twenty-five years later, to the effect that a film should indeed have a beginning, a middle and an end, but not necessarily in that order.

In place of the essentially static pattern perfected by, among others, Marcel Carné in *Le Jour se lève* (1939), *Citizen Kane* employs a dynamic approach to the role of the flashback in film structure and in so doing it inaugurates a new era of film-making. The basic form of Welles's film is strikingly similar to that of *Last Year at Marienbad* made twenty years later. Both films open with a slow, mood-evoking, semi-abstract entry into an enclosed world (Kane's 'palace' of Xanadu; the baroque hotel of Marienbad). Then follows a statement of the elements of the story (the newsreel; the play fragment). An attempt is made to fit the jigsaw pieces into a coherent pattern (the journalist collects the overlapping testimony of Kane's associates: Thatcher, Bernstein and Leland, his second wife Susan and Raymond the butler; the long attempt at persuasion occurs). Finally comes a resolution which solves nothing (the revelation of meaning – or lack of meaning – in Kane's dying word, 'Rosebud'; the entry into a fresh labyrinth). In the central portion of *Citizen Kane* each stage of Kane's career is viewed from a different angle and by a different witness and this adds to the complexity of the portrait of Charles Foster Kane that emerges. It also allows the film to move back and forth in time and to repeat some of the climaxes. In this way, for example, we see Susan's operatic *début* both from the stalls (as the audience experiences it) and from the stage (as it seems to her). *Citizen Kane* is such an important film because it destroys once and for all the fallacy of 'photographic realism' on which so much cinema is built, namely the belief that there is a simple truth about everything which can be captured just by recording its surface with a movie camera. Welles, by discarding the pretence that events in the film are seen from a standpoint of godlike omniscience and by including in his film all the obscurities and inconsistencies, achieves a remarkable advance towards true realism.

It has been argued against the film – most notably by Charles Higham – that the portrait of Kane which emerges lacks psychological depth, that we know 'despite all the commentaries, too little about Kane ... We see only a dazzlingly illuminated cartoon figure, as two-dimensional as Colonel Blimp'.[2] But in taking this line the critic is, in effect, applying nineteenth-century conceptions of character to an essentially twentieth-century work. Quite naturally the film emerges as inadequate in these terms, as indeed do most of the modern films dealt with here. One can answer Higham on his own level by pointing out that in the hollowness of Kane lies the crucial point of Welles's view of power, namely that in the pursuit of it Kane has ceased to be a person and become instead a shell, a façade. The same holds true of most of Welles's monomaniacal scorpion-like villains, right up to Hank Quinlan in *Touch of Evil*; and the reporter's failure to find a real man beneath the legend in *Citizen Kane* is totally apposite. But it is really pointless to defend the film in these terms, as its real richness lies in the perfection with which the facets of the legend are fitted together. Not only is the basic pattern of six-part narration brilliantly cohesive, the film also abounds in novel and exciting editing devices linking individual scenes and fragments across the years. There is the image of the front door of Susan Alexander's flat, as Kane's wife leaves after the confrontation which ends their marriage, dissolving into the newspaper

Citizen Kane: the pieces of a jigsaw

photograph next morning, published under a banner headline exposing the 'truth' about Kane's love life. To balance this freezing of the image there is the photograph of the 'world's best newspaper team' which comes to life six years later, when Kane re-poses it at a party to celebrate his acquisition of their services. The rapid, sharply cut set of shots wittily chronicling the decline of Kane's first marriage ('It was a marriage, just like any other marriage') contrasts with the slow dissolves whereby the face of the aged Leland is twice imprinted over these images of past events which he is describing from his wheelchair.

The visual richness of the film, ranging from the simplicity of the compositions illustrating Kane's modest home background to the empty grandeur – captured in deep focus – of his old age in Xanadu, is very apparent in the opening newsreel. Welles shows here a very modern awareness of visual and aural textures: clips taken from existing films were aged by deliberately scratching the negative or reduplicating it over and over again, and supplemented by shots taken in newsreel style by a team working with light-weight equipment. The whole was then blended together by a score drawing on the wealth of music in the RKO archives. The modern feel of the film even thirty years after it was shot derives too from the fact that Welles not only soaked himself in the films of the past before starting work on this first feature (much as directors like Godard and Resnais were to do in the 1950s) but also used sets and clips from other RKO films. There is a whole dimension of personal allusion and parodistic reference which Higham lovingly chronicles: Xanadu was painted by men from the team that made *Snow White and the Seven Dwarfs*, a window, an archway and a fireplace were taken from John Ford's *Mary of Scotland*, a doorway from *Gunga Din* and even bats from *Son of Kong*.

In this way *Citizen Kane* is, in texture as well as overall structure, twenty years ahead of its time. It is moreover a film without immediate successors. RKO cut forty-five minutes from Welles's next work, *The Magnificent Ambersons*, giving it a largely irrelevant ending directed by someone else, and from then until *The Trial* in 1962 Welles did not experience real freedom to make the films he wanted. The film which took the methods of *Citizen Kane* a significant stage further was in fact made nine years later in Japan by a man who, though deeply influenced by the American cinema, had never seen Welles's first work. Akira Kurosawa's *Rashomon* makes the same systematic use of the hypothesis shot common to the thriller (the recounting of a version of events which may or may not be the truth) as Welles's film did of the flashback. *Rashomon* presents a simple situation – a nobleman riding through

Versions of truth: Kurosawa's *Rashomon*

the forest is attacked and overpowered by a bandit who subsequently rapes his wife – but thanks to the treatment Kurosawa gives this material the film emerges as a study of the impossibility of truth. The story of the rape and its aftermath is narrated four times. The bandit claims that yielding to the entreaties of the woman he released the husband and killed him in a fair fight. The woman herself maintains that she killed her husband because he spurned her after the rape, while the husband (speaking through a medium) claims that he committed suicide after his wife had tried to incite the bandit to kill him. Clearly all of these three characters forming the central trio have reasons to reshape the truth into a version which reflects credit on them, and there is no reason why one should be trusted more than another. The one outside witness, a woodcutter, then gives his account of the facts – that the bandit begged the woman to go off with him, but that she ran away while the two men, most reluctantly, fought the duel on which she insisted. This version, perhaps the blackest of all four, shows all the protagonists in a bad light and would explain their need to lie, but doubt is cast on the woodcutter's honesty by the implication that he is a thief.

The relevance of *Rashomon* to the areas of modern cinema with which we are concerned here can be seen by a simple confrontation of two quotations: Donald Richie's account of *Rashomon* in his study of Kurosawa and Alain Robbe-Grillet's summary of his own intentions in *Last Year at Marienbad*. *Rashomon*, writes Richie, 'is about an action as few pictures are *about* anything at all. We turn the object this way and that, look at it from various angles, and it resembles a number of things but *is* only one thing, the object that it is.'[3] Of his own film Robbe-Grillet says:

We can imagine *Marienbad* is a documentary on a statue, with interpretive views of the gestures, with a return each time to the gestures themselves, such as they remain, frozen in the sculpture. Imagine a documentary that succeeded, with a statue of two people, in uniting a series of shots taken from different angles and with the help of different camera movements, and in telling a whole story this way. And at the end you notice that you have come back to where you started from, the statue itself.[4]

Both films provoke critics to the same kind of futile attempt to unravel the 'objective truth'. Richie himself devotes several pages to trying to ascertain 'what really happened in *Rashomon*', just as so many critics have striven to uncover the 'real chronology' of *Marienbad*. In fact an ambiguity is essential to both films, which are open-ended puzzles or unresolved enigmas.

If the new patterns of temporality and perspective created by film-makers like Welles and Kurosawa are in one sense the root of the 1960s' work of men like Resnais and Robbe-Grillet, an even more striking anticipation is provided by another isolated masterpiece, Jean Cocteau's *Orphée*, which, like *Rashomon*, dates from 1950. In this 'realistic documentary of unreal events'

'More real than the real': Cocteau's *Orphée*

Cocteau creates a timeless world. He takes a fantasy subject, the poet's relationship with death, and films it as if it were literally true. He deliberately disregards time, for this is 'a purely human notion' which does not really exist. Blurring the boundaries of this world and the next, he mingles the possible and the impossible, combines very obvious parts of our own world (the Rolls-Royce, the motorcyclists, the messages inspired by those sent out by the wartime Resistance) with trick photography depending on mirrors, mercury tubs and reverse projection. In his preface to the published script of the film,[5] Cocteau claims that *Orphée* contains neither symbol nor thesis, maintaining that it is 'a realistic film which brings into play (in film terms) what is more real than the real'. Cocteau's view of the cinema is remarkably like that later elaborated by Alain Robbe-Grillet in the stress placed on the realism of the unreal, which the medium makes possible. For Cocteau 'every film is realistic since it shows things instead of suggesting them by a text'. Because they are shown in a film, things 'exist in the form of facts, even if these facts derive from the unreal, which the public is not used to seeing'.

It was not until nine years after *Orphée* and *Rashomon* that the European cinema took further decisive steps forward in its self-imposed task of freeing itself from the bonds of an aesthetic based on the nineteenth-century novel

Oblique identity: *Hiroshima Mon Amour*

and the 'well-made play'. Alain Resnais's *Hiroshima Mon Amour* is a good example of the total novelty that now became possible. The film is far more than simply the portrayal of a woman remembering a past love in the context of a new one. To begin with the characters are not the realistically drawn and defined ones of traditional literature. They emerge from the 'allegorical exchange' of nameless, shapeless bodies in bed at the beginning of the film and by the end they have lost their personal identity again: 'Hi-ro-shi-ma, Hi-ro-shi-ma. That's your name ... Your name is Nevers. Ne-vers in France.' *Citizen Kane* showed the difficulties of pinning down and evaluating a complex character. *Rashomon* made clear how little the bare facts of a situation (rape and killing) tell us about the truth of the personalities involved. Now *Hiroshima Mon Amour* rejects character analysis altogether and traces simply the ebb and flow of the characters' emotional responses.

Past and present are not rigidly divided in *Hiroshima Mon Amour*: not only are the images of the earlier Nevers love fitted into a framework of the current love at Hiroshima (and accompanied by Japanese noises on the

28

soundtrack), but also the two levels overlap and colour each other. The figures of the German and Japanese lovers, fourteen years apart in time, become fused into one figure: 'When you are in the cellar (at Nevers), am *I* dead?' asks the Japanese lover; and the two love experiences interact and destroy one another. By recounting her Nevers experience to a 'stranger' the heroine deprives it of its aura of magic, but this very destruction of 'an inconsolable memory, a memory of shadows and stone' also makes her realize the ultimate futility of attempting to preserve her present relationship. A further development is in the location of the action. *Citizen Kane* took place in the real world, with Kane's past actions evoked by the words of his associates. In *Rashomon* the events are created four times by the accounts of the protagonists. In *Hiroshima Mon Amour* the transition towards interiority is completed, for the film takes place in the heroine's mind and the images of Nevers we see are her mental images, welling up into her consciousness. Hence a question mark hangs over the whole film – is all this really happening? – and it is not altogether surprising that Resnais and his collaborators, in their discussions of the heroine during the shooting, should have come to doubt the veracity of her story. At times they queried whether she was in Hiroshima at all, feeling it more likely that she was in an asylum inventing Japan; at others they accepted her present whereabouts but fancied she might be a mythomaniac making up the story of Nevers. Neither of these two hypotheses need make one change one's interpretation of the film, but clearly it is a very small step from this to the total ambiguity of much of the mid-1960s' modernist cinema.

Alain Resnais, making his feature debut with *Hiroshima Mon Amour*, is very much a part of a new generation of film-makers which includes Jancsó, Pasolini and Robbe-Grillet and might be expected to create radically new forms of cinema. What is particularly fascinating about the 1960s, however, is the way in which the new tendencies were embraced by film-makers of all ages and backgrounds. It is the older directors to whom we turn first, for they show most clearly the manner in which modern film-making grows out of the traditional forms prevalent in the 1940s and 1950s. It is only when these links with the past are fully understood that we can begin a critical assessment of the achievements of filmic modernism.

We are concerned specifically with films made since the mid-1960s, but all the film-makers treated here were active in the cinema for twenty years before this. Indeed Luis Buñuel's career goes back to the first involvement of film and surrealism in the 1920s, and one of the more exciting aspects of *Belle de Jour* is its reinterpretation of the surrealist aesthetic. Michelangelo Antonioni was intimately involved in the Italian neo-realist movement, and in his mature work we can trace the way in which predominantly social concerns have given way to more personal obsessions, as the real setting has evolved from being the context for the action and become rather the expressive image of that action itself. Ingmar Bergman began as writer–director in the 1940s and his career shows how, in a Northern context too, basically naturalistic concerns come gradually to be replaced by the kind of formal preoccupations that give rise to modernist structures. The French directors show a character-istic variety of approaches, but are equally concerned with finding new ways of using the fund of past experience. Both Jean-Pierre Melville's later gangster films and Jacques Tati's comic style as exemplified by *Playtime* make clear the manner in which traditional forms are modified as a result of reinterpreta-tion in contemporary terms. In a similar way, Robert Bresson takes traditional literary material but, by a very conscious separation of image and sound, creates totally new narrative patterns. The overall careers of all these film-makers have been dealt with at length in specialist monographs. What we are concerned with here is showing the links between them and defining – through the analysis of individual works – the particular relationship with the past and the specific modernity of each film-maker.

3. Luis Buñuel: Surrealism and Narrative

If Luis Buñuel's first works – *Un Chien Andalou* and *L'Age d'Or* – are the purest examples of surrealism in the cinema, his film-making of thirty or so years later is of no less interest and significance. Working in very varied production set-ups and with constantly changing crews and collaborators, Buñuel has created a series of films of striking homogeneity. Films like *Nazarin* (1958) and *The Exterminating Angel* (1962), both shot in Mexico, the French-made *Belle de Jour* (1967), *Le Charme Discret de la Bourgeoisie* (1972), and *Le Fantôme de la Liberté* (1974), together with the two Spanish films, *Viridiana* (1961) and *Tristana* (1970), all succeed in integrating the surrealist beliefs to which Buñuel has remained true into a narrative frame-work. We find expressed the director's lasting concern with dreams, imaginings and the workings of the subconscious, as well as his deep distrust of religion and bourgeois ways of living. The films offer seemingly spontaneous jets of images, but at the same time they tell a complex story. The vision Buñuel makes us share has the daylight quality of a waking dream, yet his films spell out the very real problems of freedom and responsibility, sex and human relationships. The refusal of surface realism is complete – though the action may be placed in a clearly recognizable world, the crucial aspect of the work is its inner progression – yet the comment on our society and conventional beliefs is unequivocal.

Perhaps the clearest example of this interaction of surrealism and narrative

A waking dream: *Le Charme Discret de la Bourgeoisie*

is *Belle de Jour*, which is a perfect demonstration of the complexity of Buñuel's art. Since it also shows the interpenetration of reality and imagination which is such a feature of modernist film-making in the 1960s, a detailed analysis of it forms an excellent starting point for our investigation. The film's tormented heroine, Séverine Sérizy, is played by Catherine Deneuve, an actress whose particular beauty and cool reserve provided a number of directors of the mid-1960s with a most effective counterpoint to images of horror and hallucination. In Roman Polanski's *Repulsion* (1965), for example, she played a young woman undergoing a mental collapse, into the subjective experience of which the director subtly entices us; while in Agnès Varda's *Les Créatures* (1966) her role was that of the wife of a writer who is eventually forced into a life and death struggle with the creations of his own imagination. But without doubt the most dazzling of all exploitations of this particular ambiguity is Deneuve's performance in Buñuel's film as a young doctor's wife who, under the name of Belle de Jour, takes an afternoon job in a brothel. The introductory note to Buñuel's published script makes clear the particular tone of the film. It explains that Séverine's story is 'interrupted a number of times by sequences which are either childhood memories or, more often, daydreams, in which certain typical obsessions appear and reappear'. Vital to our experience of the film is the fact that 'no distinction, either in the picture or in the sound', is made between these imaginary sequences and other scenes of the film which 'seem to describe objectively the relationships between the principal characters and the development of these relationships'. The crucial word here is 'seem', for, as we shall see, the film is so constructed as to throw doubt on every apparent certainty.

As soon as we begin to discuss *Belle de Jour* in these terms the very deceptiveness of the film's simplicity is apparent. Clearly there are links here with Alain Robbe-Grillet's investigations of the workings of the imagination in films like *Last Year at Marienbad* and *L'Immortelle*, but in *Belle de Jour* the imaginary scenes are, at first sight, more easily explicable in rational terms as the mental products of a woman we see to be both frigid and masochistic. For much of the film we are in no doubt about the fact that it is in her mind that the action is taking place. Again, *Belle de Jour* was adapted from a 1929 novel by Joseph Kessel – a straightforward piece of psychological analysis of a woman driven by her feelings to sin and later brought to repentance. In the adaptation which he wrote with Jean-Claude Carrière, Buñuel transposes the action to the present day, while retaining some of the period touches – the landau and the duel, for example. But these anachronistic notes set none of the problems posed by Robert Bresson's use of a similar technique in his updated adaptations of Bernanos and Dostoievski. In Buñuel's film the period elements appear only in those scenes which are most clearly subjective and, despite the director's decision to cut an early scene which offered a seemingly logical explanation of the landau (it was stated to be a first anniversary present from her husband Pierre), the anachronism causes little bother. It can quite easily be explained away as a by-product of Séverine's somewhat impoverished, book-fed imagination. Such a temptation to gloss over the complexities of the film is in many ways reinforced by the quality of Buñuel's *mise en scène*. The direction of actors and the handling of the camera is straightforward, unobtrusive, seemingly banal, with none of the flights of fancy one might expect in a film dealing with a young woman's erotic imaginings. If this is a dream, it is indeed a very wakeful one.

Yet beneath the surface *Belle de Jour* is an extremely rich and complex film, and its structure, if examined in detail, throws up a great many ambiguities hidden from us at first sight. It is significant that the film begins, as it will end, with scenes and images that are clearly imaginary. The stately procession of the landau bearing Séverine and her husband Pierre through the Bois de Boulogne takes us to a totally unexpected incident of whipping and sexual assault by the grooms, at the husband's instigation but with

Belle de Jour

34

Séverine's very positive complicity and (eventual) enjoyment. If Séverine's extreme masochism is novel, her attitude of submission is something she shares with many of Buñuel's heroines, all of whom emerge quite unscathed from sexual encounters. One thinks of Evie's matter of fact acceptance of the warden Miller's assault in *The Young One*, Tristana's returning of her uncle's kiss and, most startling of all, Viridiana's acquiescence in rape by one of the beggars to whom she has offered shelter. Buñuel is the least sentimental of directors and, just as he can make a blind beggar unsympathetic as well as pitiable, so too he views his heroines' sexual initiations calmly and without taking any stand of moral disapproval.

In *Belle de Jour* Pierre's words 'What are you thinking about Séverine?' bring us back from this detachedly observed sexuality to the comforting banality of the marital bedroom. Yet the very smoothness of the transition should make us question the truth of this scene and of the other domestic sequences that follow. On the one hand, Séverine is much more real and alive in her fantasies than in this apparent conjugal bliss, which has some echoes of the 'happy ending' of *Un Chien Andalou*, where we see the lovers finally united but buried up to their necks in sand. The playing of all the domestic scenes of *Belle de Jour* is disturbingly stiff and without any sense of real intimacy, and the transitions from them to the ski resort and then back to a Parisian taxi are also abrupt and off-putting. An ambiguity about the 'reality' of the various images runs throughout the film, as Buñuel's direction undercuts the seemingly real while giving fantasy a disquieting solidity. Just as the repetitious opening of *The Exterminating Angel*, with the guests arriving twice for the same party, prepares us for the eventual and quite unexplained inability of the guests to leave Nobile's apartment, so the beginning and ending of *Belle de Jour*, with images of overt imaginings, 'contaminates' all that lies in between.

Buñuel enjoys immensely his jokes at the expense of the serious-minded and the rational – his explanation of the repetitions of *The Exterminating Angel* (that otherwise the film would have been too short) betrays an attitude of slightly mocking humour that finds its way into his films as well as into his interviews. In *Belle de Jour* we see two apparently harmless childhood memories. The first, depicting the eight-year-old Séverine undergoing a sexual assault by a burly workman, is placed immediately after her discovery that an acquaintance, Henriette, works part-time in a brothel and just before she questions Pierre about whether he has ever been to such a place. It seems to offer a very reasonable explanation – we 'understand' now why Séverine indulges in these masochistic fantasies. The reassurance we draw from this explanatory use of a memory shot lures us into attempting to make the same connecting link for the second memory inserted a little later. But this one – the young child refusing communion – is placed with wicked precision in the middle of Séverine's first visit to Madame Anaïs's establishment. Are we to connect church and brothel in a similar causative sequence? In a context like this the reality or otherwise of the scenes depicting Séverine's work in the brothel cannot be established with any certainty. The clean and ordered world, with its charming madam and beautiful friendly whores, seems almost too good to be true. Whether it is real or simply imagined by Séverine, it does, however, serve as a remarkable mirror image of bourgeois society. The critique of accepted social values which runs through all Buñuel's work, from the indifferent aristocrats in *L'Age d'Or* to the lucidly observed slum dwellers of *Los Olvidados* and the petrified upper-class figures of *The Exterminating Angel*, finds its echo in *Belle de Jour*. Home and brothel are parallel worlds, both with their unobtrusive servants and ideals of male dominance and female elegance. In terms of the plot there is also a clear link between the young Séverine in her respectable home and the young Catherine whose mother works as maid for Madame Anaïs (both suffer unambiguous male attentions). It would seem from the published script that Buñuel intended making a similar link later in the film between the sexual perversities of the Duke and the rites of the Catholic church, but was prevented by censorship restrictions.

Despite their ambiguity the brothel scenes reveal the genuine quality of Séverine's emotional reactions and her gradual growth to awareness as she explores her own sexuality. The three initial clients all illuminate aspects of her personality. As might be expected, the first, Monsieur Adolphe, terrifies her, but she submits docilely when confronted by Madame Anaïs's firmness and his brutality. The torment into which this first act of prostitution throws her is counterbalanced by a sense of vitality. She never looks more beautiful than when, having bathed away all traces of the encounter, she burns her underwear. The subsequent fantasy, in which she is pelted with mud by her husband Pierre and their friend Husson, echoes the opening sequence of the film but in a Camargue setting. It might seem no more than a scene of total humiliation, but it is heralded by the sound of cowbells which here, as in *L'Age d'Or*, have connotations of release.

The effect throughout is lightened by Buñuel's sense of humour – here Pierre and Husson are at one moment arranged in attitudes that parody the celebrated painting of the angelus (a typical Buñuel joke at the expense of culture, like the *Last Supper* parody in *Viridiana*). Séverine's encounter with her second client, a professor as masochistic as herself, shows how little she understands her own responses. Spying voyeuristically on the scene between him and another of the girls, she is both fascinated and disgusted. How can anyone get so low? she asks Anaïs. But with the third customer, a huge Asiatic with a mysterious buzzing box (of insects?), she achieves a genuine release, and it is notable that he carries a tiny bell in his left hand which he rings as she prepares for bed. Here again the ambiguity of what really happens (we never see the contents of the box) and Buñuel's humorous touches (the Asiatic tries to pay with a Geisha Club credit card) add to the delight of the scene. At this point in the film Séverine has found an expression of her sexual feelings but only in a context removed from her home life with Pierre. His role in her fantasies is always a passive one and her sexuality is held firmly in check, reserved for her brothel work 'between two and five'.

The gradual contamination of her whole life by her sexual needs begins with the reappearance of the landau, this time containing a mysterious Duke who, as we discover later, has bizarre sexual needs. Where, in the first half of the film, there had been a sense of exploration, of extension and testing of Séverine's feelings in a startling but rationally explicable way, we are now offered a more perplexing universe where abrupt transitions and reversals are part of the basic pattern and where seeming miracles can occur. Whereas the atmosphere had earlier been abstracted and the vice banal, the mood now becomes more melodramatic and highly charged. This, after all, is the place to which Séverine comes every day in her dreams, as she tells the Duke when he picks her up for what he terms 'a kind of religious ceremony'. This latter entails Séverine representing his dead daughter and lying down naked but for a black veil inside a coffin, while the Duke busies himself curiously underneath. Buñuel views the necrophiliac aberrations of the Duke with the same detached benevolence with which he portrays the obsessive behaviour of such similar characters as Don Jaime in *Viridiana* and the uncle, Don Lope, in *Tristana* (both played by Fernando Rey).

The sequence ends with Séverine receiving the punishment she desires for her involvement and which she invariably metes out to herself in her fantasies (she is brutally kicked out into the rain by the butler), and this sudden change of mood underlines the unreality of the events. But back in the untaxing warmth of her domestic situation, Séverine imagines another sequel, a rather similar situation of an explicit if mysterious sexual game under the table with her husband's friend, Husson (Michel Piccoli), and in the presence of Pierre. This is the first time that Séverine's sexual imaginings have taken on a social dimension and intruded into the world of her family and friends, and Husson's role is a key one for an understanding of the film. Since it was he who first aroused Séverine's interest in prostitution and who gave her the address of Madame Anaïs's establishment, it would seem natural that he should figure either as an embodiment of evil (luring a young woman away from fidelity to the husband she loves) or as a liberating force (showing up the sham values of a bourgeois marriage). In fact he is neither of these, for this kind of moralizing over-simplification is precisely what Buñuel avoids in all his depictions of sexual acts and relationships.

Belle de Jour (Pierre Clémenti at right)

An even greater movement from pure fantasy to total encroachment on Séverine's settled existence is to be found in the subsequent sequence of the film. This begins with a Godardian lightness with two gangsters in the Champs Elysées (there is even a young newspaper seller calling out 'New York Herald Tribune' to recall *A Bout de Souffle*). When the gangsters go to spend their ill-gotten gains at Madame Anaïs's, a passion immediately springs up between Séverine and the younger of the two, Marcel. The playing of Pierre Clémenti as Marcel could hardly be more remote from that of Jean Sorel as the husband. In Clémenti's dynamic performance the lover emerges as a man of violent, arrogant, domineering and anti-social power, and Séverine is now faced with the problem of keeping complementary two totally opposite love relationships. Both men begin to make demands on her – Pierre expresses (not for the first time, one feels) his desire for a child and Marcel wants her totally for himself, to know her real name and to possess her for a whole night, not just from two till five. The inevitable climax of confrontation is anticipated by the appearance of Husson, who pays a visit to Madame Anaïs and comes face to face with Séverine. The meeting itself is inconclusive,

39

for it was her virtue that attracted him to her, and he retreats when she is suddenly accessible. But it does offer yet another example of the film's frequent inclusion of rationally explicable but still perplexing behaviour – Husson leaves expressing his increased admiration for Pierre and sending him a box of chocolates. Séverine seeks release in a new and extreme fantasy, a duel between Husson and her husband. This ritual is graphically prepared, with stress on the surgeon's instruments laid out in readiness, but it can offer no solution to her problems. The person to suffer here, as in all Séverine's fantasies, is herself, and when shots have been exchanged she is the one who dies, struck by Pierre's bullets as she stands tied to a tree, that same tree in the Bois de Boulogne where she had endured her first humiliation at the hands of the grooms. Séverine then tries to avert disaster by leaving the brothel and, in the scene where she takes her leave, Geneviève Page (whose performance throughout is one of the delights of the film) captures perfectly Anaïs's hesitation as she too, like Husson, is taken aback by Séverine's new openness and susceptibility.

The tone shifts back to gangster melodrama as Marcel, having learned the secret of Belle de Jour's true identity, forces himself into her home, violating her privacy and bringing together the two halves of her life that Séverine had taken such pains to keep separate. Defining Pierre as the obstacle to his happiness, Marcel coldly shoots him in the street, only to be gunned down himself in turn by the police. His last appearance, like his first, shares with that of Michel Poiccard in *A Bout de Souffle* an atmosphere of parodistic reference deriving from what must be a conscious echo of the prior deaths of a hundred film gangsters. Pierre is not killed in the attack, but emerges from the hospital paralysed, blind and mute. He seems a figure of accusation, like the crippled old mother in Zola's *Thérèse Raquin*, constantly reminding the heroine of the fruits of her guilty passion. The note of moralistic melodrama struck in these scenes, as Séverine, living now without dreams and fantasies, busies herself with tending her husband, is as convincing as that in the earlier brothel sequences. The tone is maintained as Husson arrives and insists on telling Pierre the whole truth in order, as he puts it, to release him from his remorse at being now totally dependent on his wife. With Séverine's subsequent confrontation with an utterly destroyed Pierre, the culmination of this aspect of the film is reached. If we wish to interpret the film in such a way as to see some scenes as unquestionably fantastic (e.g. the landau ones) and others as unquestionably real (e.g. the home ones), then this resolution is satisfying and the film can end here. Back in the solidly defined certainties of her bourgeois home, Séverine must face up to the fruits of her vicious self-indulgence. The wages of sin must be paid . . .

But, as we know from his other films, nothing could be further from Buñuel's basic beliefs than such an ending, and at this point *Belle de Jour* undergoes a brilliantly realised and totally unexpected series of reversals. These upset the trite and moralistic ending and throw into fresh perspective all the apparent certainties of the film. As Séverine looks tenderly at her husband, the sound of cowbells is heard. Pierre, suddenly restored to total health, asks again the question that heralded the initial transition from the opening Bois de Boulogne scene to the domestic hearth: 'What are you thinking about, Séverine?' and she replies as before, 'I was thinking of you, Pierre.' The whole sexual torment and masochistic indulgence of the film's action is erased as Pierre talks banally about their holidays and pours them both a drink. Then the circle is completed, as the sound of cowbells and hooves gives way to the harness bells of the landau which approaches, empty, on the very same avenue along which it had passed in the opening shots of the film.

Throughout this very detailed description of the structure of *Belle de Jour* care has been taken to stress the ambiguity of what we see on the screen. There is clearly a continuum linking the various scenes, and though we can say that some seem more real than others, we cannot, on the evidence offered us by the film, vouch for either the absolute reality or the total fantasy of any given shot or image. The satisfying rightness of Buñuel's surprise ending is that it underlines this essential ambiguity and thus gives the film a note of total consistency. But for all their structural rightness, these final images do not impose a point of view on us. They complete the circle and round off the film, but at the same time they throw open the interpretation of its meaning. What, in fact, does the empty landau mean? Does it simply take us back to the beginning, signifying a recommencement without progress in the *monde clos* of the heroine's imagination? Is it, by contrast, an indication of Séverine's mental collapse as she blocks out the all-too-real disaster of her marriage? Does the empty landau here constitute a symbol of Séverine's release from the obsessive fantasies we have shared? Or is the fact that Séverine's last words are to draw Pierre's attention to the landau a sign that she has reached the stage of requiring Pierre's conscious involvement now, so that the empty landau comes, so to speak, to carry him off to the realization of his own secret dreams?

This multiplicity of possible interpretations is not a sign of blurred focus, but the perfect artistic expression of Buñuel's moral preoccupations as they are apparent in forty-odd years of film-making. He talks a language accessible to Christian believers, but refuses the cliché answers of sin, guilt and retribution. He celebrates the total purity of *amour fou*, yet offers a voyeuristic, even fetishist presentation of his heroine. He shows abnormality and innocence co-existing in the same figure. Therefore it is fitting that his chosen ending for *Belle de Jour* should have connotations of liberation in the manner of *L'Age d'Or*, yet at the same time refuse resolutely to offer a reassuring image of solid, unimpeachable reality.

4. Jean-Pierre Melville: Appearance and Identity

To move from Luis Buñuel's cool dissections of bourgeois behaviour and belief to the shadowy world of Jean-Pierre Melville's gangsters might, at first sight, seem an impossible jump in style and preoccupation. Certainly it would be difficult to find immediate connections between the films each has adapted from a Joseph Kessel novel, Buñuel's *Belle de Jour* and Melville's *L'Armée des Ombres*. But in some respects at least a comparison can be fruitful, for both are very much concerned in certain of their films with the ambiguity of appearances and have dealt explicitly with the riddle of identity which a man's life may offer. In contrast to Buñuel, who returns again and again to the same themes throughout his creative life, Melville was an eclectic. In his early films he is the most chameleon-like of directors and seems to be trying on a series of masks, searching for his own style through a succession of explorations and impostures. Even his personal identity is a mask – born Grunbach, he adopted his second name at the start of his career as a homage to the author of *Moby Dick*.

Melville's work as a film-maker falls sharply into two contrasting halves. He began his feature career with two literary adaptations. The first, *Le Silence de la Mer* (1947), was a version of a short story by Vercors, in which he experimented with the use of a commentary over the images in a style which has remarkable similarities to that later perfected by Robert Bresson.

In the second Melville showed his affinity with yet another distinctive hermetic world, that of Jean Cocteau. *Les Enfants Terribles* (1949) was the product of an extremely close collaboration of writer and director and offered the opportunity for further stylistic experiment, notably• the then novel idea of using classical music (Bach and Vivaldi) as a counterpoint to the film's action. After an unsuccessful attempt at a purely commercial feature, *Quand tu liras cette Lettre* (1952), Melville made two more personal works. *Bob le Flambeur* (1955) was ostensibly a gangster film in the currently popular mode, a successor to Jacques Becker's *Touchez pas au Grisbi* and Jules Dassin's *Du Rififi chez les Hommes*, but at a deeper level it is a personal work filled with nostalgia for the Montmartre of the director's youth. In a similar way, the plot of *Deux Hommes dans Manhattan* (1958) is no more than a pretext for what Melville himself characterized as a 'love letter to New York'. These early works are independent and uninfluenced by current fashion or taste, yet somehow tentative. For all their undeniable qualities they are apprentice works, and it was only when, in 1960, he incorporated star personalities into his films that Melville's full talent made itself felt. Then he embarked on the second stage of his career which extended until his death in 1973. Having set out to make films which would be commercially successful without compromising his personal integrity, Melville took his place as one of the major film modernists.

The link with Buñuel in the use they both make of ambiguity becomes clear if we confront the first of this new series of Melville films – *Léon Morin, Prêtre* (1961) – with Buñuel's *Nazarin*, made three years earlier. Both works mark the beginning of a new creative phase in the director's career, *Nazarin* leading directly to the modernist period of Buñuel's work of which *Belle de Jour* is a fine example, while *Léon Morin, Prêtre* looks forward, in method if not in content, to Melville's maturity. Both are studies of priests which question the validity of Christian belief and vocation, and both deal with fundamental problems of appearance and reality. The central figure of *Nazarin* is a priest whose unconventional way of living among whores and thieves leads him to break with his Catholic superiors and with the idea of organized religion. Instead he sets out on an odyssey, aiming as it were to relive the life of Christ and bring God's word to the people living amid superstition and disease in the countryside. Protected by the certainties of his faith, Nazarin continues doggedly on a path that at every stage presents him with the evidence of his own defeat and failure. Trying to earn his food, he becomes a blackleg in a labour dispute and sparks off a confrontation that ends with the killing of a foreman. Trying to help the sick, he is first hailed and worshipped as a saint with supernatural powers, then later finds himself ignored as a dying woman puts her immediate physical need of her lover above his promise of eternal life.

43

Buñuel's *Nazarin*

Melville's *Léon Morin, Prêtre*

Called a heretic because of his rejection of privilege and, though carnal love is something quite alien to him, treated as a lecher because he allows two women to accompany him on his travels, he is thrown into prison amid men whose physical violence he can forgive but whose blasphemy makes him despise them. To all he meets he is ultimately irrelevant, a truth pointed out to him by a murderer in jail – the perfectly good man is akin to the perfectly evil in his meaninglessness. The lessons we are to draw from this story are left open by Buñuel, who refuses any conclusion that might turn the film from a work of art into a polemical tract. Instead *Nazarin* ends with a scene of striking ambiguity. Battered and with his head bandaged, the priest is being marched back under police escort to face discipline from his superiors in the church when he meets an old woman who offers him a pineapple. Confronted with this act of charity he feels his inner certainties crumble and a roll of drums on the soundtrack conveys only too clearly the anguish within him. But what in fact has shattered for Nazarin? His pride, which gave him his invulnerability but prevented him from loving his fellow men as individuals? His faith in the Christian God, now that he can see where an imitation of Christ leads? His belief in his own ability to live as a priest outside the

45

church, the recognition that his superiors are right in their condemnation? Is the film a profoundly Christian one, or a work of blasphemy? Buñuel exploits here the cinema's ability to present actions neutrally from the outside. The answer to these questions is vital for any interpretation of the film, but Buñuel simply shows us Nazarin's terrible vulnerability and leaves us to draw our own conclusions based on our own experience.

Melville's *Léon Morin, Prêtre* is also the story of a priest who allows his attraction for young women to go beyond what is considered seemly, but there the similarity of plot ends. Though this film too is set in a time of strife and oppression (the German occupation of France), Morin is not shown as being in any way troubled by the conflict of the times. He helps those, like the Jews, who are on the run, but he never seems to run any personal risk. Instead the film focuses on his relationship with Barny, a young woman whose emotional vulnerability has already been stressed before she enters the confessional box to shout at him that religion is the opium of the people. Caught up in a dialogue conducted in a tone she had not anticipated, led to debate theological issues and to pray and confess, she falls in love with the priest.

The film poses two questions: is Barny's conversion genuine? and what is the exact role of Morin? The first is answered fairly convincingly, in that we see clearly that her love for Morin as a man is at least as important as her belief in the words of religion he utters. But there is nothing to say that the faith he has apparently given her will not last after they have separated, and Barny's case is too special to allow us to widen out the film's meaning and to take it as a discussion of the question of conversion itself. The second question is more difficult. Léon Morin is not in any way caricatured and one can see him as a genuine priest. But since the film adopts Barny's perspective totally, giving us her dreams (in some of the visuals) and her constant interpretation of events (in the commentary), there is no way of viewing his behaviour objectively. Does he act in perfect innocence or does he consciously toy with Barny's feelings? One feels the latter, but the case is impossible to prove, since, even in Barny's account, he never does anything which unequivocally expresses a physical desire for her. The doubt and uncertainty make the film a riveting piece of viewing, but at the end one feels one has experienced less a spiritual statement than the working of a perfectly smooth-running machine (a view of the film Melville himself endorsed in interviews).

It is important to stress the profound differences between *Nazarin* and *Léon Morin, Prêtre* because they allow us to define more clearly some aspects of cinematic ambiguity. There is an extractable meaning (even if posed in terms of a question) in Buñuel's film which raises important issues. It demands that we relate the film to things outside it – to Buñuel's biography, to the surrealist movement or the art of Goya and Cervantes, and above all to our own experience. The ambiguity is the profound expression of a revolutionary art which refuses to furnish us with glib and comfortable certainties (Nazarin loses his faith), but instead drives us to relive his odyssey and reach our own conclusion. For this reason the particular open ending of *Nazarin* (like that of *Belle de Jour*) is vital to the way we, the audience, relate to the film and to change it would be to destroy the whole meaning of the work. In *Léon Morin, Prêtre* there is a much greater abstraction and distance. Melville, the chameleon who is everybody in his film and plays all the roles with equal conviction, does not invite us to look into his life for answers or to search our own souls for them. Instead he offers us a spectacle, invites us to join him, as it were, in a game of question and doubt. He uses the presentational ambiguities of the cinema as ends in themselves and for this reason the ending can be changed at will. Ultimately it does not matter whether Léon Morin is aware or not, whether the informer in *Le Doulos* phones the police or his girlfriend, whether Jeff Costello in *Le Samourai* dies solemnly or with a smile on his lips (the last two are actual changes from the script made by Melville during the shooting of the films concerned). At most one solution is more elegant than another; the meaning and experience of the film is the same in each case. Buñuel, the atheist tormented all his life by belief and blasphemy, demands a response different from Melville, the cynic who toys with the masks of faith and doubt.

Melville's work only becomes unsatisfactory if we adopt this particular perspective. In fact it is as inappropriate to look for spiritual values in his films as in Bing Crosby's performance as a priest in *Going My Way*. He is exploiting in a film like *Léon Morin, Prêtre* a type of ambiguity common to traditional cinema. Alfred Hitchcock in *The Wrong Man*, for example, deals with equally unaccustomed solemnity with such problems of identity, and innumerable thrillers play on the ambiguity of appearances. Is the wealthy heroine's husband tending her devotedly or is he trying to murder her? Hitchcock provides a perfect example of how this plot can be handled in his 1941 film *Suspicion*, and interestingly enough he too toyed with two possible endings. In the planned version Cary Grant was indeed a murderer and the final sequence showed him giving his wife the fatal glass of milk and then unwittingly posting the letter which will convict him. This was rejected by the producers, RKO, on the grounds that Grant as a star could not be depicted as a murderer. So, in its released form, the film clears him of all suspicion and reunites husband and wife. Still the ambiguity runs all through the film and Hitchcock records that the production executive who tried to remove all the scenes which implied that Grant might possibly be a murderer ended up with a film forty-five minutes long. Melville's work in *Léon Morin, Prêtre* is to be seen in this perspective, and it is only when his film-making turns in on itself, as in his gangster films, where film convention becomes the subject of the film, that he can be regarded as a modernist as the term is used here.

All the films Melville made after 1961 have been variations of one kind or another on thriller or gangster film themes, though sometimes these themes have been only one of the dominant elements. *L'Aîné des Ferchaux* (1962), for instance, an adaptation of Simenon, is as much an evocation of a dream America and a meditation on solitude and human relationships, while *L'Armée des Ombres* (1969) is a seriously intended study of the French Resistance. More central to the genre are *Le Deuxième Souffle* (1966), Melville's handling of the traditional theme of the gangster on the run, *Le Cercle Rouge* (1970), a variant of the perfect robbery idea which has had so many cinematic echoes since *The Asphalt Jungle*, and *Un Flic* (1972), the last film he made before his death. The distinctive quality of Melville's work, and in particular its modernity, is most discernible in *Le Doulos* (1962) and *Le Samourai* (1967). The debt to the past in both films is immediately apparent but totally digested. All the recurrent patterns of imagery are there – hats, guns, cars, dark city streets, nightclubs and so on – but presented with characteristic Melville detachment. Out of a form which traditionally had strong sociological connotations (the first gangster films – *Little Caesar* (1931) and *Scarface* (1932) for example – reflected the current situation before the repeal of prohibition in 1933), Melville distils a style in which behaviour becomes ritual and the action an expression of pure myth.

Melville once listed the sixty-three American directors, from Lloyd Bacon to William Wyler, who, he maintained, had created the talkies in the 1930s. It was from them that he derived the sense of cinema without which he could not have made *Le Doulos*. The film bears out this debt to the past, being that of a man totally absorbed in the medium of film and quite at home with genre requirements. It is in fact a virtuoso piece, with the action leading like a well-oiled machine to the death of all the main characters, and the *mise en scène* never deviating for a moment from its chosen style. From the title (*doulos* = hat and, by extension, police informer) to the final images of multiple carnage, the film continually refuses all resemblance to the real world and sets up instead a troubling series of resonances. Despite the nominally French setting, the decor is systematically Americanized (telephone booths, windows, bars, cabaret acts) and filmic references abound, from a police office modelled on that in Rouben Mamoulian's *City Streets* (1931) to a final homage to John Huston's *The Asphalt Jungle* (1951), when Silien (Jean-Paul Belmondo) visits his stable before going to his death. The spectator is unlikely to pick up all the allusions at a single viewing for they are never overstressed, but from the first image of a man in a soft hat and belted raincoat (Serge Reggiani) making his way through a drab but carefully lit urban landscape, the mood is that of a nightmare constructed out of the half-recalled moments of countless thrillers and *films noirs*.

The degree of stylization, with its constantly false decor and disquieting filmic echoes, is a perfect reflection of the film's theme. True to Melville's prefatory note from Céline – 'One must choose . . . to die . . . or to lie?' – the characters all present a false face, offer alibis, twist and evade the truth. When Maurice Faugel ends up in prison for a murder and his part in a failed robbery in which his accomplice and a police inspector both died, we feel sure that his friend Silien is responsible. We have seen the latter assault Maurice's mistress, Thérèse, to find the address of the robbery and later help the police to arrest Maurice. But then Silien sets out on a personal quest and, with the aid of Maurice's revolver, the loot from the murder and the false testimony of an ex-mistress, he constructs a convincing case against the successful crook Nuttheccio and his right-hand man. He shoots them both and departs with most of Nuttheccio's ill-gotten gains, leaving a carefully posed tableau of a quarrel among thieves that persuades the police to release Maurice. Silien then puts to his friend his own version of events. Flashbacks recall the suspicious acts we saw Silien commit and he puts them all into a new perspective: the informer was Thérèse and all his actions have been designed solely to save Maurice. The latter is convinced, but discovers too late that the revenge he had plotted in prison is now under way. He, Silien and the hired gunman die in the final confrontation; and now that they, like Thérèse, are dead, we cannot know whether Silien's actions or his words should have been believed, whether he was the informer or the friend.

Le Doulos is very much of its period, in that the 1960s were a time when many young film-makers were beginning to make films shaped by lessons learned from their viewing of American movies. But Melville differs from the Godard generation in that he does not simply toy with images and references in a playful, parodistic manner and out of context but creates his whole film out of the allusions. While it is a French film of the 1960s and not an American work of the 1930s, *Le Doulos* is still a real gangster film in a way that Godard's *A Bout de Souffle* is not. Moreover, viewed outside the perspectives of the gangster film and in a modernist context, *Le Doulos* takes on a new light. Silien, the key figure of the film, is a mere cipher who does not interest us as a character. There is no background to his personality, no explanation of his ruthless killing, no sense of greed or ambition. He moves between crooks and police, but this world of crime is viewed with the same neutral detachment with which Buñuel contemplates the sexual aberrations of his characters. Killers kill, informers inform, the police pursue and capture . . . all die in the end. What is fascinating is the way Silien emerges in this

The American connection: *Le Doulos* (Serge Reggiani) . . .

... *Le Samourai* (Alain Delon)

perspective as a character akin to those in Alain Robbe-Grillet's novels and films, a lone figure moving through the false décor of the imagination, a universe characterized by ritualized dress and formalized modes of contact, who struggles to impose himself on the world and his version of events. If Resnais and Robbe-Grillet had cast *Last Year at Marienbad* in the underworld instead of a baroque chateau, they would have come close to *Le Doulos.*

The stylization of this film is taken to still further extremes by Melville in *Le Samourai.* On one level the film is a masterly thriller, drawing on the conventions of the genre and offering the spectator the customary pleasure of recognizing fresh variations on the ritual pattern of events. Jeff Costello (Alain Delon) is, in this sense, the typical film killer — solitary, taciturn and doomed. After establishing an elaborate alibi he successfully carries through the contract he has been given to kill a nightclub proprietor. But in doing so he arouses the suspicions of the police, and his temporary arrest leads his employers to doubt his usefulness. Thus his meticulously planned and executed act plunges him into a world of treachery and violence, as his employers try to have him executed and the police, by bugging his room and

51

'Tender but cool': *Le Samourai* (Nathalie Delon, Alain Delon)

blackmailing his fiancée, set about breaking down his alibi. Jeff proves his superiority to the world through which he moves by eluding the police net and killing his treacherous employer, but the mechanism of the plot still leads him to his death. He has accepted a second contract – to kill the girl who is the sole witness to his crime. But meantime he has fallen in love with her, and when he goes through the ritual prelude to murder a second time, he removes the bullets from his gun. The killer becomes an acquiescent victim as the police shoot him down like a wild animal.

The script, by Melville himself, is beautifully worked out, sharply delineating the rival worlds of police and gangsters. As is so often the case in the thriller genre (in *The Asphalt Jungle*, for instance, which Melville admired so much), the police for all their logic and rationality are unsympathetically depicted. We feel (quite unjustifiably) outraged by their use of underhand methods, and are drawn insidiously into Jeff Costello's world. Whereas the acts of crime and violence are explicit, the hero's personal relationships are left deliberately ambiguous. His relationship with his fiancée, Jeanne Lagrange, who furnishes him with his alibi, is tender but cool, and Melville cast Nathalie Delon (who was at that time Alain Delon's wife) in the part because the two of

'Abstract, timeless, fantastic': Alain Delon as *Le Samourai*

them look, in his words, like brother and sister. Equally Jeff's love for Valérie (Cathy Rosier), the nightclub pianist who witnesses the first murder and for whom he throws away his life, is expressed only by glances and never verbalized.

Without in any way detracting from the impact of these conventional thriller elements, Melville has, throughout the film, subtly negated any realism which might attach itself to the happenings he records. Even to recount the plot in the terms we have just used is in a real sense to falsify the film, for Melville offers no explanation of either plot or character. The opening sequence is totally without dialogue, and only emerges as the establishing of an alibi after the police investigation begins. As we watch the film we have only the experience of seeing a succession of mysterious acts performed with utter assurance. Likewise nothing in the film is simply copied or transcribed from reality; it is made abstract, timeless, fantastic by the director's handling of it. The colour does not reproduce the world in its natural tones, but remains cold and inhuman throughout. To achieve this effect Melville chose locations and dress to fit his preconceived scheme and also deliberately removed all the colour from such everyday items as bank notes or bottles.

The stylization of dress is equally rigorous. Though the film is nominally set in the Paris of 1967, Jeff Costello wears the traditional garb of the 1930s' gangster – soft hat and belted raincoat. As a result, when he moves apparently unnoticed through the chic glass and stainless steel interior of a modern nightclub, the film becomes virtually a pure fantasy.

Where Melville differs from the 1930s' Hollywood directors to whom his film-making owes so much is in the very conscious and deliberate way he uses this filmic iconography. To quote just a single example at random: Jeff, who wears his hat throughout, signifies his acceptance of the death in store for him when, for the first time, he hands over the hat at the desk and fails to pick up the ticket. We become very aware too, as the film progresses, that the unfolding of events is not contrived to simulate the hesitancies and contradictions of real life, but is submitted to an external pattern. Details are repeated exactly to form patterns, and the whole ending of the film reproduces the opening – once more we see Jeff Costello set off to kill someone whose identity we do not know. *Le Samourai* draws more on our memories of films we have seen than on our direct experience of life. Jeff's confrontations with his employers are shot in images which clearly recall the conventional handling of the gunfight in Westerns, and Jeff's speed of response makes him an invincible epic hero in the mould of the classic Western gunfighter. In this way Melville offers us not the realistic portrait of a 1960s' assassin, but an idealization and abstraction. The tone is caught by the echoes of Akira Kurosawa's period films in the title, *Le Samourai,* and in the invented 'quotation' from the Book of Bushido with which Melville prefaces his film: 'There is no greater solitude than that of the samourai, unless perhaps it be that of the tiger in the jungle.' It is in this perspective of stylization that the echoes of Jean Cocteau's world become so totally acceptable. Melville had retained an admiration for the work of Cocteau since they collaborated on *Les Enfants Terribles,* and here in the figure of Valérie he created a variant on the Princess played by Maria Casarès in *Orphée.* On a banal level merely the eyewitness with whom the killer falls in love, Valérie, a beautiful black woman clad only in white, becomes a personification of the death Jeff longs for and moves towards throughout the film.

The use of abstraction to create ambiguity links the work of Melville with his younger compatriots such as Agnès Varda, whose film *Le Bonheur* has the same disturbing lack of sociological and psychological explanation. In a similar way, Melville's cool treatment of the theme of madness aligns him with such directors as Polanski, Jessua and Ferreri. Though *Le Samourai* seems to offer a detached view of its hero, it is in fact the world as seen through Jeff's eyes that we experience in the film. The opening image of Jeff stretched out on his bed is not a static shot that pins him down coldly like an entomological specimen. On the contrary, by combining here a track back and simultaneous zoom forward Melville manages to create a very ambiguous initial sense of unease and involvement. The cold, austere and clinical look of the film mirrors Jeff's view of life. We experience through him the events of the film and so the killings occur without pain or remorse, everyday acts (dressing, stealing a car) take on an air of ritual, and personal contact is remote and impassive. On the surface Jeff Costello is merely a violent killer in a conventional mode, but through him Melville can express a distinctively modern form of perception of the world – the schizophrenic as exemplary hero. Echoes of Albert Camus' sense of tragic absurdity are as real to *Le Samourai* as those of Jean Cocteau's cult of death. We view Paris and violence in this film much as we experience the Algerian landscape of *L'Etranger* – through an apparently detached narration which reflects the deadened perception of the protagonist. Ultimately, Jeff Costello is less a successor to Baby Face Nelson and Legs Diamond than a creation in the tradition of Jean-Paul Sartre's Roquentin, Albert Camus' Meursault, and Mathias, the hero of Alain Robbe-Grillet's novel, *Le Voyeur.*

5. Michelangelo Antonioni: Figures in a Mental Landscape

Jean-Pierre Melville's career shows the kind of mutation which traditional forms may undergo when transplanted into a new context – in this case the way in which, in a gangster film, all defined time and place may be pared away so that the habitual expression of ritualized violence now occurs in an equally ritualized ambience. Something of the same development can be seen if we relate the use of setting in the Italian neo-realist cinema to the handling of background and location in modern cinema. A film-maker whose career makes this change clear is Michelangelo Antonioni, an international figure, who began his career as assistant to Marcel Carné on a quintessentially French film, *Les Visiteurs du Soir*, in 1943, worked in Britain and the United States in the 1960s, and has had as much influence outside Italy as within it.

Antonioni is a particularly good example for our present purposes because he was deeply involved in neo-realism in the 1940s (as critic, screenwriter and documentarist) and his colour films of the 1960s – in particular *Blow-Up* – are crucial to any definition of film modernism. But concentration on Antonioni should not make us forget the other contemporary film-makers who have trodden the same paths. As early as 1953, Roberto Rossellini's *Viaggio in Italia* (known as *Voyage to Italy* and *The Strangers*) offered some anticipations of Antonioni's methods in *L'avventura*, principally the use of a basic journey structure and a presentation of inner conflicts through the

Cronaca di un amore

interaction of man and landscape. Such an attempt to relate in new ways the object seen and the eye that observes also has connections with a number of films that fall outside the scope of this study in that they replace narrative with documentary discovery: Rossellini's own *India* (1958) and Chris Marker's *Lettre de Sibérie* (1957) or *Description d'un Combat* (1960). Similarly the decision to fragment the narrative by treating a group of characters within a restricted compass which we find in Antonioni's *Le amiche* (1955) is akin to that in Federico Fellini's *I vitelloni* (1953), and the quasi-symbolic use of settings (windy beaches and midnight city squares) in both films was to be schematized by Agnès Varda in *La Pointe Courte* (1956).

In so far as Antonioni's roots lie in neo-realism, they lie in a form of cinema concerned primarily with socially defined characters. Against a background of the violence of war and its immediate aftermath, these characters were observed, from the outside, in their personal and economic relationships. There was a sense of actuality, but a generalized one, for the direct link of art and life was muffled by the process through which experience was turned into film. Neo-realism built its aesthetic on a reconstruction of life which involved

57

the whole conventional apparatus of professional cinema: Cesare Zavattini worked for six months elaborating the script of *Umberto D*, and Vittorio De Sica spent weeks turning Carlo Battisti into an actor so that he could play the role for which his physiognomy made him so well suited. As a result *Umberto D* is, for all its stylistic difference, as much a prestructured and acted film as a Hollywood work of the period.

Antonioni's early films as a feature director are as pessimistic as any neo-realist work of the 1940s. The plot structures are basically circular, bringing the characters back to their starting point after offering them no more than a brief and illusory spell in which to examine the possibilities of freedom. In his feature debut, *Cronaca di un amore* (1950), the investigation of a seven-year-old death revives the relationship of a couple who were once lovers, but leads ultimately only to a second crippling fatality. In *Le amiche* Rosetta fails her suicide attempt at the beginning, but the events of the film only demonstrate to her the necessity of a second (and this time successful) attempt. In *Il grido* (1957) Aldo's long odyssey through the Po valley merely brings him back to the scene of his lost happiness and to his own death. One is struck by the way the violence which Antonioni inherited from neo-realism is invariably turned inward here and by the ambiguity of the numerous deaths. These films show too the beginnings of a progression which is continued in Antonioni's later work. The characters are psychologically rather than socially defined and the emphasis has shifted from events themselves to the effects of these events on the characters. The pattern changes, during these films, from a police-style investigation which throws up hypotheses if not proofs (in *Cronaca di un amore*) to a personal quest which offers insight but no hope for the individual concerned (in *Le amiche* and *Il grido*). As they move away from the opening disaster both Rosetta and Aldo come to understand their own predicament, but can see no option but to choose death. The role of decor reflects this shift of interest. From being a defining element of the social gulf which keeps the lovers apart in *Cronaca di un amore*, in *Il grido*, with its rain and desolation, it becomes an expression of the hero's state of mind.

With the 'trilogy' formed by *L'avventura* (1960), *La notte* (1961) and *L'eclisse* (1962) the outward violence is gone, but the doubt and uncertainty remain. Elements which might generate suspense or melodrama – such as the search for the missing girl Anna in *L'avventura* – are allowed to peter out. In the case of *Il grido* Aldo's difficulties could in part be attributed to poverty or inarticulateness, but here social problems have receded into the background and the characters are both affluent and assured. The interest moves to interior probing, though Antonioni's analysis of the sentiments refuses all explanation. *L'eclisse* ends not with a statement of the lovers' incompatibility but with a seven-minute abstract sequence of apparently disconnected images,

Disconnection: *L'eclisse*

which express anguish and solitude of a quite unverbalized kind. Open-ended plots were common in neo-realist films, particularly those of De Sica and Zavattini, and their purpose was to leave the solution to the audience: there could be a satisfactory outcome for the characters (and for those who shared their situation in real life) only if social conditions in Italy were changed. In Antonioni's trilogy, on the other hand, the open-endedness derives from the shift in focus from society to the relationship between individuals depicted in all their complexity. These characters are not dramatized (for Antonioni has a dislike of the conventional dramatic line and refuses to concede the continued validity of the old laws of drama), but they are displayed with all their inconsistencies and sudden emotional changes. These emotions are not pinned down with theatrical dialogue or organized with pre-scripted precision, but captured spontaneously as character confronts character in settings which, with the wide screen format, acquire a new visual expressiveness. The problem of the director, writes Antonioni in the preface to his published screenplays, is 'to catch reality an instant before it manifests itself and to propound that movement, that appearance, that action as a new perception. It isn't

L'avventura: a voyage into self-discovery

sound: words, noise, music. It isn't an image: scenery, an expression, a motion. But an indecomposable whole.'[1]

The films of the trilogy take the cinema of psychological analysis an important step forward in capturing the ambiguity of gesture and personal response. Their influence is borne out by the way in which, within ten years of its first release, *L'avventura* had taken on the appearance of a narrative of classical simplicity: what had once seemed startling and revolutionary now seems a normal and quite acceptable story line. The disappearance of Anna (Lea Massari) troubled critics and audiences in 1960 because it came after she had been established by all the conventional methods as the leading character. The film opens indeed with a shot of Anna coming towards the camera to justify her way of living to her father, whereas Claudia (Monica Vitti) makes her first appearance as a fleeting background figure glimpsed only momentarily, and clearly the heroine's friend. We share Anna's experience, her reuniting with her lover Sandro (Gabriele Ferzetti) and her dissatisfaction with her holiday, her surroundings and her life. We are therefore as disconcerted by her disappearance as Claudia and Sandro are, and it is only as our attention gradually shifts to their growing relationship that we cease to

60

be disturbed by the failure to find an explanation. At the end of the film the investigation of Anna's disappearance can be seen merely as a voyage into self- and mutual discovery by her lover and her best friend. The enigma of Anna remains, and Antonioni has used the disorientation he created in us in order to make us share more fully the confusion of his characters. He has not imposed a view on us, and the ambiguity of the film goes beyond the sense that the dawn reconciliation of Claudia and Sandro (after she has discovered his betrayal of her) is no more than a provisional ending. *L'avventura*'s power resides in the way it allows us to feel the mixture of emotions within the characters.

The distance which already separates Antonioni at this stage of his career from Hollywood methods of narration is shown with striking clarity if we compare the disappearance of Anna in *L'avventura* with the killing of Marion (played by Janet Leigh) in Alfred Hitchcock's *Psycho*, which was made the same year. Marion too has been established as the central figure in the film and the showerbath murder as devised by Hitchcock comes as a brutal shock that leaves us helpless by its unexpected violence and its seeming irrelevance to everything we had been concerned with in the film up to that point. But Hitchcock does not now leave us to explore the meaninglessness of human action. At his supreme best here as a manipulator of audience response, he goes on to torment us further. When we have had sufficient time to reorient ourselves and identify afresh with the reassuringly banal private detective, Arbogast, he too is brutally murdered, so that we could hardly be more tense when the third possible victim (Marion's sister Lila, an equally vulnerable figure) enters the dark house.

The shift of interest in the film from the outsiders (Marion, Arbogast, Lila) to the insane killer Norman Bates is, as Robin Wood points out, a 'descent into the chaos world',[2] but controlling this chaos is the omnipotent author, Alfred Hitchcock, who shapes our glimpses of it in such a way that we can have only one reaction (horror) and plays on our uncertainties with a virtuosity deriving from his own detachment from the events narrated. *Psycho* is in this sense the least ambiguous of films (every spectator is made to share the same experience) and though we may dismiss the psychiatrist's explanation at the end as, dramatically, a mere breathing space to bring us back to earth and, stylistically, a typically Hitchcockian joke (the false reassurance), we do emerge with the certainty that the horror and death we have just experienced vicariously are rationally explicable. For this reason the analogies Wood draws between *Psycho* and the horrors of the concentration camps are invalid. It is precisely our inability to put Belsen or Auschwitz into any kind of rational framework which is the most tormenting aspect of the concentration camp horror. In the case of *Psycho*, on the other hand, no one can emerge

The end of words: *Zabriskie Point*

from the film without an awareness of having been manipulated, and the existence of the director as puppet-master outside or above the action puts the horror into too comforting a perspective.

Since 1964 Antonioni has worked exclusively in colour and his films have taken on a new dimension. For one thing the puritanism that characterizes his earlier work has gone. The problems of communication and mutual awareness treated in the trilogy are concerned solely with the couple: the interaction is depicted in all its complexity but the ideal towards which the characters are groping might be described as the achievement and maintenance of monogamous fidelity. In the colour films this is no longer the case, and a new moral awareness is apparent in such scenes as the group in the little hut in *Deserto rosso* (*Red Desert*, 1964) playing sexual games and discussing aphrodisiacs, the casual amorality of *Blow-Up* (1966), especially Thomas's amusing sexual encounter with a pair of teenagers, the orgy amid the desert sands imagined by Daria in *Zabriskie Point* (1969) as she makes love to a boy she has met only a few hours before, and the pick-up of the young French girl by Jack Nicholson in *Profession: Reporter* (*The Passenger*, 1975). Topicality is a feature of all three films: strike pickets and cybernetics in *Deserto rosso*, pop groups and drug parties in *Blow-Up*, a campus riot in *Zabriskie Point*, and gun-running in *The Passenger*. Clearly in this context the treatment of violence becomes crucial, and the films show a steady escalation from the menace contained in the polluted factory smoke at the beginning of *Deserto rosso* to the repeated explosions and slow-motion ballet of the destruction of the entire contents of the luxurious Palm Springs house at the end of *Zabriskie Point*. The colour tends to smooth over the rough edges of the reality so that a new tension between the violence and the beauty develops. Like Jacques Tati, Antonioni does not deny that the modern urban environment is beautiful; he merely stresses that this beauty is not enough, that it solves nothing.

The balance of character and setting changes once more with these films, the interest shifting more and more to the latter. In the earlier films the backgrounds were vitally important – the rocky islands of *L'avventura*, the millionaire's house in *La notte*, the stock exchange in *L'eclisse* – but they were viewed objectively and the connections between milieu and the relationships (which formed the focal point of the films) were left for the audience to make. In the colour films, however, there is a move to greater subjectivity. In *Deserto rosso* for example, the heroine Giuliana is defined less by her relationship with her lover or her husband than by reference to the setting, which does not determine her behaviour but undoubtedly serves to reveal it. For this reason distortion away from a realistic perspective becomes more and more apparent and, as the director says, reality becomes abstract and the subject colour. Sometimes in *Deserto rosso* Antonioni can find in real life the visual effect he needs – for example the pink sand which we see as Giuliana tells her small son a story. More frequently he uses photographic means of distortion, the zoom lens, for instance, which he uses to bring people and objects together in a two-dimensional composition. Most questionably of all he also uses the traditional methods of the French 1940s' cinema – painting fruit grey and a rubber plant white to convey the heroine's desolation – in a film which elsewhere obeys other conventions. When in 1969 he went to the United States for *Zabriskie Point*, he could find examples of the transformation of environment into a virtually theatrical decor all around him, and his advertising hoardings which are so much more real than life and his television commercials with their talking puppets amid plastic settings seem hardly exaggerated, though they serve as a perfect image for the values of the materialist society which the young reject.

Blow-Up is in many ways an archetypal modern film, containing the customary paradoxes of images and sounds and a narrative that throws up as many questions as answers. In view of the emphasis put on the compositional elements it might seem that one could analyse Antonioni's colour films without reference to the narrative element, but an examination of *Blow-Up* shows how crucial the residual thread of story is. Certainly it is important for the director himself when he is at work on a film. He has recorded in an interview[3] how he once stopped at a bar in a village near Valdagno and became aware of how photogenic it was. But as he moved around the room he realized that he was uncertain of how to frame a shot of it. Without a story his visual imagination was working in a vacuum, and it was only when there was a girl at the bar – a possible character and hence a nascent story – that the shapes began to take on meaning. There is a story in *Blow-Up*, but one with false starts, queries, doubts and contradictions. Just as the images approximate to a subjective experience, so too the story corresponds more to the way we think and feel than to the conventional rules of drama. As in Alain Resnais's *Muriel* and Jean-Luc Godard's *Une Femme Mariée*, we find all the surface detail of a modern city – in this case, a Rolls-Royce and an antique shop, black nuns and gays with white poodles – used to convey not reality but the author's vision. The connections out to a wider social or political context are missing – the demonstrators whom the hero meets carry banners simply saying 'No' or 'Go away', and for the rag students at the start and finish of the film their own activity is an end in itself and the cause for which they are collecting irrelevant.

In *Blow-Up*, Antonioni's first film since *Il grido* without Monica Vitti, we have for once a man as the centre of attention. The character Thomas (played by David

Blow-Up: the image of modernity

Hemmings) offers perhaps the easiest way into the film. The opening is deliberately disconcerting: we see Thomas emerge in ragged clothes from a doss house, then drive home in a convertible Rolls-Royce. Visually the incongruity persists as he photographs the elegant model Verushka while still in his old clothes. Yet another view of him emerges as he deals casually and brutally with five less experienced girls modelling ready-made clothes. Therefore by the time we come to the crucial central scene in the park, we are intrigued by his behaviour and caught up in his actions. This sequence, in which he observes and photographs an apparently ordinary pair of lovers enjoying the solitude of the park, seems innocuous, but ends with an extreme reaction on the part of the woman concerned. When she realizes she has been photographed, she pursues Thomas to his studio and offers herself to him in exchange for the negatives. This naturally makes Thomas feel that there is more to the situation he has photographed than has emerged from his cursory examination of the prints, and from this point onwards – diverted only by an orgy with a pair of teenagers, a pop concert and a drug party – Thomas is completely caught up with the secret he is convinced must lie hidden in the photographs he has taken.

Blow-Up: the artist as voyeur (Vanessa Redgrave, David Hemmings)

If it is not possible to equate Thomas with the director (in that he does not function fully as an artist), his response to this particular incident in his life is explicitly compared to the creative methods of his painter friend Bill. As the two of them look at a five- or six-year-old canvas, Thomas's immediate reaction is to try to buy it. But for Bill there is another level of response. As he explains: 'They don't mean anything when I do them – just a mess. Afterwards I find something to hang on to – like that – like – like . . . that leg. And then it sorts itself out. It adds up. It's like finding a clue in a detective story.' This is a perfect description of Thomas's reaction to his own photographs of the park, but his attempts at rational elucidation are based not on a creative probing of experience, but on a totally chance and random act of photographing. Real creativity is something Thomas lacks – his book of photographs, for example, is a superficial response to the problem of violence and he wants peaceful images at the end simply so that it 'rings truer'. But an intellectual probing alone cannot solve anything. As he endlessly scrutinizes and enlarges his prints the evidence of a murder emerges and when he returns to the park, there – against all the rules of probability – is a corpse lying in the grass to confirm his hypothesis. But this whole structure of supposition

66

turns out to be without actual proof – while he is away his prints and negatives are stolen and when he returns to the park with a camera, the corpse has gone, so that he is left at the end doubting the power of his own senses.

Despite the failure of his attempts to dominate the situations in which he finds himself, the role of Thomas is crucial to the meaning of the film. On one level he is a typical Antonioni figure – the failed artist as voyeur. He uses a wide variety of methods to capture the images he is seeking – pretence, sexual stimulation, aggression, stealth – but reality in its full multi-dimensional aspect always eludes him. He remains a voyeur, spying on the old men in the doss house, just as he will spy on the couple in the park or on his friend Bill and his mistress making love. His relationships with the women who cross his path make this particularly clear. His photographs of Verushka are the images of a fake, non-consummated act of sexual intercourse, the two teen-agers strip each other naked for him in the orgy scene and the girl from the park offers him the sight of her breasts as an enticement to hand over the negatives. The climax of his professional career in this respect is the moment in the park at night, when he finds himself confronted with a corpse but without a camera to photograph it. The click on the soundtrack at this point seems an ironic comment on his predicament. But there is more to his role as a photographer than the simple voyeuristic elements. *Blow-Up* is partially a film about the act of photography itself in its various forms – snap shooting, composing images in *cinéma-vérité* style or with carefully posed models. Also it is about the mechanics of photography – developing, printing, enlarging – the emergence of an image on photographic paper and the interpretation of it. Thomas attempts to pin down reality through photo-graphy. But as he gets closer and closer to the images of murder which he is convinced lie somewhere within the shots he has taken in the park, he accumulates 'evidence' which is no more than a grainy pattern of greys – akin to Bill's paintings and no more 'proof' of anything's existence than a non-figurative art work is.

Ultimately *Blow-Up* is an examination by Antonioni of a life and a meaning which are just out of reach. As he himself expressed it: 'I want to re-create reality in an abstract form ... I'm really questioning the nature of reality. This is an essential point to remember about the visual aspects of the film, since one of its chief themes is "to see or not to see properly the true values of things".'[4] For this reason any interpretation of the film we may make depends on whether or not we adopt the hero's point of view. In his own eyes Thomas is a man in search of a romantic idyll who uncovers an unexpected crime. The greenness of the park is translated into black and white images and these are probed, blown up and investigated. The story emerges from them as if in answer to his desires, takes shape, twists and then vanishes, as the evidence

67

contained in the photographs is stolen and the all-too-tangible corpse disappears. Photography is a way of making reality give up its secrets: the murder really happened – the scoop every photographer dreams of – and the camera's presence brought it to light.

But as soon as we look at events from outside, the inconsistencies of this interpretation become apparent. Why did the shooting take place there, in the open? Why did the woman's accomplice carry out the killing after they had been discovered? Why did he not attempt to kill Thomas too? Is it likely that, letting the woman pursue Thomas on her own, he would leave the body in full view? Would not somebody have found it in the afternoon? The events are too far-fetched to be real and can only be occurring inside Thomas's head – the click as he looks at the body becomes evidence to support this view. The murder is invented, the image of the gun emerges because Thomas wills it, to prove his view, to show that he can stamp his imagination on reality. The ambiguity is there and the film can be interpreted from either inside or outside the character. But it is only in the latter perspective that the appearance, at the beginning and end of the film, of the group of Felliniesque students makes sense. In their mime at the end the structuring of the film round the themes of reality and imagination becomes clear. They are miming with an imaginary ball, yet we hear the noise made by their rackets; their game can arouse as much enthusiasm in a willing audience as a real tennis match and they can make even an outsider like Thomas join in their game. Yet the ball Thomas feels obliged to throw back does not exist, and the life into which he returns as he leaves them obeys a quite different logic.

6. Jacques Tati: The Open Window of Comedy

Jacques Tati's constant concern throughout his career as a film-maker has been with realism in comedy, with toning down, by means of observation and understatement, the wild exaggerations customary in slapstick and the circus tradition. This concern, which finds expression in all aspects of his stylistic approach, allows us to take further the comparisons between modernist cinema and the film-making methods of the 1940s which have already been touched upon in the discussion of the roots of Michelangelo Antonioni's style. For, if the latter represents one extension of attitudes and approaches which we can see clearly in the films of the Italian neo-realists, then Jacques Tati's work is undoubtedly another. It constitutes, in this sense, the authentically realist comedy which Italy failed to produce within the neo-realist movement in the 1940s.

Although, as will be seen, there is considerable justification for such a comparison between Tati and the Italians, certain important initial distinctions need to be borne in mind. First, in his attitude to the studio reconstruction of reality, Tati is very much a part of the French tradition exemplified by Marcel Carné in *Quai des Brumes* or René Clément in *Gervaise*. In *Jour de Fête* (1949), Tati set his brilliant mimed performance as François the postman in an authentic rural setting, but by the time he came to make his masterpiece, *Playtime*, in 1967, he had reverted to the more characteristic French approach of putting realistically observed characters into a specially

Jacques Tati in *Trafic*

contrived setting. Of course neo-realism in Italy was also based on the concept of the reconstruction of reality rather than the simple reproduction of it in newsreel fashion, but the whole idea of 'Tativille' on which so much time and money was spent in the preparation of *Playtime* would have been quite alien to an Italian film-maker of the 1940s. In Italy at that time the action of a film was customarily invented or reconstructed, but almost invariably in an authentic setting, with authentic faces. Here in *Playtime*, by contrast, the method used to create an illusion of life is the reconstruction of everything, setting as well as action, characters as well as plot.

An even stronger difference between Tati and neo-realism lies in the attitude of mind brought to bear on the problems of modern life. In Italy neo-realism was a cinema of attack, of social criticism, a cinema that asked questions and probed the all-too-easy customary official evasions. Tati shares the intense moral concern of a film-maker like Cesare Zavattini, but the whole political dimension, so important to neo-realism as a movement, is lacking. He is closer to a modernist like Alain Robbe-Grillet in that he is totally a-political and wants to observe but not analyse or evaluate social behaviour. In his world there are no villains and no dilemmas seeking a social resolution and, as he sees it, his purpose is 'not to criticize but to bring a little humour'.[1] Unlike the neo-realists he does not want to change life but simply 'to make people participate a little more'. He does not attack the Americanization of French life (typified by the titles, *Trafic* and *Playtime*, and by such locations as the drugstore and the Royal Garden Hotel in the latter film) and has no axe to grind about modern architecture (his buildings are impeccably tasteful, even beautiful). Instead he merely comments on the use people make of these resources and the way in which they allow themselves to be dominated by their surroundings.

Bearing in mind these qualifications it is still possible to see Tati's work, and *Playtime* in particular, not as the continuation of the French comic tradition – which tends to be that of boulevard wit *à la* Audiard or rustic comedy in the manner of Fernandel – but as the culmination of the kind of concern with comedy which – in Italy – in the best work of Luigi Zampa, Luciano Emmer and Renato Castellani, ran parallel to neo-realism proper. Like these directors and their writers – men such as Sergio Amidei and Cesare Zavattini – Tati draws his inspiration directly from life seen and overheard on the streets, but he is far more audacious in the extent to which he allows the observation to influence the shape of his films. In this way he fulfils some of the theoretical requirements of neo-realist comedy much better than the Italian film-makers themselves. Perhaps the nearest Italian film to *Playtime* is Luciano Emmer's *Sunday in August* (*Domenica d'agosto*, 1950), which deals with the adventures of no less than 102 characters on a single summer's day. In Emmer's film, however, the incidents are all embryonic dramas: a man is arrested for armed robbery, a meeting occurs that may well flower into love, a policeman discovers that his girl-friend is pregnant, and so on. But in Tati the de-dramatization is complete and *Playtime* contains nothing even remotely dramatic in this sense: we simply see people failing to meet, taking photographs, eating or working. Thus, just as the films of Emmer and Castellani represent an enormous leap forward if we compare them to the escapist 'white telephone' fantasies of the Fascist era, so too Tati in *Les Vacances de Monsieur Hulot* (*Mr Hulot's Holiday*, 1953) continues and in *Playtime* transcends this line of development after it had petered out in Italy in the early 1950s. This is in fact one measure of Tati's importance in world cinema. Like Jean Renoir in a work like *Toni* in the 1930s and Luchino Visconti with *Ossessione* in 1942, he establishes a link between two dominant traditions of European film-making – the Italian and the French. It is the nature of this synthesis he contrives out of the best of two contrasting approaches to cinema and, in particular, the lessons he draws from them about narrative structure that earn Tati his place among the film modernists and make his works rank among the most original and audacious experiments in film construction of the post-war period.

71

Modern times: Tati in (*above*) *Jour de Fête*, *Les Vacances de Monsieur Hulot* and (*opposite*) *Mon Oncle*

Like most modern artists, Tati is well aware of the historical context of his work. Looking at the history of film comedy he sees a process of what he has called 'democratization' at work. The first comic films were music hall acts, like those of Little Tich, simply recorded by the camera. This conception of comedy as a virtuoso solo effort reached its height with Keaton and Chaplin, then gradually gave way to comedy based on team work: the double act of Laurel and Hardy or the quadruple chaos of the Marx Brothers. If this process is to be continued, comedy must in the future belong to and derive from everybody in the film. In conformity with this view, performers and audience are linked in a spectacle in *Parade* (1974), his nostalgic return to the circus. Whether or not this pattern accounts adequately for the whole development of film comedy, it certainly underlies the widening focus of Jacques Tati's own work since 1949. In *Jour de Fête*, his first feature, he created an unforgettable comic character – François the postman – who is worthy of comparison with Buster or Charlie. But Tati felt that this type of performance – the contrived and artificial act of a brilliant mime – left little scope for further development. He therefore created Monsieur Hulot, 'a man you can meet in the street, not a music-hall character', a kind of comic Everyman as it were, who fits into the community and whose behaviour is never more than slightly exaggerated. In the course of the four films he has subsequently made featuring this character, Tati has striven to redress the balance between the 'funny man' and his environment, with the result that Hulot has been pushed further and further into the background. From being the clearly defined central character of *Les Vacances de Monsieur Hulot*, he became the foil of the gadget-ridden Arpel family in *Mon Oncle* (*1958*) and is only an episodic character in *Playtime* and *Trafic* (1971). His first appearance in *Playtime* is symptomatic: our attention to the figures in the foreground is disturbed by the sound of an umbrella being dropped somewhere, but by the time we actually catch sight of him, Hulot is already striding off with his inimitable loping gait.

As Hulot himself grows less important, so the minor characters increase in richness and variety. In Tati's own words: 'Instead of it being Hulot, as in *Les Vacances de Monsieur Hulot*, who does or executes just about the whole number of gags that there are in the film, I leave these gags, as you might say, to others, choosing the character best qualified to realize them ... The real gag, the true gag, for a head-waiter is to have it done by a real head-waiter.' In consequence Tati's films take on an ever-widening social world: the tiny village of *Jour de Fête*, the seaside hotel and its tourists in *Les Vacances*, the contrasting districts – old quarter and modern factory – in *Mon Oncle*, the whole modernized Paris of the future in *Playtime* and the European community in *Trafic*. The angle of vision has changed too, perhaps to reflect a development of French life itself over the past twenty-five years. In *Jour de Fête* modern life, in the form of a film on American postal methods, makes only a temporary impact on an unchanging community, but in *Playtime* we never get outside modern man's steel-and-glass prison and catch only fleeting reflections of the past (traditional Paris in the shape of the Eiffel Tower or Notre Dame is seen only momentarily, mirrored in the plate-glass doors of the hotel or airport).

While the level of achievement reached by Tati in his first five films is consistently high, two of them are cast in a traditional mould and as such constitute remarkable works of comic imagination, but in no way enlarge our conception of what comedy is. *Jour de Fête* is, in this perspective, simply an outstanding variation on the traditional notion of the funny man, and *Mon Oncle*, in which Tati feels that he 'wandered' a little from his real preoccupations, is built on conventional comic juxtapositions such as modernity and traditional values, Arpel and Hulot, inhuman order and well-meaning chaos. In *Les Vacances de Monsieur Hulot*, *Playtime* and parts of *Trafic*, on the other hand, we find the wholly original Tati concern with the utilization of the cinema's 'possibility of opening a terrace on to life to make all its riches known'. The basis of this, as of any kind of comedy, is observation, and Tati has said that he constantly goes out walking so that he can observe people's behaviour and listens to conversations in pubs and at football matches in

Observation: *Playtime*

order to capture natural dialogue. What is novel in Tati is the moral value he gives to such observation. For him, watching the foibles of humanity is our best defence against the pressures of modern life: 'You see, people often complain about the lack of humanity in modern architecture. They imagine themselves to be overwhelmed and crushed by these massive constructions. But if they knew how to observe, they would learn that life is the same there as anywhere else. A few added comforts are not going to change the nature and character of individuals. And it is the continuous performance offered by the behaviour of these individuals which must make our life amusing.'

From this derives the revolutionary nature of Tati's comedy: the way in which he allows the process of observation as such to determine the visual quality of his films. From using the camera at first in a conventional way to record an invented performance based on accurate observation, but stylized and hence divorced from reality (as was the case with François in *Jour de Fête*), Tati has moved on to the much more difficult and original idea of giving his audience a direct look at the behaviour itself in its context. This is what lies behind his definition of the cinema as a window opening on to life. *Playtime*, as he told one interviewer, 'is an open window. And through this window the spectators are going to see what happens. I hope they will recognize people they know: a neighbour, a tradesman, a colleague. It is such people, who are just like the ones you come into contact with every day, who are the heroes of *Playtime*, not Monsieur Hulot. Monsieur Hulot does not detach himself from the group. He is on the same level as the rest of the characters, the comic actor is not the only one to be funny. If you know how to look, the most serious people are sometimes the funniest.' The notion of the window is clearly fundamental to *Playtime* and throughout the film one has the impression of eavesdropping, of seeing human activity in a frame that shows up its absurdity. In this way the spectator becomes akin to the most pathetic character in the film, the unfortunate waiter who tears his coat and subsequently becomes a repository for all the staff's torn and soiled clothing, and is therefore forced to watch the festivities from outside. A sheet of glass allows us to be, at one and the same time, part of a scene and detached from it. Often, simply by cutting off one element, such as the sound, the glass permits us to enjoy a scene in quite a new way. The all steel-and-glass world of *Playtime* gives rise to a number of gags of this kind: the workman needing a light, Hulot chasing a reflection, the little man walking into a door, all the play with the non-existent Royal Garden Hotel door and so on.

The patterns of narrative Tati adopts also reflect his concern with preserving the essential quality of the observation. In *Playtime* the plot itself could hardly be simpler. It deals, the director tells us, with 'a group of American women who are visiting Europe at the rate of two capitals a week. Whereas they had expected to find picturesque old houses in Paris, they in fact encounter exactly the same motorways, the same street-lamps, the same office blocks, the same cars as elsewhere. But finally they do discover Paris: through its inhabitants.' To use such a slender plot line to support a film running two and a half hours in its original French version is clearly to make considerable demands on an audience, but these difficulties are deliberately imposed by Tati. He could quite well have built up the role of Hulot by giving him most of the gags, or have contrived some dramatic build-up or comic surge of incident. But all these things have been done before, by other film-makers, and instead Tati has preferred to use his powers of invention to weave together a succession of disparate and hardly developed little incidents involving a large number of characters over the period of twenty-four hours or so. Characters come and go, gather and disperse with their movements corresponding to the natural rhythms of life rather than to the needs of an imposed dramatic structure. Tati had already used this idea of construction in parts of *Mon Oncle*, an example being Hulot's disastrous attempt to restore the Arpels' ornamental bush. Hulot begins this before the reception but is unable to complete his work and returns to it only much later when most of the audience will have completely forgotten the whole incident. In the context of an otherwise normally structured comedy this kind of episode seemed disorienting and out of place to many spectators and critics, and even in the case of *Playtime*, where the avoidance of dramatic devices is deliberate and systematic, there are still those who complain at the lack of tension and order.

In fact, despite the appearance of random fragmentation, *Playtime* has a very deliberately designed shape. It begins slowly and Tati has said that at the beginning of the film he wanted the decor to be 'fairly cold, so that people would feel somewhat imprisoned by it and adapt badly to it'. For this reason, the opening airport sequence is presented in such strikingly enigmatic terms that we come to imagine that we are in a hospital. This not only gives rise to some good gags, it also underlines the impersonal, clinical atmosphere of modern architecture (no one feels at home in a hospital waiting room). This early sequence has too the elaborate manoeuvring of a large number of characters in a vast set which remains a constant feature of *Playtime*. These characters often reappear after half an hour or so, still engaged on the same activities long after we have forgotten their very existence. This was a deliberate attempt at realism of plot on Tati's part: 'All the time it's like that in life ... It was interesting to base a whole construction on this, taking into account these natural time schemes.' This gives the film its particular fragmented rhythm and incidentally illustrates a use of the time possibilities of the two and a half hour film which no other film-maker has explored.

In the first half of *Playtime* the characters are disoriented – the American women by their arrival in a new city, Hulot and his business colleague by their failure to find each other in the glass-walled labyrinth of office buildings. The audience too is disconcerted by them, for it takes time to feel at home in this kind of setting. But in the second part of the film, when the characters all gather at the Royal Garden Hotel to dine, the barriers between them are broken down. With this change comes an alteration of tone and tempo, and what had been measured and serious in the first part now degenerates into more hectic farce. It is hardly by chance that Hulot's contact in the hotel is the doorkeeper and that together he and his friend contrive to smash the plate-glass door and thus allow life to flow through the disintegrating decor of the hotel. As the formal atmosphere is destroyed, the old Paris of the boulevard cafés is recreated by the people who become masters of an environment which no longer overawes them. The quality of light is most important here. The drugstore, for example, which had earlier been filled with a bilious green neon glare, now becomes warm and lively in the early morning light. In a similar way, towards the end of *Playtime*, the problems of traffic jams and hold-ups dissolve into a game, as the cars attempting to go round a traffic island take on the appearance of toy vehicles on a children's roundabout. In this transformation of life into a ballet there are some echoes of the early René Clair, and

The airport sequence in *Playtime*

certain scenes in *Playtime*, like parts of *Le Million*, could be more aptly described as choreographed than as simply directed. But unlike Clair and so many other French directors, Tati does not work from a written text or fixed pattern of dialogue, but from directly observed reality.

Tati's discontinuous treatment of narrative is echoed in his handling of his characters. Hulot's diminished role in *Playtime* is compensated for by the existence of a whole horde of double or false Hulots. Some of these are developed into real characters (like the chap at the exhibition, for whom Hulot is mistaken by the irate German manufacturer), others, like the Negro Hulot, are mere silhouettes. Tati once admitted that for Hulot to appear in other films, to figure as an extra at a bus stop for instance, was a great dream of his (one which François Truffaut has since turned into a reality). This kind of openness between films and within the narrative structure itself is, for Tati, the way comedy will develop in the future: 'The day people laugh heartily at this sort of comic structure they will find it very difficult to laugh at a single character for an hour and a half.' This approach to time and fictional character corresponds closely to Tati's use of the technical resources of the cinema: content and style are exactly complementary. As his work takes on a new and widened scope, there is a steady growth of technical sophistication, from the fairly primitive black and white of *Jour de Fête* to the colour, 70mm format and stereophonic sound of *Playtime*. The latter is, however, in no way a denial of the past, for *Jour de Fête* itself was both planned and shot in colour and only the failure of the particular colour process employed was responsible for the eventual emergence of the film in black and white.

In any case Tati's approach to the physical dimensions of the wide screen is quite his own. In his view, it is ideal for conveying minute happenings – the most exciting thing to do with a cinerama screen and full stereophonic sound would be to use them to depict the dropping of a pin. Symptomatic of Tati's style, of his refusal of exaggeration and the obviously striking effect, is the use he makes of the lengthy long shot which compels the audience to scan the screen seeking out the unobtrusive detail which is the real crux of the scene. The silent comedians, particularly Buster Keaton, were well aware of the enormously enhanced impact obtained by doing stunts which, though extremely dangerous, were shown not to be faked by being recorded in a single, unbroken take. In another context, André Bazin has commented on the effectiveness of the same device in drama (as when we see the child and the hungry lion together in the same shot). Tati, with his dislike of the close-up and refusal to cross-cut in order to underline his effects, applies the same procedure to very different ends in his own more delicate and unspectacular comedy. His comments on the model aeroplane in *Playtime*, whose wings begin to sag as the ventilation fails, are most interesting in this connection: 'If

Playtime: the unobtrusive detail

I had taken a close-up of the plane, everyone would have seen it, but it's not a gag simply for the sake of a gag, it's a plane which melts because the people are hot, so you have to see them sweating at the bar at the same time, that's part of the whole thing. You have cause and effect in the same scene.'

For Tati, film is not a literary medium but a means of expression 'written in images' with the construction deriving directly from the visual observation. Like Resnais or Eisenstein, he conceives film as a total art form fusing colour, sound and image, and the idea of making a film according to *cinéma-vérité* techniques would be quite alien to him. Yet throughout a career that has given the cinema its most beautiful comedies, visually that is, since the great days of Buster Keaton's *The General*, he has maintained and deepened his concern to create a realistic form of comedy. As a result of his efforts, he has evolved a comic vision which makes the same demands on audience concentration as the dramatic style of Bergman or Bresson – and offers the same quality of personal expression in return. Instead of being a mere escape from the burdens of living, comedy becomes with Tati a profound meditation on the issues of contemporary life. A style rooted in the slapstick exuberances of Mack Sennett's Keystone Kops is transformed into the consciously wrought expression of a modernist viewpoint on narrative.

81

7. Robert Bresson: An Anachronistic Universe

The predominant traditions of European cinema have been realist and literary. We have seen how the realist tradition exemplified by Italian neo-realism is subtly transformed into a totally modern style in Jacques Tati's work by the decision to base the whole structure on the act of observation. As radical a renewal of the literary tradition can be seen in the films of Robert Bresson, particularly his work since 1966. This renewal draws its force from the selection and juxtaposition of elements taken from both literature and reality. Bresson's literary connections were apparent from the very beginning. His first film, *Les Anges du Péché* (1943), had dialogue by the dramatist Jean Giraudoux, while his second, *Les Dames du Bois de Boulogne* (1944), was derived from an episode in Diderot's novel *Jacques le Fataliste* and had dialogue by Jean Cocteau.

Subsequently Bresson began to show a new distance from his literary sources, a change marked by his rejection of the professional screenwriter (he has himself scripted all his own films since 1950). *Journal d'un Curé de Campagne* (*Diary of a Country Priest*, 1950), the first of his adaptations of a work by Georges Bernanos, followed the pattern which had already been established by Melville in *Le Silence de la Mer* and which Bresson was to perfect in his later films. Instead of dramatizing the story in conventional ways by padding it out with invented scenes, Bresson maintained a literary

Mouchette

style of narration by placing great emphasis on the spoken commentary. The images were played against this and often took a subordinate role, as at the very end of the film, where the *curé*'s crucial dying words are heard while the screen depicts simply a cross. *Journal d'un Curé de Campagne* has an austerity more characteristic of the director than of the writer, and when he returned to Bernanos some sixteen years later to make *Mouchette* (1967), Bresson was able to rearrange his material in much more fragmentary and diverse ways without in any way betraying his source.

Important as Bernanos is as a literary influence on Bresson, Dostoievsky is more crucial still. Both *Une Femme Douce* (*A Gentle Creature*, 1969) and *Les Quatre Nuits d'un Rêveur* (1971) are direct adaptations of Dostoievsky stories, and *Pickpocket*, though technically an original script, is clearly inspired by *Crime and Punishment. Pickpocket* dates from 1959 and is very much in tune with the new approach to narrative to be found in Antonioni's *L'avventura* and Alain Resnais's *Hiroshima, Mon Amour*, both of which were shot the same year. It would be foolish to push too far the similarities between works by such diverse directors, but all three films do share certain stylistic methods which may be taken as characteristic of modern film-making – a

Pickpocket: 'a prison without bars'

refusal of psychological explanation, a stylization of acting and an interest in novel combinations of image and music. Though all three were shot largely on location, the events are in each case submitted to a rhythm consciously imposed by the director, not one deriving directly from the patterns of everyday living. In ethos too the films are linked. The conception of redemption through love, seen as outweighing social pressures, criminal instinct and national differences, finds expression in the final images of each film – the dawn reconciliation of Claudia and her faithless lover in *L'avventura*, the kiss of Jeanne and Michel through the bars in *Pickpocket*, and the final duologue in Resnais's film.

Pickpocket is shaped as a narrative round Michel's clash of wills with the Inspector, but typically the latter's motivation in trying to help the young pickpocket is left unexplained. The real focus of the film is the development within Michel, as events (the series of petty and humiliating defeats) break down his defensive shell of assumed superiority and make him open to Jeanne's love. Here, though he is transposing nineteenth-century ideas into a contemporary context, Bresson makes more use of abstraction than of the anachronism he employs so potently in the 1960s. In his hands the characters have the blood drained from them and become mere automata obeying a

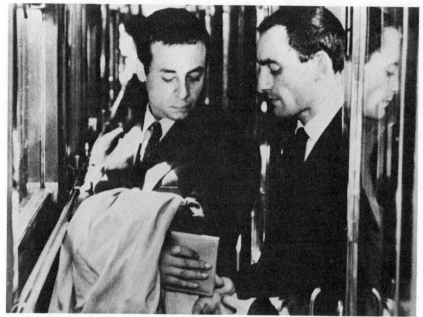

Pickpocket

superior will. They do not converse in the normal sense of the word – they utter epigrammatic phrases which express no more than their own isolation and which are answered, more often than not, by the person to whom they are nominally addressed simply turning his back and leaving. Much of the shooting for *Pickpocket* was done on location, but one has no sense of the characters being free to choose their own paths. The way in which an external rhythm is imposed on the characters is typified by the brilliantly realized scenes of the pickpockets at work, where every gesture is preplanned and executed to order so as to constitute part of an apparently empty ritual. The characters themselves are continually pinned down by the camera on a staircase, in the corner of a room or at an angle of two walls, and every setting takes on the air of a prison without bars. Most remarkable is the handling of the horse-racing sequences at Longchamps: we hear the sounds of horses' hooves, but see only the vacuous, immobile faces of the punters, as much trapped in their private obsessions as the thieves who prey on them. Nowhere is there a sense of real open air, of horses, movement or excitement.

Just as physical space is denied its openness in the film, so too is the drama deprived of its climaxes. In place of the smoothly satisfying progression and resolution of a conventional plot we find a narrative characterized by sudden

85

changes of mood. Michel expresses his confidence that his mother will recover and the film cuts to her funeral, and follows his moments of triumph as a thief with instant exposure and arrest. The fragmentation is deliberate and total. When Michel spends two years abroad, we cut from him leaving to him returning, still wearing the same suit and the same dejected expression. Structurally the futility of Michel's life is summed up in the circularity of the film's action. The failed arrest at the beginning leads only to the police success at the same race-course at the end. Michel is trapped in a prison of compulsive behaviour more real than the bars of his cell and the whole film is ultimately a vast *temps mort*, a detour that takes in exile and imprisonment for him and abandonment and an illegitimate pregnancy for Jeanne, only to bring the two of them back to a love they could have enjoyed to begin with.

If *Pickpocket* is an ideal film in which to trace the literary side of Bresson's art, the manner in which he relates fictional events and patterns to the everyday world, his subsequent Dostoievsky adaptation, *Une Femme Douce*, shows equally clearly the paradoxes of his particular realism. Dostoievsky's story *A Gentle Creature* is subtitled *A Fantasy*, though the author admits in a prefatory note that he personally considers it to be 'highly realistic'. The basic situation of a man watching over his dead wife's body, the description of a tortured relationship which has ended with the woman's suicide and the whole sequence and development of the husband's groping steps to self-awareness are all, for the author as for us, very real indeed. What is striking about Dostoievsky's note, however, is his realization that there is something fantastic in the idea of a narration that probes the mind and consciousness of its hero and posits, so to speak, an imaginary stenographer to record the man's private thoughts and self-questioning at this moment of crisis. One of the profoundest affinities linking Dostoievsky and Bresson is just such a recognition that the recounting of the most realistic happenings may be essentially fantastic. This is a very necessary element in any investigation of Bresson as a film-maker, for though he is often considered a realist, it is increasingly clear that such a label can all too easily blur the true meaning of his work. His particular brand of realism, like that of Franz Kafka, employs intensely realistic detail, but only in a framework of fantasy. No prison escape could be shown in more meticulous detail than that of Lieutenant Fontaine in *Un Condamné à mort s'est échappé* (*A Man Escaped*, 1956) – yet for Bresson the film would fail if spectators could not sense the fantastic element, the hand of God over the prison directing everything.

The same disturbing ambiguity is to be found in Bresson's attitude to the notion of spectacle. At first sight he would seem to rank himself wholeheartedly in the realist camp by his total rejection of everything that smacks of the theatre. In his first two films, it is true, a theatrical element is

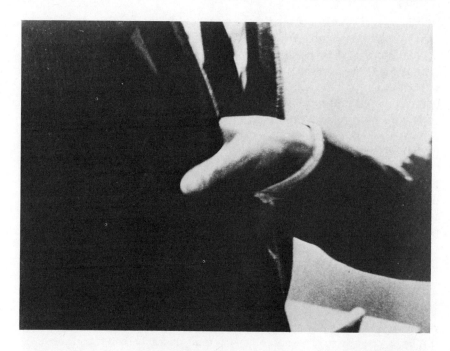

Hands: *Pickpocket* and (*below*) *Au Hasard Balthazar*

still detectable – in the dialogue for instance. In *Les Dames du Bois du Boulogne* it was possible for Maria Casarès to give an outstanding performance (though at the expense of a continual battle with the director), but since then Bresson has banished professional actors from his films. The players walk through his films with a measured tread and downcast eyes, expressing nothing of themselves as they intone their words exactly in the manner prescribed by Bresson. If a subject offers the possibility of spectacle, as did *Procès de Jeanne d'Arc* (*Trial of Joan of Arc*, 1962) or *Lancelot du Lac* (1974), this is totally ignored, and if there is a chance of suspense, it is stamped on from the outset (Bresson's prison film reveals the outcome of the hero's efforts in its very title: *A Man Escaped*). In *Une Femme Douce* the director has his heroine quote Hamlet's advice to the players, which begins with the very Bressonian injunction: 'Speak the speech, I pray you, as I pronounc'd it to you . . .' He also includes a long passage from the play in order, it would seem, to show that a filmed version of a work conceived for the theatre is inevitably bad. By staging the extract in the most artificial manner and filming it without imaginative insight, Bresson proves his point, but only at the expense of showing just how narrow his field of vision is. If Bresson's cinema is in this way an anti-theatrical one, it remains intensely dramatic. In virtually all his films there is a sharp clash of character, though this is frequently concealed behind a formal and apparently arid mode of speech – the politeness of Hélène and the lover on whom she takes revenge in *Les Dames du Bois de Boulogne*, the interchange of parishioner (the Countess) and confessor (the young priest) in *Journal d'un Curé de Campagne* or that of judge and accused (Cauchon and Joan) in *Procès de Jeanne d'Arc*. The sparsity of normal colloquial dialogue both heightens the mystery of Bresson's films and lays stress on the role of gesture. Hands are for him as important as faces – Lieutenant Fontaine preparing his escape, the thieves in action in *Pickpocket*, the ritual dealings of pawnbroker and client in *Une Femme Douce*.

Faced with the complexities of life or the inconsistencies of a literary narrative, Bresson's overriding impulse is to pare away the irrelevancies and bring the central issues into sharper focus. The visual texture of his films is vitally important and in the course of his whole career as a film-maker he has used only five directors of photography: Philippe Agostini for the first two studio-lit films of the 1940s, the veteran Léonce-Henry Burel for the studies of sainthood from *Journal d'un Curé de Campagne* to *Procès de Jeanne d'Arc*, Ghislain Cloquet and Pierre Lhomme for the studies of female victims and Pasqualino De Santis for his more recent version of the Arthurian legend, *Lancelot du Lac*. When Bresson has changed photographers it has generally been in the cause of a major development of his style, yet he has always sought total clarity in his images. The mystery present in every Bresson film derives not from any blurring or distortion, but from the very sharpness with which contradictory elements are seen and presented.

The same search for clarity can be found in Bresson's treatment of his source material. In his awareness of darkness and evil, Bresson has affinities with the novelists he has adapted, Bernanos and Dostoievsky. But from them, as from the Diderot novel, *Jacques le Fataliste*, or the trial records of Joan of Arc, he takes only the clear outline of a clash or evolution. All the surface realism, the dirt and disorder, and even the psychological motivation of the characters is left aside. In this respect one need only compare Guy Frangin's pallid, schematic performance as the husband in *Une Femme Douce* with Dostoievsky's richly tragi-comic portrayal of a blustering 41-year-old ex-officer, expelled from his regiment for cowardice. Bresson is ultimately concerned with the supernatural – the workings of God's will – but he seeks to present this simply through a greater concentration on selected aspects of the real, and not by recourse to any of the cinema's more obvious potentials for fantasy. In Bresson there is nothing to compare to the miracles in Pasolini's *Gospel According to St Matthew* or the appearances of the devil in Buñuel's *La Voie Lactée*. In his view, it is when we stare long and intently enough at faces, hands or objects that the mystery of God's presence becomes clearest to us.

Bresson's strength as a director lies in his ability to select and juxtapose elements drawn from reality to achieve just this effect. To convey a person jumping to his death one can simply show (as Pasolini does in *Medea*) a long shot of a man at the top of a cliff, then a close-up of his anguished face, then another long shot of a dummy being dropped from a great height. Bresson's handling of a similar situation at the beginning and end of *Une Femme Douce* is very different in its visual sophistication: a shot of a table slowly tipping over in front of an open window, a white scarf drifting slowly to the ground, over which is laid the sound of screeching brakes. The elements used are equally 'real', but the whole incident is given a new poetry and mystery. At the same time the effect of such an extreme selection is to isolate incidents still further from the flow of everyday life. In Bresson's work since 1965 – the series of studies of female victims which treat, as it were, versions of the Jeanne story in *Pickpocket* – the physical barriers, the prison bars and garret rooms, have disappeared and the characters move with ostensible freedom through light and sunshine. But by his control of speech and gesture, by the lighting he employs and by the situations he creates for his characters, Bresson subtly conveys the oppressiveness of life, whether rural (*Au Hasard Balthazar* and *Mouchette*) or urban (*Une Femme Douce* and *Les Quatre Nuits d'un Rêveur*).

In a similar way he has moved away from the use of explicit symbols and now employs images in which the symbolic meaning is latent. Just as the

Une Femme Douce

isolation of objects helps to turn the world into a prison, so the dislocation of chronology which selection entails contributes to the timelessness in Bresson's work. There has never been any attempt to fit his stories into a sociological framework – we never learn, for instance, the political motives and implications inherent in the execution of Joan of Arc. The director is happy to take the mechanics of a plot originally set in 1774 (*Les Dames du Bois de Boulogne*) or 1876 (*Une Femme Douce*) and transpose it without major modification to a contemporary setting. Indeed the resulting strangeness has a natural place in a Bresson film, which customarily surprises us not by any twist of the plot but thanks to the sudden and unexpected juxtapositions: nuns and gangster elements combined in *Les Anges du Péché*, the priest being hailed as a brother by the foreign legionnaire in *Journal d'un Curé de Campagne*, or the emptying of slop pails being given a Mozartian accompaniment in *Un Condamné à mort s'est échappé*. Bresson has never been afraid of anachronism – there are several straightforward instances of it in *Procès de Jeanne d'Arc* – and all his more recent films explore the possibilities offered by a complex double time scale.

In this respect the richest of Bresson's films is *Au Hasard Balthazar*, his first original script since *Pickpocket* and the film which in 1966 marked the beginning of the third major stage in his development as a film-maker. Any film which takes a donkey as its central character is bound to be unusual, and the particular tone of *Au Hasard Balthazar* is caught on the soundtrack during the credit sequence, when phrases of a Schubert piano sonata alternate with the braying of an ass. The film itself follows Balthazar from the time when he is still unweaned to his death, years later, on a hillside amid a flock of sheep. The donkey's story is interwoven with that of his first owner, Marie, and the people around her in the small border town in which she lives: her parents, her childhood sweetheart Jacques, the vicious Gérard who comes to dominate her totally, an alcoholic tramp Arnold and an avaricious corn merchant. Balthazar is not, however, used simply as a pretext or linking device for a conventionally structured slice of rural life. His personal story is at least as important as that of Marie which runs parallel to it.

An added difficulty of the film at a first viewing is the way it is shaped as a succession of jumps and elusive fragmentary scenes. The film needs to be seen more than once if the full meaning of the opening scenes of Marie's childhood is to be uncovered. Since the framing of the various shots isolates certain elements without overt explanation, the objects on which the camera concentrates — hands, a bench, a stable door, the impassive Balthazar himself — become charged with a very ambiguous significance. The natural climaxes, such as the death of a child, are underplayed to such an extent that one wonders whether they really happen or not. At the end of the film, for example, Marie's mother says that she has gone away and will never return. Everything seems to indicate that she has died, but Bresson does not state this unequivocally. Direct statements about the plot are therefore very difficult to make, because we can never be quite sure of anything. They also run the risk of being misleading, since the whole impact of the film derives from the way in which seemingly essential information is withheld, so that to interpret the plot is to distort the experience of viewing.

Moreover, the action does not flow in a predictable fashion. Each new scene is so arranged that it negates the assumptions aroused by its predecessor. The children's father says that they cannot possibly have Balthazar and the very next shot shows them taking him away with them; Gérard says contemptuously to Marie's father 'I'm not a thief' and the film cuts to him detected in the act of stealing; Arnold vows to give up alcohol and immediately we see him getting drunk in a bar. At the moment when we feel sure that the police have come to arrest Arnold for a murder they (and Gérard) suspect him of having committed, we learn with surprise that he has inherited a fortune. When we anticipate that the baker's wife will punish Gérard for betraying her trust, she rewards him with the gift of a motorbike and a transistor radio. This world of reversals and upsets, where a summer holiday ends in tragedy and a quiet drive along a country road leads to a pointless accident, is one in which Gérard, the film's evil genius, is totally at home. He submits all those around him to his whims and cruel practical jokes, putting oil on the road, tormenting Balthazar, seducing Maria and beating up the defenceless Arnold. Bresson's vision of a world without grace is a bleak one. While the other characters are fixed in their attitudes and vices – total submission, inordinate pride, drunkenness or avarice – Gérard alone moves with apparent freedom, unpunished and hiding his spite behind a choirboy's seemingly innocent face.

Where Bresson's earlier films experimented so as to counterpoint music or commentary with the images, *Au Hasard Balthazar* finds its pattern of contrasts and discontinuities more within the events themselves. The film seems situated totally out of time through the setting of explicitly modern touches (transistor radios, motorbikes, leather jackets) against traditional images (the donkey and the rural background). There are many enigmatic allusions to Christian imagery: a bunch of irate farmers pursuing Balthazar are caught in a grouping momentarily reminiscent of the Garden of Gethsemane; Arnold is kissed by Gérard and his lieutenants as he sets out on his lonely donkey ride to his death. But at the same time there is nothing ethereal about the film. In its concentration on hands, in its images of the cruelty inflicted on Marie and Balthazar (as in the powerfully structured seduction scene), it is a very tactile work. The violence of the car crash and the smashing of the café contrast with the impassive response of the witnesses. The film is set in the open air and the images capture the full beauty of rural landscapes in the sunlight, yet the characters are prisoners, closed in on themselves and constructing their lives around their vices.

Only twice in the film – when Arnold is leading tourists through the countryside – do the themes of *Au Hasard Balthazar* become explicit. Then there is talk of art ('I don't paint the waterfall, I paint what it tells me') and a discussion of the connection between criminality and responsibility. About the actions of the main characters, however, we are left to draw our own conclusions, for they are presented without psychological explanation or overt comment. Marie is as consenting a victim as Joan of Arc at her trial, but hers seems an unlikely path to sainthood. Just as her father refuses, through pride, to defend himself against charges which he knows to be false, so Marie, through her total submission, acquiesces in her own moral degradation. She claims to have discovered reality, but she has no defence against the forces which Gérard represents – she submits to his brutalities without complaint and prostitutes herself to the corn merchant without protest. The path she follows can only lead to death.

Au Hasard Balthazar and (*below*) *Mouchette*

The curious anachronism at the heart of the world which Bresson puts before us is apparent when we set Marie's story against that of the donkey. Balthazar too is at the mercy of events, though his stoical resistance takes him through a wider range of experience. But how are we to fuse the various images of him that we see in the film? We observe him suffering and abused, but also hear him described as the lover – 'as in mythology' – of Marie (by Gérard), as the most powerful brain of the century (in the circus where he works for a time) and as a saint (by Marie's widowed mother). Balthazar's death from a customs officer's bullet while he is being used by Gérard for smuggling is a fittingly ambiguous ending for a film which, despite Bresson's refusal of sentimentality, is strangely moving as well as visually compelling.

8. Ingmar Bergman: The Disintegrated Artist

Up to now we have been concerned almost exclusively with two aspects of modern cinema: the links of film and reality, as reflected in the style of the work (the refusal of verisimilitude, the search for new formal tensions, etc.), and the nature of the response demanded of the audience by the mixture of distance and involvement. There is, however, a third element that must be considered, the expression of the author's personality and his involvement in his creation. A more directly personal note is a characteristic feature of most 1960s' film-making, not merely the modernist segment of it. In part this derives from the new economic structure of the industry, for both the old studio system and the division of labour it entailed (especially the separation of the roles of writer and director) ran contrary to any idea of autobiographical film-making.

This is not to say that a personal style was not possible – one can always recognize the stamp of a Ford or a Hitchcock – but often this personal stamp is to be found at least partly in the tensions set up between the creator and his material (the imposed star, the genre conventions, the obligatory happy ending, etc.). The case of *Citizen Kane* is very interesting in this connection. In many ways the first genuine work of modern cinema, it is at the same time very much a Hollywood film of the 1940s. As such its authorship is to some extent open to doubt, and recently Pauline Kael has argued eloquently, if not totally convincingly, that the true author of the film is not the director, Orson Welles, but the scriptwriter, Herman J. Mankiewicz.[1] Welles is a man of enormous personality and has a very European conception of the director's role, yet to some degree *Citizen Kane* must be seen as a collaborative effort. This is a useful reminder of how rare direct and untrammelled personal work was in all Hollywood-style production systems.

The new personal tone of the 1960s' film-making can be seen in two very different directors whom one might term, borrowing Stephen Spender's definition, contemporaries rather than moderns: Federico Fellini and François Truffaut. Every image in a Fellini film is another contribution to his continuing portrayal of the Romantic artist as showman and clown. His 1972 film, *Roma*, is a typical example. Here Fellini evokes the idea of Rome as conceived by a child growing up in the provinces, reconstructs the Rome he knew in the late 1930s and creates his vision of the present and anticipation of the future. But all these conflicting images are presented as they are filtered through his own experience. In this way the film becomes not a distanced documentary on the Italian capital, but a dual portrait of the city and the *cinéaste*, drawing its strength from the confrontation of the two. But the portrait of Fellini that emerges is totally unproblematic. He is nearer to those Renaissance painters who filled the walls and ceilings of innumerable villas and palaces with exuberant portraits of their mistresses and friends, barely disguised as figures of classical or biblical allegory, than to such self-analytic film-makers as Bergman or Godard, whose films question their own creative impulses and artistic drives. In a very different style, François Truffaut, a miniaturist with Hitchcockian pretensions, has also given a barely disguised personal biography in a series of films, the Antoine Doinel sequence made with the actor who has become virtually his alter ego, Jean-Pierre Léaud. *Les Quatre Cents Coups* (*The 400 Blows*), *L'Amour à Vingt Ans* (*Love at 20*), *Baisers Volés* (*Stolen Kisses*) and *Domicile Conjugale* (*Bed and Board*) trace a path from adolescent uncertainties to married bliss which may not correspond to the outward facts of Truffaut's life, but certainly represents its inner development in a spontaneous and totally unselfcritical manner.

Both these directors have on occasion borrowed modernist devices. The structure of Fellini's $8\frac{1}{2}$ is very much post-*Marienbad*, and Truffaut employs the Bressonian pattern of a detached narrator–presenter for his own performance as Doctor Itard in *L'Enfant Sauvage* (*The Wild Child*). But despite their complexity the films of these men lack the kind of ambiguity we have been looking at here – they are films of certainty, rather than questionings of reality. Fellini's *Juliet of the Spirits* is an excellent example of a film that, for all its surface flamboyance, remains a narrative in the traditional sense. Fellini is a director who imprints his own vision on every foot of his films, and this one is particularly personal in that it is both for and about his wife, Giulietta Masina. The film presents the fictional Giulietta's real and fantasy life during a period of crisis leading up to her husband's decision to leave her for a young Swedish model. The real life takes on a fantastic aspect (especially in the handling of her next-door neighbour Susy, played by Sandra Milo, who becomes a symbol of female sexuality), and the images representing Giulietta's memories and fears crowd the scene with an almost tangible presence. But we do not lose ourselves in this maze of often dazzling visual imagery – there is never any real ambiguity as to what is real and what imaginary – and we are always carried along by the flow of the action cunningly constructed by Fellini, the master storyteller who mixes dream, nostalgia, sentiment and satire with a comforting certainty.

The works of the modernists we have dealt with so far are personal, but they do not treat the figure of the artist as a problematic one in all its dimensions. Antonioni is perhaps the director who comes nearest. It is possible to find parallels between his life and his work which are at times as close as those of Fellini or Truffaut – the new element of hope embodied in the figure of Monica Vitti, for example, which is missing from his work before 1960. In reply to an interviewer's question about whether he used the scripting period as a time to familiarize himself with his characters, he expressed great surprise: 'But the characters are not strangers that I may or may not be on intimate terms with; they emerge out of me – they *are* my intimate inner life.'[2] But Antonioni never treats an artist figure of full stature, equating himself totally with a single character in one of his films. The artists are generally dismal ones – the failed painter in *Le amiche*, the architect who has sold out for money in *L'avventura*, the trendy photographer in *Blow-Up*. Even the successful Giovanni Pontano in *La notte* is on the verge of becoming a mere publicist for a big businessman. As a result we never feel that Antonioni is fully exposed in his depictions of any of these figures (he is so clearly an artist on a different level) and sometimes, as in *Zabriskie Point*, there is so vast a moral and intellectual gulf between him and his creations that he reverts almost to the very unmodern position of possessing a godlike omnipotence *vis-à-vis* his characters. If we turn, however, to the artist figures depicted by Ingmar Bergman in his films of the past decade we are faced with an almost indecent sense of direct communication with a creator who has stripped himself morally and emotionally naked.

Bergman's progress from naturalistic dramas like *Port of Call* in 1948 to the modernist complexity of *Persona* (1966) was not by any means a steady and consistent one. His work has an amazing richness and diversity, and the artist theme with which we are concerned here is only one of the many he has explored in depth during almost thirty years of film-making. His work in the late 1950s, for instance, offers examples of the kind of 'contamination' of reality which so interests Alain Robbe-Grillet. Orson Welles in *Citizen Kane* and Alf Sjöberg in his adaptation of Strindberg's *Miss Julie* (1951) had pioneered the device of allowing the older narrator to appear in the same image as the scenes of his or her earlier days. In *Wild Strawberries* (1957) Bergman used this idea extensively, and the particular quality of the effect he sought is well captured by the narrator's words in the published script: 'I don't know how it happened, but the day's clear reality flowed into dreamlike images. I don't even know if it was a dream, or memories which arose with the force of real events. I do not know how it began either, but I think it was when I heard the playing of a piano.' This is no mere pastiche of Proust, for new tensions are created by the aged narrator's appearance in this 'twilight world of memories and dreams which are highly personal' and by the encounters he experiences there, for, as he discovers, 'one cannot easily converse with one's memories'.

Bergman himself did not develop further the particular stylistic patterns of *Wild Strawberries* and its final note of serene acceptance is foreign to his later work. A film which anticipates more of the 1960s' anguish is *The Face* (known in the USA as *The Magician*), made in 1958 when the director was forty. The film is set in 1846 and opens with a motley band of travellers – Vogler's Magnetic Health Theatre and a dying actor they have picked up in the forest – being compelled to halt their journey at the mansion of Consul Egerman, who confronts them with his friends, the police chief and the sceptical Royal Medical Counsellor Vergérus (Gunnar Björnstrand). The party of travellers, led by Albert Emmanuel Vogler (Max von Sydow) and including his assistant Aman, his old granny and his business manager Tubal, is naturally anxious. They are wanted by the police elsewhere and without the goodwill of the authorities they are helpless. The special performance arranged at the Egerman house and its aftermath develop into a battle between Vergérus and Vogler, rationality and magic, reason and illusion. Vogler is defeated and his trickery unmasked, but not before he has made a deep impression on Egerman's wife and terrified Vergérus. Finally, at the moment of his profoundest humiliation comes an unexpected reversal – a summons to give a special command performance before the King in Stockholm, which allows Vogler to make a triumphant departure. *The Face* uses all the devices and mechanics of the horror film – shots of gallows in the forest, unexpected apparitions and dead men coming back to life, a severed hand, an eyeball in an inkwell. The horror is personal in so far as Bergman is recreating terrors akin to those all children know and which he himself experienced in the nursery of the Lutheran parsonage in which he was brought up:

The Face: the landscape of horror

The nursery had an ordinary black blind, which when drawn brought everything alive and a little frightening, when the toys changed and became unfriendly or just unrecognizable. It was a different world without mother, a noiseless isolated lonely world. The blind did not exactly move and no shadows showed on it. The figures were there, nevertheless. No special little men or animals or heads or faces, but *something for which no words exist.*[3]

But the desire to horrify is secondary to the consideration of the phenomenon of illusion. Another of Bergman's early memories is of his grandmother's flat in Uppsala, where he used to play under the table. One day, when he was five, he heard the piano being played in the next flat, 'waltzes, nothing but waltzes and on the wall hung a large picture of Venice. As the sunlight moved across the picture, the water in the canal began to flow, the doves flew up from the square, gesticulating people were engaged in inaudible conversation. The bells were not those of Uppsala cathedral but came from the very picture itself, as did the piano music.' Here, in *The Face*, questions about what is real and what is false occur throughout. Granny is a witch but, as Tubal explains, her tricks aren't funny any more because they can't be explained. Vogler is an illusionist, using trickery, sleight of hand, his magic lantern and hypnotic powers to dazzle his audience, but to the authorities he has to declare himself a fraud. As Aman puts it, 'A game, nothing else. We use various kinds of apparatus, mirrors and projectors. It is very simple and quite harmless.'

But what is Vogler to himself? Here again the article written in 1956 from which quotations have already been taken gives a clear idea of Bergman's own identification with his magician: 'When I show a film I am guilty of deceit. I am using an apparatus which is constructed to take advantage of a certain human weakness, an apparatus with which I can sway my audience in a highly emotional manner . . . Thus I am either an imposter or, in the case where the audience is willing to be taken in, a conjurer. I perform conjuring tricks with conjuring apparatus so expensive and so wonderful that any performer in history would have given anything to own or make use of it.' Albert Emmanuel Vogler has an impressive façade – his silence, his beard and his hints of mysterious healing powers make him a Christ-like figure. But the beard is false and his muteness feigned, just as his assistant Aman is really his wife Manda. His powers may desert him, he is stripped naked and his illusions are unmasked, yet in his clash with the force of rationality he has fought as an equal. And just as Vergérus can disguise his terror by falling back on his social front, his position as a man of authority, so too can Vogler, when the summons to Stockholm gives him back his faith in himself.

The Face represents an early stage of Bergman's self-examination as an artist. The film is shaped as a comedy and Vogler's anguish is balanced by the healthy sexual appetite of the young Sara and the coachman Simson and by the pompous Tubal's defeat at the hands of the housekeeper. The choice of a conventional form and the very directness of the equation Bergman = Vogler weaken the film's impact, so that it becomes less a universal statement about art and illusion than an undistanced confession of the fear of artistic impotence. When, after the torment of his trilogy on the silence of God – *Through a Glass Darkly*, *Winter Light* (or *The Communicants*) and *The Silence* – Bergman returned to the theme of the artist in *Persona* (1966), the perspective had changed. In the autobiographical note, *The Snakeskin* (written for the presentation of the Erasmus Prize in 1965 and reprinted as a preface to the script of *Persona*), Bergman takes stock of his position. After twenty years of satisfying his basic hunger to communicate and thereby, almost incidentally, acquiring fame, money and success, he has begun to feel the need to establish the reason for his artistic activity. The new curiosity has brushed aside the fears expressed in a film like *The Face* and is driving him forward into new forms of expression:

I feel like a prisoner who has served a long sentence and suddenly tumbled out into the booming, howling, snorting world outside. I am seized by an intractable curiosity. I note, I observe, I have my eyes with me, everything is unreal, fantastic, frightening

The Face

or ridiculous. I capture a flying particle of dust, perhaps it's a film – and of what importance will that be: none whatsoever, but I *myself* find it interesting, so it's a film. [4]

The first product of this new involvement with the life around him and with his own artistic drives was *Persona*, Bergman's major contribution to modern cinema in the sense in which the term is used here.

Persona is a film which has been subjected to a wide range of interpretation. For Robin Wood the two women in the film are 'real', and the film describes 'the process whereby the protective façades people erect to defend themselves from reality are broken down'.[5] Peter Cowie, in contrast, sees the film in Jungian terms as 'the exchange between the outer mask (*persona*) and the soul-image' and in this light the two women are 'states of mind, the discordant halves of a single personality'.[6] This ambiguity as to the reality status of the two main figures is typical of the film's complexity and any attempt to offer a summary of the action is hazardous. *Persona* deals – ostensibly at least – with an actress, Elisabeth Vogler (played by Liv Ullmann), who, we are told, was playing in a production of *Electra* when she suddenly stopped speaking for a minute or so. Next day she refused to talk at all, and when the film opens she has maintained her silence for three months. The film focuses largely on her relationship with the nurse assigned to her, Alma (played by Bibi Andersson), whose incessant chatter is a perfect foil for her silence. The two women go off to an isolated piece of coastland together, grow very intimate, confront each other violently, and eventually their personalities seem to merge in some inexplicable way. In Bergman's original script it is clear that Alma finally goes back to her banal existence and that Elisabeth returns to the stage, but in the finished film the ending is an open one: the two women separate, but we have no means of knowing where they are each heading. Interpretation of the film in terms of psychological conflict or as an examination of erotic behaviour (it contains a description of an orgy and hints of lesbianism and even vampirism) in no way bring out its full richness and originality. It is better to follow Susan Sontag and assert that *Persona* 'takes a position beyond psychology – as it does, in an analogous sense, beyond eroticism'.[7] If, instead of adopting either of these approaches, we examine the film as a self-questioning about art and communication on the lines of the Erasmus Prize statement, many of the obscurities vanish and a coherent pattern of meaning can be discerned.

The fact that Elisabeth is a great artist is commented on several times in the film, as when Alma expresses her admiration for artists: 'I think art is tremendously important in life – particularly for people who are in some kind of difficulty.' There are many details which link *Persona* with *The Face*, which is unquestionably a Bergman self-portrait. The heroine's name is

Persona: the mask of silence broken

Vogler; her face at the beginning (when she is without her Electra make-up and has not yet blossomed forth as a woman under the influence of Alma's presence) is as naked as that of Albert Emmanuel Vogler when he removes his beard; equally she uses silence as a mask against the intrusion of the world. But where the earlier work simply toyed quite self-consciously with the mechanics of film style, *Persona* confronts the whole notion of film itself. It is pointless to talk, as some critics have done, about the naturalism of the early scenes without noting the totally theatrical claustrophobia of the hospital (no exteriors, no noise, no other nurses or patients) and without giving full weight to the framing of the action with sequences depicting, among other things, film running through a projector and breaking or burning. This particular device also occurs in the middle of the film at a moment of crisis, when we least expect it, and it is accompanied by snatches of an old comedy film, fragments of cartoons and odd and frightening flash images. There are also shots of a boy, who is perhaps Elisabeth's son, lying in bed in a morgue-like room and reaching out to touch the hugely enlarged, projected image of a face resembling hers. All these, which might seem to be alienating devices, are in fact used to involve us more deeply in the film, for they shift the action from

103

some naturalistic setting in an alien country 'out there' to the cinema screen and hence to our own consciousness. When the boy stretches out to touch his mother's portrait, it is towards us – the audience – that his hand comes.

Clearly, if *Persona* is to be seen as an examination of artistic communication it is largely a paradoxical one, since the artist figure in the film, Elisabeth Vogler, maintains an almost unbroken silence throughout. But the twin problems of language and silence are central to any discussion of contemporary culture. George Steiner, in his collection of essays on the subject, poses the key question for the artist: 'Are we passing out of an historical era of verbal primacy, out of the classic period of literate expression – into a phase of decayed language, of "post-linguistic" forms and, perhaps, of partial silence?'[8] Bergman himself, in the statement already referred to, offers the film-maker's answer when he deals explicitly with this aspect of modern experience and self-doubt. For him, from the beginning, cinema was 'a language that by-passed words', which offered the possibility of communicating with the world around him 'in a language that is literally spoken from soul to soul, in terms that avoid control by the intellect in a manner almost voluptuous'.[4] Bergman is not one of those film-makers he speaks of who 'live their films and would never abuse their gifts by materializing them in reality',[4] but in *Persona* he shows his understanding of an artist who rejects the theatre and lives out the drama directly instead of mediating it through the words of a Greek tragedy. Elisabeth Vogler has rejected the social role of the actress: 'In the second act she stopped speaking and looked around her in something like surprise. She wouldn't take a prompt or cue from the other actor, she just kept quiet for a minute.' *Persona* traces her progress after she turns away from acting to try to bridge the abyss between what she is for herself and what she is for others. Yet, as the doctor points out to her early in the film, the maintenance of silence is as much a role as was Electra: 'You can keep quiet. Then at least you're not lying. You can cut yourself off, close yourself in. Then you don't have to play a part, put on a face, make false gestures. Or so you think. But reality plays tricks on you. Your hiding place isn't watertight enough. Life starts leaking in everywhere. And you're forced to react. No one asks whether it's genuine or not, whether you're true or false. It's only in the theatre that's an important question. Hardly even there for that matter ... I think you should keep playing this part until you've lost interest in it. When you've played it to the end, you can drop it as you drop your other parts.'

At this point in his original script Bergman intended to place a break in continuity. In the film this is reserved for later, and instead we have a sudden transition to Elisabeth and Alma by the sea, at the doctor's seaside cottage. The roles of nurse and patient have vanished and the two women are dressed alike and look almost like sisters. Elisabeth is still not speaking and she is

Persona: the merging of personalities

unmoved by words on the radio or in her husband's letter. But she is hypersensitive to images: the picture of her son, the television shots of a Buddhist monk burning himself, and the photograph of a child being marched away by the Nazis in the Warsaw ghetto. Through her reaction to the latter we understand something of the horror at the violence of life which has driven her to silence. In this she is strongly contrasted with Alma, whose image of happiness is banal (marriage and children) and whose deepest experience is a personal one evoked purely verbally (the orgy on the beach described with astonishing erotic force by Bibi Andersson). Elisabeth – through her silence – shapes a relationship with Alma which, from her side, is strong but distanced, personal but not sexual. It is Alma who responds to this by falling in love, dreaming of Elisabeth coming to caress her and reacting with violence when she feels herself scorned. The involvement of the two women has grown so intense that Elisabeth can now communicate directly, speaking 'from soul to soul' and without words. By breaking off the film as the violence of their interaction is about to reach its peak, Bergman jolts us out of any comfortable identification with his characters and prepares us for the second half of the film in which the emotions are more powerful but presented in a totally non-naturalistic style.

These strange and haunting scenes which have troubled so many critics cannot be written off as mere imaginings. Alma's earlier dream of sexual union with Elisabeth was shot with diffused light, accompanied by the sound of ships' sirens and by gestures which were gentle, almost balletic. The later sequences are by contrast brutally direct and have an immediate emotional impact even if they disturb us intellectually. What they represent is not some sort of mystic fusing of identity or demonstration of supernatural psychological insight, but the communication of the experiences which have led Elisabeth to impose silence upon herself. Each is narrated in a different non-naturalistic style and together they constitute a presentation of the artist's spiritual anguish which is far more profound and touching than the direct confession of *The Face*. On the surface Alma, under the influence of the other's silence, re-enacts to Elisabeth the latter's own experience. But as, at this stage in the film, the setting and the characters are no longer realistically defined, the two women become merely figures through which Bergman communicates directly with us, the audience.

The pattern of these latter scenes is a logical one. The hollowness of Elisabeth's relationship with her husband – 'You mustn't touch me, it's shame, a dishonour, it's all counterfeit, a lie. Just leave me alone ...' – is verbalized by Alma as she fulfils Elisabeth's role by making love to the husband in Elisabeth's presence (the latter's face in huge close-up dominates the screen). Her relationship with her son is expressed in the sequence in which Alma tells of her horror – 'I find him disgusting with his thick mouth and ugly body and wet appealing eyes. I think he's disgusting and I'm afraid.' This is narrated twice in identical words and an identical sequence of shots, except that the first time the camera is directed at Elisabeth and the second time at Alma. The latter tries to avoid the power of Elisabeth, but the communication continues. In a room we have not seen before Alma, now back in her nurse's costume, utters a seemingly random jumble of phrases ending 'Words, many words . . . incomprehensible disgust . . . an insupportable pain' – Elisabeth's experience as an actress mouthing words that have become meaningless. An enigmatic scene in which Elisabeth seems to be sucking blood from Alma's arm may express her sense of being parasitic on life. Another pause and then the final confrontation: Alma, back now in the hospital, makes Elisabeth repeat the single word, 'nothing'. Elisabeth's progress to silence has now been communicated in full and her role is complete – she packs her bags and departs. We see again the shot of her as Electra, but this time immediately after the vacant face of a carved wooden ship's prow. Alma is left with her dream and the drab reality of a bus ride, and the film ends, as it began, with images of the boy reaching out to touch his mother's face, the film breaking and the lamp being extinguished.

In *Persona* the act of artistic communication is presented with its full force, but not romanticized: the ending of the film, when the performance is complete, is totally flat and empty. The film is not the most explicit of Bergman's portrayals of the artist's plight, but it is the most significant in that the personal anguish is transmuted into a universal vision.

Part Three: Fusions

9. Film Narrative in the 1960s

The work of men like Bresson, Antonioni and Bergman shows the way in which comparable modernist structures were reached by film-makers starting out from very different positions in the realist or literary cinema of the 1940s. By the mid-1960s the work of these older directors had been reinforced by a whole new group of film-makers, dominated by those born in the years 1921–23. This group includes the Frenchmen Alain Resnais, Alain Robbe-Grillet and Chris Marker, two Italians, Francesco Rosi and Pier Paolo Pasolini, the Hungarian Miklós Jancsó and the Polish-born but French-based Walerian Borowczyk.

Despite their differing nationalities these directors have enough in common for us to talk of a new generation of film-makers. They all came to feature film-making comparatively late, having made a reputation for themselves in some other capacity first, and had had some prior film experience before they turned to directing. Francesco Rosi, whose career was in many ways the most conventional, had been assistant and screenwriter on a number of significant features, including some of those directed by Visconti. Miklós Jancsó had worked as newsreel director and documentarist, and Alain Resnais had made some of the finest French short films of the 1950s, including *Nuit et Brouillard* (*Night and Fog*) in 1955. All these three made feature debuts in the late 1950s, Rosi with *La sfida* and *I magliari*, Jancsó with *The Bells Have Gone to Rome* and Resnais with *Hiroshima Mon Amour*, though only the latter is an authentically modern work. Chris Marker too, though he began as a writer (poet, novelist and critic), made a number of documentaries based on his travels in the 1950s, while Walerian Borowczyk, who trained as a graphic artist, had by 1965 established himself as one of the most original talents ever to work in the field of film animation. Alain Robbe-Grillet and Pier Paolo Pasolini, both writers of international reputation, had experience of work as scriptwriters for other film-makers before going on to direct films from their own original screenplays in the early 1960s. To this group, which dominates a whole area of modern film-making, one might add two younger film-makers (both born in 1928): Marco Ferreri, who began his career with two features in Spain, and Agnès Varda, whose first work, *La Pointe Courte* in 1955, anticipates many aspects of the style later perfected by the film's editor, Alain Resnais.

All these film-makers are concerned with the evolution of a wholly personal style and their work has a remarkable homogeneity. Often there is a strong literary bias, natural in the case of such writers turned directors as Pasolini or Robbe-Grillet, but to be found too in all Resnais's features (which have been made in collaboration with distinguished novelists) and in the films of Borowczyk, Marker and Varda, who write their own scripts. To balance this concern with literary values there is a direct response on the film-maker's part to the world around him. Rosi's roots are in neo-realism and both Resnais and Jancsó were originally documentarists. The directors of this group use the cinema to report on their travels (Marker), to re-interpret recent political events (Rosi), to confront contemporary myths (Resnais in *La Guerre est finie*) or offer a series of examinations of national history (Jancsó's work since *The Round-Up*). In contrast to the younger Godard generation, whose work overlaps with theirs in time, the film-makers of this group make films which exist on a single level of reality and within just one set of conventions. There is little of the toying with fragmentation and alienation techniques so common with younger film-makers. In a totally individual and carefully worked out style they each offer re-interpretations of conventional narrative and of such themes as history, myth and fairytale. Eschewing naturalism, they stylize the performances of their actors and aim at new fusions of past and present, real and imaginary.

In the area of the non-fiction film a fine example of the fusion of literary style and contemporaneity is furnished by the work of Chris Marker in such documentaries as *Lettre de Sibérie, Description d'un Combat* and *Cuba Si*. In the fiction film, the boundaries between which they work may be defined as, at one extreme, Francesco Rosi's studies of recent Italian history and, at the other, the purely literary approach favoured by the ever-increasing number of

109

Chris Marker's *Le Joli Mai*

novelists attracted to the cinema and typified by Marguerite Duras and Susan Sontag. Rosi has said that he makes films in order to participate in the development of the society in which he lives, and this aspiration is the motivating force behind such reconstructions of Italian history as *Salvatore Giuliano* (1962) and *Il caso Mattei* (1972). Both these films deal, not with political theses, but with political enigmas observed, ten years on, in all their complexity and contemporaneity (and hence in all their ambiguity). Rosi customarily spends many months on firsthand research and uses real locations – Montelepre for *Salvatore Giuliano* and the site of the actual air crash in *Il caso Mattei*. Yet the resulting films, though authentically documented, are by no means documentaries in the conventional sense. They are vigorously paced and handled with journalistic panache, so as to present a vivid portrait of men of action seen within the social context in which they functioned.

Rosi was born in Naples and a concern with the problems of Southern Italy is to be found in much of his best work. Both *Salvatore Giuliano* and *Il caso Mattei* deal with underdevelopment, the one at home in Sicily, the other in the oil-producing states of the Middle East. While in no way blurring the issues or disguising the gulf between rich and poor, Rosi shows the lives of both bandit and industrialist to be an inextricable tangle of conflicting involvements and motivations. The complex formal structures Rosi chooses reflect this sense of ambiguity – in *Salvatore Giuliano*, for example, he starts with the body of the dead bandit in July 1950 and then moves to and fro through the preceding five years of Italian history to probe and partially explain this death. In both films an historical character emerges in a new light – the legendary bandit demystified and seen as a semi-anonymous figure in a white coat manipulated by political forces he does not understand, and the remote industrialist given an added human dimension thanks to Gian Maria Volonté's outstanding performance. Blending the real and the reconstructed, analysis and myth, truth and supposition, Rosi has succeeded – in *Salvatore Giuliano* and *Il caso Mattei* – in posing fundamental questions about the structure of contemporary Italian society.

At the opposite pole to Rosi's immensely vigorous and extrovert directorial style is the literary cinema practised by Marguerite Duras and Susan Sontag. Duras had long been connected with the cinema before she turned to directing. Four of her novels have been filmed (by directors as diverse as René Clément and Peter Brooks, Jules Dassin and Tony Richardson) and she herself scripted Resnais's *Hiroshima Mon Amour* and Henri Colpi's *Une Aussi Longue Absence* before working closely with Paul Seban on the screen version of her play *La Musica* in 1967. Sontag is the author of two novels, *The Benefactor* and *Death Kit*, but is perhaps best known as a critic of contemporary culture in her essays, collected as *Against Interpretation* and

Ciphers: Marguerite Duras's *Détruire Dit-Elle*

Styles of Radical Will. Both women made a film début in 1969 and have since continued to work in the cinema, Duras as director of *Détruire Dit-Elle* (1969), *Jaune le Soleil* (1971), *Nathalie Granger* (1972), *La Femme du Gange* (1973) and *India Song* (1975) and Sontag with *Duet for Cannibals* (1969) and *Brother Carl* (1970). A confrontation of their first films opens up interesting perspectives on the literary extremes of modern cinema.

Détruire Dit-Elle exists, by intention at least, on several levels. To begin with it is a literary film in what is now an accepted mode: in an unspecified time and place a handful of semi-anonymous characters meet to interact and exude anguish. The film's impact derives largely from its Pinteresque dialogue, full of studied repetitions and non-sequiturs. Duras indeed spent six weeks rehearsing the actors in the delivery of their lines, compared with a mere two in actual shooting. The similarities with Resnais's films are obvious: a unified acting style reminiscent of *Muriel,* a hotel setting in the manner of *Marienbad,* and lines about marital happiness which echo Duras's own script for *Hiroshima Mon Amour.* The characters seem at times to be the products of each other's imaginings: they speak each other's lines, describe each other's feelings and prompt each other's responses. Yet for Marguerite Duras the

113

Literary cinema: Susan Sontag's *Duet for Cannibals*

meaning of the work lies elsewhere; she sees it as a political work, so that the easily missed allusions to the slogans of May 1968 ('Nous sommes tous des juifs allemands' or 'La lutte continue') are for her crucial to the film. The difficulty with an interpretation of the film in political terms is that the basic pattern becomes too simplistic and the characters, as abstract ciphers, fail to engage us emotionally. *Détruire Dit-Elle* states a thesis, instead of realizing it fully through the audio-visual resources of the cinema.

Duet for Cannibals, Susan Sontag's first film, is an equally literary work and also a typical product of the cinema's present internationalism: a Swedish-language film made by an American director and featuring an Italian actress. Ostensibly about politics, it is in essence a study of personal relationships and thus provides a neat antithesis to Duras's film. The central figure –the political exile Bauer – was originally conceived as a psychiatrist, and the film concentrates on the themes of authority and humiliation, cruelty and collusion. A young student and his fiancée are caught up in the fantasy world of Bauer and his Italian-born wife Francesca, who act out a complicated series of games based on the notion of dominance, exorcizing their own madness and paranoia and constantly interchanging roles. The younger pair are unable to tear themselves away from their complicity in the Bauers' fantasies until both husband and wife have successfully acted out a death fantasy. Yet even then as they drive off, the ominous faces of the 'dead' couple still watch from the window.

Ultimately these two films call into question the whole notion of film as a director's medium. The kind of literary cinema they represent creates totally personal works – both directors make a film exactly as they would write a novel – but the result is an introspective exercise, not a spectacle designed to communicate with an audience (which, for all their modernity, both *Last Year at Marienbad* and *Persona* are). These films are deliberately de-dramatized to the extent that the dominance of the central figure is simply stated, not realized in emotional or dramatic terms. There is a gap between what the film represents for its maker and what is actually conveyed to the audience, a gap which the presence of a director should fill. The visual flatness of both films is emphasized by their intended Bressonian austerity. Such literary film-making is fascinating but strictly limited, for it lacks the unmistakable if indefinable touch of pure *mise en scène* which a true director like Resnais or Jancsó imparts to all his films.

Of wider interest than the film work of either Sontag or Duras are the films of a third woman director, Agnès Varda. In five features made between 1955 and 1969 she explored virtually the whole range of styles and approaches which preoccupy this generation of film-makers. A literary concern is there from the start, for she made her first film, *La Pointe Courte*, as a kind of film equivalent to William Faulkner's *The Wild Palms*. The film demonstrated the effectiveness of juxtaposing lovers conceived in very literary terms with an apparently unrelated, realistically observed setting (in this case a very ordinary fishing village), and opened the way for Alain Resnais's work. Varda's second feature, *Cléo de Cinq à Sept*, made seven years later in 1962, revealed a characteristic obsession with time, in this case equating real time with film time, so that we experience the crucial two hours of the heroine's life in an actual ninety minutes of viewing. Varda's best known film is *Le Bonheur* (1965), in which the characters are mere ciphers whose behaviour is submitted to the requirements of a highly structured plot. The abstraction with which the director handles the central philosophic notion of happiness – ignoring all consideration of psychology, sociology and morality – is as startling as the manner in which Jancsó treats historical forces in his Hungarian films. In *Les Créatures* (1966), too, the characters are mere puppets in the film-maker's hands, as Varda explores the idea of depicting 'real' characters in conflict with the phantoms of their own imagination, somewhat in the manner of Alain Robbe-Grillet.

Varda's fifth film, *Lions Love*, which she made independently in Hollywood in 1969, shows a concern with direct cinematic allusion and with spontaneity much more characteristic of the younger Godardian generation than of

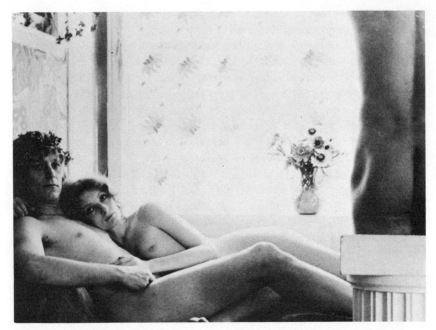

Agnès Varda's *Lions Love*

Pasolini or Borowczyk. Like many of Jean-Luc Godard's films, *Lions Love* is a collage, in this case built up of four distinct themes. First there is the central trio – Viva, Jerome and James – living together in an experimental *ménage-à-trois* and acting their lives, not simply living them. The manner in which Varda fuses the semi-improvised texture of their dialogue into the pre-scripted framework of her film is masterly. Interwoven into their story is that of a New York film-maker (played by the director Shirley Clarke) who comes to Hollywood to make a film and meets with failure. Her suicide attempt is set against the shooting of Andy Warhol and the television version of the assassination of Robert Kennedy (Varda bought the eleven-hour CBS tape of this and set her film in the first week of June 1968) and, as a unifying background to the whole film, there is Varda's own documentary on Hollywood, a city of the past which paradoxically lives only in the present.

Though on the surface a chaotic movie, *Lions Love* was strictly organized and indeed Viva, used to Warhol's methods, found it positively Hollywoodian. In fact it is far freer in its narrative structure than any of Varda's other features and recovers some of the spontaneity evident in the early short *Opéra Mouffe* (made in 1958). Like that film *Lions Love* builds up

116

a picture of a whole milieu in a loose, thematic way which gives Varda a chance to break down the narrative by including fantasy passages, amusing inventories of places and emotions, reportage and a few chastely posed nude shots. The whole film is constructed around a typical Varda juxtaposition of reality and dream. It begins with a play excerpt – *The Beard* in a theatrical production – and ends with the same passage parodied by Viva and the boys. The true and the false are constantly intermingled: Hollywood is defined as a place you always seem to be getting to but never reach, Viva lives in a totally artificial environment (even some of the trees in the garden are fakes), and the Kennedy assassination is contrasted on television with the 1937 Frank Capra movie, *Lost Horizon.* The most striking proof of Varda's intention is the way she includes in her film the (real) scene of Shirley Clarke breaking down because she cannot play her part adequately, but throughout the actors are constantly reminding us that we are watching a film, and we also see Varda directing and hear the technicians talking.

If Varda's career is thus in many ways an exemplary one and shows how the modernist concerns of this generation merge with those of the next, it is the eclectic Marco Ferreri, who later went on to make the exuberant *La Grande Bouffe* (*Blow Out*), who offers the best anthology of the themes and obsessions of this filmic modernism. Indeed *Dillinger e morto* (*Dillinger is Dead*), which he made in 1968, contains so many characteristic ideas that it seems at times almost like a modernist parody. The opening sequence, for example, which equates modern man in his social role with a man in a mask moving through an atmosphere of poison gas, is an explicit statement of the meaning conveyed by the yellow smoke at the beginning of Antonioni's *Deserto rosso.* Like the latter film, *Dillinger e morto* is a work which uses colour – particularly red – in place of words to convey its meaning. The hero (played by Michel Piccoli) is defined as a solitary consumer, watching the television set that pours a meaningless flood of images into his room and endlessly preparing and eating food. The relationship set up between his methodical preparation of his evening meal and his cleaning of an old revolver he has found in a cupboard (wrapped up in newspapers reporting the death of the one time public enemy John Dillinger) is one of the most striking of the film's many bizarre touches.

In *Dillinger e morto* all the hero's deeper urges are thwarted. He tries to preserve his world by recording it on film and tape, but the images and sounds he captures are fragmentary and meaningless, like the Algerian footage shot by Bernard in Alain Resnais's *Muriel.* Equally his attempts to enter into a relationship with the images are frustrated, like those of the soldier in Godard's *Les Carabiniers.* The character's sexuality too is deadened – he has to smear the maid with honey before he sleeps with her and he approaches his

117

Dillinger e morto

wife only with a toy snake. The violence has great overtones of parody – as when he paints the gun red with polka dots – and turned inward (as when he mimes suicide) – a tone very much akin to the ending of Godard's *Pierrot le fou*. If the notion of the mask and the ambiguous relationship of real character and projected image call to mind the Bergman of *Persona*, the meticulousness of his behaviour hints at the underlying violence, as in Jean-Pierre Melville's *Le Samourai*, while the refusal of psychology or explanation is as great as that in Varda's *Le Bonheur*. The character seems trapped, but this is the evening of his release, when he beds the maid, shoots his wife and breaks with his ordered existence. So the end of the film shifts from reality to myth, to an orange sunset and those cliché symbols of escape, the sailing boat and the beautiful young girl representing (as in Fellini's *La dolce vita*) essential innocence. Ultimately the sheer abundance of echoes and parallels linking *Dillinger e morto* to other (and possibly greater) films tends to work against the film's impact. But it does evolve its own pattern of progress from observed life to imagined myth, from temporality to timelessness, and so reminds us that one fundamental quality of modern cinema is the new relationships set up between the film and the reality it purports to represent.

118

10. Alain Resnais: The Simultaneous Experience

Any consideration of modern cinema must confront the notion of time, for in some shape or other temporality and simultaneity underlie the basic preoccupations of modernism. This is an area of art in which the cinema is uniquely well-equipped to play a part, and it is precisely because it excels in the representation of new temporal concerns that it is possible for us to see the cinema, as the art historian John Berger does, as '*the* art form of the first half of our century'.[1] Similarly, Arnold Hauser is surely correct when he asserts that the time experience of the present age consists above all in 'an awareness of the moment in which we find ourselves'. For the social historian, everything that is topical, contemporary, or bound together with the present moment is of particular value and significance to us, so that 'the mere fact of simultaneity acquires new meaning' and our intellectual world is 'imbued with the atmosphere of the immediate present'.[2]

The traditional language of art bases its conventions on concepts such as logic, narrative and perspective, and draws much of its power from the observation of external facts. As such, it cannot cope adequately with the inner experience of simultaneity. While our factual, external logic tells us that an object cannot be in more than one place at one time, our emotional response is more complex, and drives us to assert that we do indeed visualize objects existing in different places simultaneously and experience varying, even contradictory, states and conditions at one and the same time. The new technologies of the twentieth century have in common that they enhance this sense of the interconnection of opposites and the annihilation of the limitation of time and space. Television offers obvious, everyday examples of this. A dozen people offered the television director's choice of images from half a dozen camera sources each showing the same event from a different angle would create such radically different versions of the event that it would no longer be possible to talk of the event as having an objective existence. The television viewer sitting at home watching live happenings in another part of the world is almost literally in two places at once, if the images on the screen have sufficient power to absorb his attention. In a similar way, film can confront the experience of simultaneity in a direct and natural manner.

Most of the possibilities of what Hauser called 'the thoroughly subjective and apparently irregular character'[3] of filmic time are of course quite lost in the average film, which does no more than try to capture some equivalent of the time scheme of the conventional novel or play. But the French cinema of the mid-1960s does offer numerous examples of a more experimental approach. The ways in which past, present and future may be dissolved into a simultaneous experience become very clear if we look at three 'futuristic' films made in France at this time: Chris Marker's *La Jetée* (1964), Jean-Luc Godard's *Alphaville* (1965) and Alain Resnais's *Je t'aime, je t'aime* (1968). The cultural climate in which all three film-makers have come to maturity is one which fosters experiment and an eclectic approach to film and contemporary culture. It allows them, for instance, to reveal quite unselfconsciously a serious interest in comic strips, which in England would then have been regarded as an intellectual aberration.

In the case of Marker, Godard and Resnais there is, however, none of the direct allusion to comics which one finds in films like Alain Jessua's *Jeu de Massacre* (1967) and Roger Vadim's *Barbarella* (1968) or in the paintings of Roy Lichtenstein. The interest stems rather from an overriding interest in the possibility of shaping in new ways the cinematic images and sounds with which these directors are dealing. In this context, the strip cartoon is as natural an analogy as painting or literature, but the influence, such as it is, remains a subterranean one, though the authors offer us a few signposts (the names of Lemmy Caution's three failed predecessors in *Alphaville*, for example, are Dick Tracy, Flash Gordon and Henri Dickson). Resnais's career as a maker of art films prior to *Hiroshima Mon Amour* is very illuminating in this connection, particularly his short film based on Picasso's *Guernica*. This painting of 1937 sums up, as Sigfried Giedion points out, 'the entire experience of three decades', embodying 'the principle of simultaneity, the penetration of inner and outer space, the working of curved planes and different textures'.[4] At the same time Picasso is using the film and cartoon

Time and memory: Chris Marker's *La Jetée*

methods noted by Wylie Sypher:[5] close-up and cinematic perspective, black and white imagery and deliberate distortion and exaggeration. It is perhaps because the painting fuses in this way three of Resnais's major preoccupations of the 1950s – the worlds of painting, film and the comic strip – that the translation into filmic terms was so successful.

The circularity of plot in all three of the futuristic films with which we are concerned here is particularly clear in Chris Marker's *La Jetée*, which begins and ends on the main pier at Orly airport, 'a few years before the outbreak of the Third World War'. The nameless hero is (like Charles Foster Kane, oddly enough) a man haunted by an image of childhood, but in his case the image is not one of life (the sledge and snow of Kane's lost childhood paradise) but one of death: a man's body falling and the frightened face of a woman. It is because of the strength of this memory that the man is used by scientists concerned with the survival of the human race after the holocaust as a guinea pig in their experiments in sending a man through time. Marker shows little interest in what might seem an important element in his subject – the mechanics of time travel – and the scientific logic of the film is hardly

121

convincing. What concerns the film-maker is rather the mechanics of film as applied to the story of a man wandering in time. The film's closest analogies therefore are not with *Things to Come* or *2001: A Space Odyssey*, but with a work like Resnais's *Hiroshima Mon Amour*: it is a love story of nameless individuals existing outside time against a background of war and horror that fuses past and present into one flow.

Marker's total novelty lies in his use of stills to tell this story. The device proves totally apposite, providing the necessary breaking of the naturalistic illusion most economically, and conveying beautifully the sense of images oozing into the man's consciousness from 'the museum of his memory'. The relationship of man and woman reaches its peak in a seemingly endless series of slow dissolves of the woman lying sleeping, which culminates in the truly magical moment when she opens her eyes (the film's only fragment of natural movement). The use elsewhere of frozen images, combined with an inventive soundtrack which eschews dialogue in favour of a detached narration supplemented by whisperings, heartbeats and a music track of particular subtlety, succeeds in conveying the novel time experience which is the core of the film: two people who are 'without memories or projects. Their time simply builds itself around them, with, as its only landmarks, the taste of the moment they are living and the signs on the walls.'

Like Marker, Jean-Luc Godard in *Alphaville* shows very little interest in the specifically science-fiction aspect of his subject. Indeed it is crucial for the meaning of the film that while the subject is nominally futuristic, the shooting was done in present-day Paris and the hero is a figure from the pulp fiction of twenty years ago, Lemmy Caution. This blending of three time levels allows Godard great freedom, and he can solve the problem of interplanetary travel, for instance, with a laconic assurance: he simply begins and ends with Lemmy (played by Eddie Constantine) driving his white Ford Galaxie 'across inter-sidereal space'. Whereas *La Jetée* often echoes and develops themes from *Hiroshima Mon Amour*, *Alphaville* is much nearer to *Last Year at Marienbad*. There is at least one direct parodistic reference, when, at the hotel inhabited by Lemmy's predecessor Henri Dickson, someone reads from a novel about the Red Star Hotel: '... in no way can it be compared to our splendid ... passages, all glittering ... with luxury and light. It is merely a huge, tall, narrow labyrinth ...'

While this kind of allusion is admittedly on the same level as the film's joking references to *Le Jour se lève*, to Céline's novel *Voyage au Bout de la Nuit*, to the pop art environment and the comic strip heroes, there are affinities which lie deeper. Both films exemplify the surrealist concept of love which underlies much of the poetry of Paul Eluard (from whose *La Capitale*

Godard's *Alphaville*: Lemmy Caution and Natasha

de la Douleur Godard quotes extensively here and who, incidentally, provided the commentary which was so vital a component of Resnais's *Guernica*). In both *Alphaville* and *Marienbad* we find too the theme of a man coming to take a young woman away from an enigmatic father/guardian figure and a suffocating environment to which she clings; and some of Lemmy's words as he pursues his relentless quest along the endless corridors of the computer centre could have been uttered by the protagonist of Resnais's film: 'I had the impression that my life here was gradually ... becoming ... a shadow, a twilight memory.'

Another shared element is the nostalgic quality with which both directors imbue the images of their films. In *Alphaville* it seems most fitting that the villain should be called Nosferatu (after Murnau) and that his daughter Natasha (Anna Karina) should initially remind Lemmy of 'one of those old vampire films they used to show in the cinerama museums'. If Resnais looks back to Feuillade and the old serial days, Godard shows a close affinity with Cocteau in scenes like the questioning of Lemmy by the all-powerful computer Alpha-60, which could almost have come from *Orphée* or *Le Testament d'Orphée*: 'What is the privilege of the dead?' – 'To die no longer.' 'What transforms the night into the day?' – 'Poetry.' *Alphaville*, like *Last Year at Marienbad*, derives much of its ambiguity from the realization that, on the one hand, the most complicated of labyrinths is, as the Greeks asserted, a straight line, and on the other (to quote the lines of Eluard used by Godard in his film): 'One need only advance to live, to go / Straightforward towards all that you love.' Most important for our present consideration of the film is the role it assigns to time. Alphaville, the modern city of light and logic, is for Lemmy no more than Zeroville because it is a world of the eternal present and 'the present is terrifying because it is irreversible ... because it is shackled, fixed like steel'. The computer Alpha-60 proclaimed its view of time early in the film: 'No one has lived in the past and no one will live in the future. The present is the form of all life, and there are no means by which this can be avoided. Time is a circle which is endlessly revolving. The descending arc is the past and the rising arc is the future ...' This circularity is beautifully illustrated in *Alphaville* by the recurrent imagery of the city and its buildings, the symmetry of which is aesthetically most pleasing. But the fact that this order is achieved only by the destruction of human life and response as we know them is what Godard emphasizes.

When the past is negated and any hope for the future proscribed, the dictionary replaces the bible as bedside reading and even it can be changed daily as the authorities succeed in erasing for ever such words as 'robin redbreast', 'to weep', 'autumn light' and 'tenderness'. The result is a society in which the connections necessary to make life meaningful are inevitably eliminated along with the past. Isolated words and details can be comprehended, but the whole is now elusive. People may know the number one, but they cannot proceed to the equation one plus one equals two because they have forgotten the meaning of plus. In *Alphaville* as in *Je t'aime, je t'aime* there is a strong element of the fairytale. Lemmy's corpse-ridden progress through the city leads not to the logical outcome – disaster – but to total success: with fists and gun he defeats the logic of science, wins the beautiful Natasha and saves the world from destruction. But the ending is such an obvious evasion that it has a double-edged impact on a contemporary audience. This ambiguity is sharpened by the fact that the bleak Alphaville of fiction from which the hero makes his escape is all too recognizably the Paris of the present in which it was filmed, and the horrors of the city of the future are in retrospect no more frightening than the current reality described by Godard in *Bande à Part* or *Masculin-Féminin*.

Whereas both Marker and Godard deal, in other films, with subjects quite alien to the temporal concerns of the two works discussed here, all of Alain

Resnais's work can be seen – and indeed most usually has been seen – as part of a single meditation on time and memory. The constant mention of his name throughout this chapter shows clearly how relevant all his work is to any discussion of a concept like simultaneity: the past of Nevers temporarily swallowing up the Japanese reality in *Hiroshima Mon Amour*, this year and the last indissolubly linked in *Marienbad*, the remembered experience tested out against the present in *Muriel*, the anticipations and imaginings built into the immediate experience of the hero of *La Guerre est finie*, or the linking of Trotsky in exile and the fate of the pathetic Serge Alexandre in *Stavisky*. *Je t'aime, je t'aime*, his fifth feature and in many ways a summation of a decade of film-making experience, provides an equally striking example of the particular qualities of his handling of the problems of time and narrative. In it Resnais continued his customary practice of working closely with a scriptwriter – in this case the novelist Jacques Sternberg – and none of the scenes or dialogue in the film were composed by him. Yet it is easy to trace direct similarities with previous works: the relation of the lovers to their environment, the use of music, the importance of the editing, and so on. The film also has a wealth of semi-private allusion, hitherto equalled only in the director's most personal short *Toute la Mémoire du Monde*, being full of discreet appearances by his friends and former collaborators. More importantly for the present discussion, it also helps us clear away some of the clichés that have accumulated round his work and makes us re-examine the notions of time, past and memory in relation to his films.

Je t'aime, je t'aime is the story of a man, Claude Ridder (played by Claude Rich), chosen by a group of scientists to undergo an experimental journey through time. They project him one year back into his past, but instead of returning as planned after one minute, he finds himself condemned to relive, in disjointed, fragmentary form, the progress of his relationship with Catrine (Olga Georges-Picot) and the events leading up to his suicide attempt one month previously. Though it is, in this way, ostensibly about travel through time, *Je t'aime, je t'aime* – like *La Jetée* and *Alphaville* – is not really a science-fiction film. There is no interest in the actual mechanics of time travel: the very shape of the machine and the use of a mouse as Ridder's companion on his journeying both point to an ironic attitude to the whole mystique of science in our computer age. Ridder sets the tone better during his first trip to the research centre. On being told that something extraordinary may happen to him, he asks whether they intend to turn the Mercedes into a pumpkin. There is more than a touch of the fairytale, the 'once upon a time', in the opening of *Je t'aime, je t'aime*, recalling that ten years earlier Resnais told an interviewer that *Alice in Wonderland* would make a good film subject.

Je t'aime, je t'aime lacks totally the kind of ambition that characterizes

125

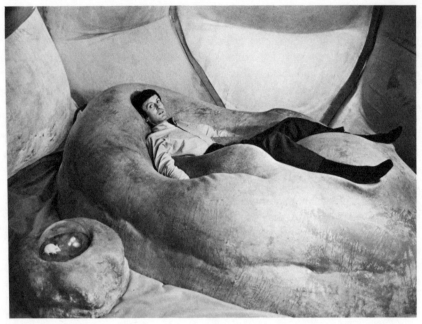

Time travel: *Je t'aime, je t'aime*

Stanley Kubrick's *2001*. The words used by one of the scientists to describe their project of sending a man back one year in time, but for one minute only, fit the film exactly: 'All that isn't very spectacular. We are still groping, but one day we shall go further. For that reason we need to begin with a short trip, with an experiment which may seem uninteresting.' Indeed the strangeness of this film, like that of *Muriel*, comes largely from its concern with banality, the science-fiction framework having been chosen to make this stand out more clearly. Resnais and Sternberg refuse to accept the conventionally dramatic moments of a life as the most significant ones. Normally in the cinema flashbacks are chosen to contain just those incidents which are most striking and are ordered so as to give these a vigorous emotional impact (*Le Jour se lève* is a classic instance of this approach). But in *Je t'aime, je t'aime* we often have scenes of trivial happenings, images of Ridder waiting for nothing in particular, meeting people whose impact on his life is negligible or experiencing situations that have no bearing on his pressing problems of the moment. The moments of crisis which do occur are all fragmented (and so deprived of their conventional dramatic impact) and left ambiguous. It seems improbable that Ridder in fact killed Catrine, but this would be impossible to

126

Je t'aime, je t'aime: varieties of time

prove on the evidence given in the film, and similarly Ridder's final fate is left in the balance: he is dying, but not dead, when the film ends. He himself is as ordinary as the life depicted in the film, a man without strong passions, drives and beliefs who allows himself to be trapped in a relationship with a woman who makes him unhappy and whom he cannot satisfy. Ridder is in fact far closer to the mediocre Alphonse of *Muriel* than to Diego, the active and enterprising hero of *La Guerre est finie.*

The role of time in Alain Resnais's work is often misinterpreted and *Je t'aime, je t'aime* is a film that almost invites one to apply to the director the label he abhors, that of '*cinéaste* of memory'. In fact this is to falsify the film totally. The time travel section of the film contains incidents and scenes spread over a sixteen-year period in Claude Ridder's life, and these are all relived in a non-chronological sequence within the framework of a single afternoon, that of 5 September 1967. Yet there is no sense of a past here, for, as Resnais himself has pointed out: 'Just because we get into someone's head and memory that doesn't mean we are in the past.' One fragment of time succeeds another – all part of a life already lived – but Ridder himself is never conscious of moving from one to the other. Each incident is relived

127

Je t'aime, je t'aime: the presence of the past

unselfconsciously, as it happened; that is to say, it is experienced as part of a continuous present. On occasion Resnais has gone so far as to claim that he has never used a genuine flashback in any of his films. Certainly in his films we never have objective statements of the way things actually happened. Always the scenes that appear to be simple flashbacks are very much a product of a character's conscious effort to recall his or her past. The Nevers episodes of *Hiroshima Mon Amour* are all part of the heroine's experience in Japan, and the apparent flashbacks of *Last Year at Marienbad* are hypothetical shots of what may have happened or of what the narrator claims happened. *Muriel*, though it deals with the impact of the past on the present, unfolds in a rigidly chronological manner, and the shots that have the appearance of flashbacks in *La Guerre est finie* are nearly all flashes forward in time, Diego's anticipations of what will happen. *Je t'aime, je t'aime* fits this pattern and is much more meaningful seen as the examination of a man's life than as any sort of real journey into the past.

The construction of *Je t'aime, je t'aime* – like that of any other Resnais film – rests on a pattern of contrasts. The totally chronological and unemotional opening is played against the disjointed memories of Ridder, the seriousness of the scientists against the fairytale atmosphere of their time machine, the banality of the images against the lyricism of Penderecki's music. Even Ridder's fate in his unhappy travels through time finds a parallel in the adventures of the mouse, which shares his experience (even intruding into one of his memories) and ultimately makes a successful return to the present. The emotional core of the film lies not in the contrast of past and present but in the evocation of Ridder's life, particularly his relationship with Catrine. Though the material extends over some sixteen years, there are certain privileged moments to which Ridder returns again and again. His work, which occupies so little of his vital energy, is largely ignored in this reconstruction of his life and most of the women he has known make no more than fleeting appearances.

Almost always the central concern is Catrine, so that even the scenes showing Ridder with Wiana Lust, a close and sympathetic friend for several years, are largely taken up with discussion of her. The moment to which the scientists send him back — four o'clock on 5 September 1966 — is a moment of no particular significance to him, having been chosen arbitrarily by the scientists. But perhaps under the influence of this moment of seaside holiday on a beach in the south of France (to which Ridder tries vainly to return when he realizes he is lost in his wanderings) many of the scenes depicted are of holidays with Catrine. The crucial and ever-recurring scenes, however, are those of his first meeting with the young girl, their early months together, her death in Glasgow seven and a half years later and his subsequent confession (or invention) of his complicity in her death to Wiana. These scenes have a total authenticity, but the film is punctuated too with images of Ridder's dreams or imaginings, particularly daydreams about women.

This story could have been told in the order in which the events occurred — as an experiment Resnais actually edited a chronological version of the material so as to form a coherent narrative without the framework of time travel. Not surprisingly he found that in this form the film lacked the emotional impact which now derives from the interplay of the events as they present themselves to Ridder. The arrangement of these events — which allows the film to present in a mere ninety minutes the density of Ridder's long entanglement with Catrine — is Resnais's principal contribution to the scripting of his film. Jacques Sternberg has explained that originally there were five hundred pages of script, half of which Resnais had immediately to discard. The arrangement of the remaining two hundred and fifty pages was carried out by Resnais in a very short time, virtually by instinct. As Sternberg says, 'He must have known why he wanted one scene to follow another, but I don't think he could have managed to explain this logically — his reasons would have been very private ones.'[6]

It is this patterning of events, by which sixteen years of a man's life are relived virtually simultaneously, that makes *Je t'aime, je t'aime* so personal and audacious a film. Like *Alphaville* it also shows the relevance of the surrealist heritage of the 1920s to the modern cinema. Whereas Godard drew much of his inspiration from the poetry of Paul Eluard, so too Resnais here fulfils his old dream of constructing a film according to the principles of automatic writing advocated by André Breton and illustrated (in Resnais's eyes) by the paintings of Max Ernst. The particular importance of surrealism to the notion of simultaneity we have been examining here becomes immediately apparent if we consider Breton's definition of the movement – in the First Surrealist manifesto – as being based on 'the belief in the superior reality of certain forms of association heretofore neglected, in the omnipotence of the dream, and in the disinterested play of thought.'[7] The striking explorations of the time potential of the film which we find in the works of film-makers like Godard, Marker and Resnais are thus not works existing in a void, or solely in the context of the director's own personal obsessions, but are a part of a continuing interaction of contemporary modernism with its own artistic past.

11. Alain Robbe-Grillet: The Reality of Imagination

For Alain Robbe-Grillet, who was already the author of four remarkable and controversial novels before he turned to the cinema in 1961, novel writing and film-making are two separate and complementary occupations. The one is carried on in privacy and in solitude, the other in the full glare of publicity, with a group of collaborators. The novelist struggles to build a world out of abstract symbols – words – while the film-maker, by contrast, strives to sever the photographic image's too close link with reality and so create an autonomous work. Because of this distinction, Robbe-Grillet has found no difficulty in continuing his literary activity alongside his film work, publishing two further novels, *La Maison de Rendez-Vous* (*The House of Assignation*) in 1965 and *Projet pour une Révolution à New York* (*Project for a Revolution in New York*) in 1970. It would be wrong therefore to read into his progress as a novelist from *Les Gommes* in 1953 onwards a move towards the cinema as a more natural or congenial form of expression. Nevertheless his early novels – *Le Voyeur* (*The Voyeur*, 1955), *La Jalousie* (*Jealousy*, 1956) and *Dans le Labyrinthe* (*In the Labyrinth*, 1959) – together with the collection of essays published under the title *Pour un Nouveau Roman* (*Towards a New Novel*) do make his basic preoccupations clear and offer a useful introduction to his films.

In his critical writing Robbe-Grillet is anxious to relate his work to literary tradition. He claims to be a realist, but denies that for contemporary man objects and settings can have the solidity they acquire in a Balzacian novel. While offering thorough and meticulously detailed descriptions, he refuses to give objects any meaning which is not conveyed in terms of colour, dimension, angle, etc. The world of Robbe-Grillet is not humanized, but we are aware of the fact that it is seen through human eyes, even if the narrator is never explicitly mentioned. Since the world becomes in this way shaped by a man's thoughts and distorted by his passions, the comforting boundaries between fact and fiction vanish. As in *Les Gommes*, where a character whom we know to be lying has to tell his invented account of events a number of times, so that gradually this fiction has 'assumed enough weight in his mind to dictate the right answers to him automatically; it contrives of its own account to secrete its own details and hesitations – just as reality would in such circumstances'.[1] In Robbe-Grillet's work the relationship of art and reality is redefined, and he devotes a whole essay to denouncing as empty formulae and outdated notions the conventions of the nineteenth-century novel: character ('a mummy, but still enthroned in the place of honour'), story ('to tell a story well is to make what you write resemble the pre-fabricated synopses people are used to'), commitment (for the artist, art must be 'the most important thing in the world'), and the critical distinction between form and content ('the work of art contains nothing, in the strictest sense of the word').[2]

Robbe-Grillet's approach has important implications for the cinema. In an early essay of 1956 he analyses the contrast between film and novel in terms of their ability to present objects. In a novel, a vacant chair has no existence of its own, it merely becomes a sign denoting absence or expectation. In a film, however, we actually see the chair, and it retains its reality, so that its meaning becomes just one of several attributes. Seven years later, when Robbe-Grillet again confronts the cinema after having worked on his first film, the perspective has changed and he gives two reasons why the cinema attracts novelists. First, the film, possessing a soundtrack as well as a set of images, allows its author to play on two senses at once, the ear and the eye. Secondly, the images themselves, enabling fictional situations to be acted out by real people in real surroundings, permit the artist to present 'with every appearance of unquestionable objectivity what, moreover, is only dream or memory, in a word, what is only imagination'.[3] Images in a film have the same essential ambiguity as passages of description in a novel because they make it possible for a film-maker to show an image which 'stops you believing in something at the same time as it affirms it'.[4] Just as description and the film image are used to undermine the claims of the real world, so time is presented in such a way as to destroy chronology. Robbe-Grillet says explicitly of *La Jalousie* that the story was constructed in such a way that any attempt to unravel a 'real' chronology was bound to result in contradictions, and the same is clearly true of all his films. The result is a new conception of temporality, demonstrated already in the opening pages of *Les Gommes*:

'Unfortunately time will soon no longer be master. Wrapped in their aura of doubt and error the day's events, however insignificant they may be, will in a few seconds begin their task, gradually encroaching upon their ideal order, cunningly introducing an occasional inversion, a discrepancy, a confusion, a warp in order to accomplish their work.'[5]

One role of time in Robbe-Grillet's novels and films is to show us the present unfolding, creating itself. This gives a world where, as the computer Alpha-60 affirms in Jean-Luc Godard's *Alphaville*, 'the present is the form of life, and there is no means by which this can be avoided'. Through the novels one finds a gradual abandoning of the normal variations of tenses, which serve to divide the story into past, present and future, the real (indicative) and the imagined (subjunctive), in favour of a narrative which uses the present tense exclusively. In his later novels it is this technical device which gives the sense of works unfolding as they proceed and creates the labyrinthine quality which is their most evident characteristic. One can say of Robbe-Grillet's work from *Les Gommes* to *Project pour une Révolution à New York*, from *L'Année Dernière à Marienbad* (*Last Year at Marienbad*) to *Glissements progressifs du plaisir* and *Le Jeu avec le Feu* what Jorge Luis Borges says of the work of his fictional Chinese writer, Ts'ui Pen, in the story *The Garden of Forking Paths*. Whereas 'in all fictional works each time a man is confronted with several alternatives, he chooses one and eliminates the others', here, on the contrary, 'he chooses – simultaneously – all of them. He *creates*, in this way, diverse futures, diverse times which themselves proliferate and fork.'[6] In literature the use of the linguistic device of the present tense narrative can be startling and at first sight disconcerting – one scholar alone managed to unravel Ts'ui Pen's labyrinth. Yet the limitation is only apparent, and in the cinema it takes on a new resonance for, as Robbe-Grillet never tires of telling his interviewers, the essence of the film image is that it is always in the present. If one ignores the temptations of trying to reconstruct a 'real' chronology and accepts the order of events on the screen as the only one that matters, then all of Robbe-Grillet's films, including *L'Année Dernière à Marienbad*, can be seen to have a simple and satisfying emotional shape.

The scripting of *L'Année Dernière à Marienbad*, which was directed in 1961 by Alain Resnais, reflects Robbe-Grillet's conception of a modern work of art as a questioning of reality rather than simply a reflection or imitation of it. The film is one of those rare works – like *Umberto D* or *Les Enfants du Paradis* – which grow out of a perfect balance of writer and director. It has often been analysed and found totally baffling, but this is simply because critics have tended to base their judgments on the cliché view of Resnais as the *cinéaste* of memory. In the context of Robbe-Grillet's work it is far more

Eternal present: *L'Année Dernière à Marienbad*

explicable, and the usual insoluble questions about time and place disappear, for there is no past or future in any of his films or novels, only an eternal present. As far as *Marienbad* is concerned, this love story 'that we are being told as if it were a thing of the past was in fact taking place under our very eyes, here and now'.[7] Equally the distinction between what is real and what is false is meaningless, for the film reflects an inner reality. Its chronology and logic are therefore those of the mind, not of clocks.

The stylistic effects that have troubled some critics and seemed to others a clue to the true meaning – the statuesque gestures, theatrical diction and remote baroque setting – are merely used as alienating devices. The core of the film lies elsewhere, as is shown by the fact that the makers at one time contemplated translating it into a story of tramps set in the *métro*. The visual style and intellectual coldness, which set the film apart from Robbe-Grillet's other films, come from Alain Resnais. In place of the white, over-exposed shots of the heroine ecstatically welcoming the narrator with open arms, Robbe-Grillet had prescribed in his script 'a realistic scene of rape in a rather melodramatic style'.[8] Similarly Delphine Seyrig is not the kind of heroine he had envisaged: 'I had imagined someone less intelligent, more carnal. I had thought of an actress like Kim Novak, if you like, who is much less expressive than Delphine Seyrig and who would have been a sort of incomprehensible fleshly statue.'[8]

The peculiar richness of *Marienbad* comes from its double authorship. Robbe-Grillet's own films lack the polish and visual sophistication of Alain Resnais's direction; they are more direct, more realistic and more blatantly erotic. Each of them has its own particular focal point: the cliché Orient with its mosques and mysterious women in *L'Immortelle*, the role of the author *vis-à-vis* his creations in *Trans-Europ-Express*, the labyrinth in *L'Homme qui ment*, the use of colour in *L'Eden et Après*, of objects in *Glissements progressifs du plaisir* and the house of assignation in *Le Jeu avec le Feu*. But all of them, like Robbe-Grillet's novels, are marked by scenes of sex and violence of a kind notably absent from *Marienbad*. The Oedipal undertones of *Les Gommes*, the unseen sex murder of *Le Voyeur* and the sexual jealousy of *La Jalousie* find their echo in the feigned rape sequences of *Trans-Europ-Express* and the erotic posing in *L'Immortelle*. In Robbe-Grillet's view what differentiates men from animals is that for them 'the sex act passes via their heads'.[9] When a man has a relationship with a woman 'he already begins to imagine her, make her conform, model her in his head'.[9] If the erotic material of *L'Immortelle* (*The Immortal One*, 1963), his first film as a director, seems stereotyped, it is because, as he sees it, 'this black underwear, these slit skirts, these chains, all these popular erotic images . . . are part of a collective erotic material'.[9] If the conception of Leila in the film is ambivalent and her attitudes

The director's double: Robbe-Grillet (*right*) in his own *Trans-Europ-Express*

contradictory this is because 'woman is at one and the same time an object, with all that that implies in the way of submission and slavery, and at the same time a sort of queen who rules over the world of men'.[9]

It is clear that Françoise Brion, who brought the abstract heroine of Robbe-Grillet's script to life, is meant to embody the cliché erotic woman of the narrator's sexual imaginings. But just as women are turned into sexual objects by passing through men's minds, so inanimate images and objects are brought to life in the same way. In *La Maison de Rendez-Vous*, for example, the narrator clearly reveals his obsessions: 'The leather whip in the window of a Parisian saddler, the bare breasts of a dressmaker's dummy, a half-clad figure on a poster, an advertisement for suspenders or for a perfume ... impose on me their insistent, provocative décor.'[10] Indeed, if one wanted a single image to stand as an example of Robbe-Grillet's stylistic approach, one could choose an erotic moment, such as the final nightclub scene in *Trans-Europ-Express*: a naked woman with her hands behind her back, draped in chains, motionless but revolving on a turntable to a soundtrack of erotic breathing. It is an image central to Robbe-Grillet's vision, summarized so well in an account of Raymond Roussel:

Everything is shown in movement, and yet immobilised in the very middle of this movement by the description that leaves all the gestures . . . in suspense, perpetuates the immanence of their end and deprives them of their meaning. Empty enigmas, time standing still, signs that refuse to be significant, gigantic enlargements of minute details, tales that turn in on themselves.[11]

The erotic elements of *Trans-Europ-Express*, Robbe-Grillet's second feature (1967), are encased in a complex narrative structure. The film is full of multiplied images: mirrors and reflections, photographs and postcards, parallels and doubles, similarities of names and so on. For example, the girl is called Eva and the nightclub Eve, all the whores in the brothel windows are the same girl, gangsters masquerade as policemen and a policeman is mistaken for a gangster, rendezvous leads to rendezvous and the password about the *abbé* Petitjean is endlessly repeated. In this connection the role played by Robbe-Grillet in the film calls for comment. At the very beginning we see three people – played by Alain Robbe-Grillet, his wife Catherine and Paul Louyet – board the Trans-Europ-Express and begin the task of fabricating a film script. This has led some critics to maintain that the director plays himself in the film, but this is simply not true. At best the author–director in the film is a double who bears a superficial resemblance to the author of *La Jalousie*. His name in the film is Jean, just as Catherine Robbe-Grillet plays a secretary called Lucette and Paul Louyet a producer, Marc. The director's name serves to link him closely with the leading character of the film (played by Jean-Louis Trintignant) whom he christens Elias but who refers to himself throughout as Jean. Hence, in place of a simple Hitchcockian appearance by the director, we have the typical Robbe-Grillet situation of the real author imagining a film director, Jean, who closely resembles him and who in turn imagines a character, Elias, who looks like Trintignant but calls himself Jean. To complicate things still further, Trintignant makes at least one appearance as himself and at the end is seen in a pose that has definite echoes of his previous role in Claude Lelouch's *Un Homme et une Femme*. All this should make us beware of the logical equation Robbe-Grillet = Robbe-Grillet, and it is far better to adopt the totally sceptical attitude of Gilles Jacob, who had the splendid idea that if this is really a film about dope peddling, then the guilty party is clearly that man with the false moustache who pretends to be a film director so that he can smuggle cocaine in his tape recorder . . .

There is no better example of Robbe-Grillet's idea of time than the plot 'imagined' by the fictional film director in *Trans-Europ-Express*. Here, as in the novels, we find a use of the present 'which is continually inventing itself as if it were at the mercy of the writing, which repeats itself, bisects itself, contradicts itself, without ever accumulating enough bulk to constitute a past'.[12] This latter aspect is particularly noticeable in that the inconsistencies in *Trans-Europ-Express* are resolved by the suggestion that scenes we have seen

137

Trans-Europ-Express

which do not fit should simply be removed from the film, either by cutting the images at a later stage or by erasing the sound (i.e., winding back the tape recorder). While this will clearly help the imaginary Jean to create a consistent film, in *Trans-Europ-Express* we see the 'false' scenes later discarded play as real a part as any other. The murder of Eva, for example, to which Elias is driven when she betrays him to the police by stealing a key from his pocket, constitutes the climax of the action. But her theft is logically impossible, since we have already seen Elias hand the key in question to an accomplice. For the authors in the film to say subsequently that they will scrap the first scene in no way resolves the complexities of our response to the murder.

Elsewhere in the film the authors show themselves to be as fallible as anyone else. They are unable to account for the actions of their characters on several occasions and sometimes confuse matters even more by their interventions, as when Lucette insists on a scene of Elias throwing away a parcel which he did not have with him in the first place. Robbe-Grillet could have said specifically of this film what he said of modern narratives in general, namely that 'it is not only that they don't aspire to any other reality than that involved in reading, or seeing, them, but also that they always seem to be challenging themselves, casting doubt on themselves all the time they are constructed. Space destroys time in them and time sabotages space. Description repudiates all continuity.'[12] In *Trans-Europ-Express* we find a story in the course of composition, groping and weaving its way along, frequently coming to a dead end or having to retrace its steps, and finally being scrapped by its 'authors', not because it is too absurd, but because it is too real. Reading a newspaper account of a crime identical with the one he has just imagined, the director, Jean, decides that the film cannot be made: 'You always have trouble when you use real stories.'

The method of construction also has clear similarities with the work of a composer like Pierre Boulez who, in a 1970 programme note on his own composition *Eclat/multiples*, wrote that 'the work is conceived as a succession of mirror images in which developments reflect each other or, so to speak, the multiple reflections of the original musical images interfere with each other and create divergent perspectives, such as Paul Klee imagined in certain of his paintings'.[13] Robbe-Grillet likewise begins with a statement of the constituent elements, the tone row as it were, out of which the film will be constructed. To take again the example of *Trans-Europ-Express*, the elements can all be derived from the three-part title and the opening scenes. *Transes* is the name of the detective story in which the hero hides his gun, and from this come all the gangster aspects presented in parody form in the film. *Europe* is the title of the nudie magazine flicked through by the film director and stolen by Elias. In the latter's hands it is transformed into a collection of sado-masochistic studies, thereby anticipating the erotic development of the film towards (simulated) rape and (real) murder. *Express* is both the French magazine (*L'Express*) in which Elias conceals his copy of *Europe* and the train itself, which provides a linking thread through the film as well as the setting for much of its action. This silent world of glass, mirrors and shiny metal takes on an unreal air and gradually assumes a quasi-symbolic meaning, as is shown by the intercutting of trains and railway lines in the scenes of Elias's sexual activity.

Another significant aspect of *Trans-Europ-Express* is the choice of Antwerp as the train's destination. In French this city is 'Anvers', which is phonetically identical with *envers* meaning 'the wrong side' (as in *à l'envers*, meaning upside down, topsyturvy). The notion of an *envers*, a distorted mirror image, occurs throughout the film as a basis of construction: the hero stays at the Hotel Miro; the journeys, characters and incidents are frequently repeated; and shots of scenes often turn out to be shots of mirrors reflecting the action. Through all Robbe-Grillet's work the situations multiply: four endings are tried out in *L'Année Dernière à Marienbad*, there are three car crashes in *L'Immortelle*, Elias has two games of rape and makes three journeys on the express, and so on. Gradually, too, the elements become distorted under the pressure of emotion, and one can no longer talk of mere repetition or coincidence. The whole second half of *L'Immortelle* is a contaminated version of the first: Leila is seen plotting with her husband and with the antique dealer, the visit to the mosque is replaced by a ghostlike appearance, and the erotic dance becomes an invitation to rape and murder. The pattern of *Trans-Europ-Express* is even more complex, for Elias moves from simulated rape sequences accompanied by the music of Verdi's *La Traviata*, which we find both sexy and funny, to a quite frightening murder to which the same music now seems a bitterly ironic counterpoint. But while the emotional impact of Elias's actions becomes more real, the plot itself becomes more and more illogical and unbelievable, full of inconsistencies and loose ends.

The basic contradictions out of which *Trans-Europ-Express* builds its powerful impact are reflected in the film's style. Robbe-Grillet uses the familiar conventions of film realism as the basis of his visual approach: location shooting at railway stations and in the cramped space of a real train compartment, non-actors (like himself), interiors shot with natural light, even if this means the whites are bleached out. Yet the musical accompaniment is derived from a Verdi opera, and the story which is told could hardly be more far-fetched. Elias constantly reminds us that we are watching a film (as when he comments that a waiter is merely a film actor pretending to be a waiter, or when he tells his story to the young Matthias adding, 'that's as far as we've got so far'). The authors too constantly intervene to call our attention to the fact that we are watching their story, but their control over and understanding of their characters is limited. The difference in levels of reality which should separate them from the alleged creatures of their imagination is missing: Elias returning to Paris turns up on their train going to Antwerp, and at the end they can read an account of their own plot in a newspaper they buy on Antwerp station.

Thus we follow for ninety minutes an action we know to be false and impossible, though its setting seems totally real. Since the world of the film is a *monde clos* of the imagination, the ending has to be auto-destructive: the lovers can leave the hotel of Marienbad only to enter a new labyrinth, the narrator of *L'Immortelle* can find only his own death, and the 'authors' of Elias and Eva destroy them by scrapping the story, only to find them there at the station, seemingly mocking them, at the end. The films of Robbe-Grillet can in fact end only where they begin, for, as the actress says at the very beginning of the play sequence of *L'Année Dernière à Marienbad*: 'This whole story is already over now. It came to an end – a few seconds . . . more — It has come to a close.'

12. Miklós Jancsó: Dialectic and Ritual

Of all the film-makers active through the 1960s and in the early 1970s, none has in his mature work followed a path more rigorous and certain than that of Miklós Jancsó. Yet Jancsó's début in the Hungarian cinema of the 1950s was inauspicious. Unlike Alain Resnais, whose documentary work retains its power and fascination twenty years later, Jancsó was a prolific maker of short films who was unable to find his own style until he made *My Way Home* in 1964. It was his next feature film, his fourth, *The Round-Up* (1965), that established him as a director of world class. Jancsó's earliest ambition was to become a stage director, and his first films seem to have been hampered by an uncertainty of choice between the rival claims of realism and formalism. On the one hand, as a member of the generation which was in its early twenties when the war ended, he was driven by a desire to confront the real problems of the people. Yet, as is shown by *The Confrontation* (his own lucid analysis of this age group's attempt to change the world), this impulse, though genuine, was confused and contradictory. As an artist too Jancsó was attracted less by socialist realism (though he admired such films as Mark Donskoi's Gorki trilogy and Jean Renoir's *La Grande Illusion*) than by the notion of allegory. His first feature film, *The Bells Have Gone to Rome* (1958), and a number of his documentaries attempt an allegorical expression of reality which is at odds with the basic realism of the film image.

141

The Round-Up

In the European cinema of the early 1960s Jancsó could find many other directors following, more successfully than he had so far been able, an analogous line of development, and he has spoken of being influenced by Ingmar Bergman, Andrzej Wajda and Jean-Luc Godard among others. But his admitted master was Michelangelo Antonioni, as is very clear from his second feature, *Cantata* (1962). Together with his inseparable scriptwriter Gyula Hernádi, Jancsó studied *La notte* over and over again, examining the style, the dramatic structure, the utilization of space, actors, movements, gestures, dialogues. The long take – what the French call the *plan séquence* – he learned from Antonioni, but he has used it not to depict, as the Italian director does, the anguish and alienation of affluent bourgeois society, but as a tool for revealing the class struggle in filmic terms. Jancsó's modernity as a film-maker lies in his rejection of the technique of cross-cutting, indeed of *montage* as a whole, in favour of a style which, as he says, shows more respect for the audience in that it allows the spectators to reflect on the action as it unfolds. Yet, though in this way he drew inspiration from a wide range of foreign artists, Jancsó is an authentic national film-maker. He found his own style fully only when he chose as subject for *The Round-Up* the problems of the Hungarian national character, using an historical setting as a means of procuring himself the necessary distance for a proper investigation of it.

This distance is perhaps the most immediately striking thing about *The Round-Up* for an outsider. The film is rooted in the history of 1860, and is intended as a real comment on the events it describes and on the aspects of Hungarian character which these lay bare. On the one hand is the legendary figure of Sándor Rózsa, a hero of the struggle for freedom, still worshipped by his followers. On the other is Gedeon Raday, the commissioner who fights the rebels in the name of the Austro-Hungarian empire. Raday's methods in the film – part mediaeval, part psychological – follow the pattern set out in contemporary records of his campaign. Such a fortress as the nameless prison in the film did indeed exist (at Szeged) and the key figure of the guerrilla Janos Gajdor is historical. But throughout the film Jancsó shows a total refusal of petty realistic detail. Names, references to antecedents, explanations of the action are either deferred or deleted altogether. The various visual elements are picked out and differentiated with all the clarity we expect in a Hollywood Western: the shackled peasants and their black-caped persecutors, the horsemen in their army uniforms, the white walls of the prison, and above all the emptiness of the plain itself. (In a different sense from the one originally intended, one can apply to Jancsó the words about Velasquez quoted at the beginning of Godard's *Pierrot le Fou*: he too is 'the painter of the evening, of the plains, of the silence'.)

The effect of this isolation of the iconographic elements is one of abstrac-

The mechanics of terror: *The Round-Up*

tion, which is reinforced by the perfection of the mechanics of the action by which Raday sets about his double task, first of ascertaining whether Sándor is among the prisoners assembled within the prison walls, and then of separating his supporters from the ordinary peasants among whom they are initially indistinguishable. Jancsó has said that even at this stage in his career his work was not rigidly pre-scripted: 'As a matter of fact we don't write the scenario, we only talk about it and record our conversation on tape. There is hardly any difference between the dialogues of *The Round-Up* and the dialogues we recorded when discussing the situations of the film.'[1] But the chain of betrayals and treachery which Raday sets under way is perfect and unbroken, and the whole *mise en scène* is extremely formal. The grouping of visual elements within the wide-screen frame is calculated to the last millimetre, and the coldness of the film emphasized by the way in which the relation of figure to landscape or the precise alignment of a rank of soldiers takes precedence over any identification with the psychology of oppressor or oppressed.

As a result of these formal tensions, we enter in *The Round-Up* a nightmare world, detached and remote from the everyday, where actions are charged with ambiguous significance. The first sequence, in which a man walks away

145

from the fortress only to be shot down by the soldiers, makes clear the first paradox: despite the seemingly limitless plain in which the prison is set like an island, there is no hope of escape. Yet throughout the film it is precisely on this hope of escape and survival that Raday plays. French critics have evoked the name of Kafka to describe the atmosphere of *The Round-Up*, and have compared the role played in the action by Sándor – ever present in the minds of his guerrillas despite his physical absence – to that of Godot in Samuel Beckett's play. This, rather than any attempt to draw direct parallels between *The Round-Up* and the Nazi concentration camps of our own century, is indeed the perspective in which Jancsó's work should be seen. The impact of the film is in no way lessened by this distancing from actuality: we experience fully the mechanics of an implacable terror and are witness to the manoeuvring of human beings like chess-men in a game whose rules we only dimly grasp.

Most of the elements out of which Jancsó was to develop his mature style over the next six years are to be found in *The Round-Up*. First of course, the reinterpretation of the Hungarian past:

Ever since I was a boy, I've been bedevilled by the problem of what Hungarians are really like. Here is this small nation in Europe, with its strange and contradictory history, with its senseless nostalgias and unrealistic dreams which, when I was a boy, exerted a mass effect ... A people who seldom waged a fight for a sensible purpose – although when they did, they did so with their heart and soul – and apathetically resigned themselves to making sacrifices during the two world wars. [1]

Visually the recurring symbol of this national concern is the Puszta, the Great Hungarian Plain which serves as setting for so many of Jancsó's films. Against this background the characters are manipulated like marionettes, typed as oppressors or oppressed, manoeuvred, aligned, choreographed. An increasingly fluent and mobile camera captures the balletic movement of these puppets, creating its own choreography to match that of the actors. But though one is tempted to see Jancsó's films in visual terms, it must not be forgotten that they are very much *sound* films. Though dialogue is sparse and seldom explicit, much of the meaning of the films is carried in the silence or song which accompanies the images.

Such a simple enumeration of constituent elements, though useful as a starting point, tends to ignore the striking development in the director's work up to *Red Psalm* – a development which has marked parallels with that of Alain Robbe-Grillet over the same period. The latter has moved from the rigidly pre-scripted *L'Immortelle* to the improvisation around a set of themes apparent in *L'Eden et Après*, a change typified by the manner in which women are depicted. Françoise Brion, caught continually in the same erotic pose, reveals the closed obsessional view of the narrator in *L'Immortelle*, whereas the nakedness and sensual movement of Catherine Jordan in *L'Eden et Après* is that of a genuine release from conventional restraints. In Jancsó's work can be seen a similar movement from the frozen rigidity of defeat in *The Round-Up* to the joyous sense of liberation in *Red Psalm*, pointing to a continual extension of the film-maker's power. In Jancsó's case there is, for almost every new film, the addition of a new technical resource which, exploited to the full, leads to a reinterpretation of the basic motifs. Again the change can be seen very clearly in the use made of the image of the naked women. In *The Round-Up* this is purely a symbol of oppression – the shock image of a girl forced to run naked between two lines of soldiers armed with canes. In *Red Psalm*, on the other hand, the nakedness of the peasant women is a sign of their freedom, a mark of tenderness and an assertion of faith in the new order of society.

Jancsó is by temperament a prolific film-maker who has recently evaded the constraints imposed by Hungary's small annual output of films by working abroad. If we ignore these 'foreign' films – the Franco-Hungarian *Sirocco* (1969), which starred Jacques Charrier and Marina Vlady, and the three Italian works of the early 1970s, *The Pacifist* (with Monica Vitti), *Technique and Rite* (a reinterpretation of the story of Attila), and *Rome Wants Another Caesar* (about the rise of Octavian) – we are still left with a core of essentially Hungarian films which constitute a major contribution to world cinema. *The Red and the White* (1967) adapted the style formed to capture the claustrophobic oppression of the prison in *The Round-Up* in quite new ways. To treat this subject – Hungarian involvement in the Russian Civil War of 1917 – and to capture the pulse of a conflict in which ruthless groups of men achieved supremacy and killed their opponents coldly only to be overcome in turn by a fresh wave of the enemy, Jancsó sought and obtained a new fluidity of camera movement. Also, in the brief scene where captured nurses are compelled to dance in costumes of the now vanished past, there is an anticipation of the role music and dance is to play in Jancsó's later work. In *Silence and Cry* (1968), a study of repression in the Hungary of Admiral Horthy in 1919, after the defeat of the first aspirations to revolution, the action is more confined. This is in fact a Kammerspiel film, like many of Bergman's later works, but without the psychological dimension. Here no explanations are offered as to why this unheroic family should shelter the Red deserter István, why the two women should be engaged on poisoning the husband of one of them, or indeed why the deserter's presence should be tacitly accepted by the otherwise ruthless police chief (are they brothers, or cousins?). To compensate for the restriction of action and explanation, Jancsó, working here for the first time with the young cameraman János Kende, used a freer lighting style and a zoom lens to penetrate among the actors in a way scrupulously avoided in the more distanced *The Round-Up*.

The Confrontation (1968) is set in 1947 (when Jancsó was twenty-six) and

Silence and Cry

examines the 'pure and naïve faith in the future' which characterized the young people of the time as they attempted to build a better world. The film's basic development has the characteristic Jancsó fluidity, as it describes what happens when a group of students from a people's college set out to confront the staff and pupils of a nearby Catholic school. In the process they discover their identity with and separation from the police and the party, try out violent and non-violent tactics, elect and depose successive leaders. Jancsó's method of handling the complexities of popular democratic organization and the ambiguous relationship of students and authorities is strikingly original. *The Confrontation* is both his first work in colour and the first in which song and dance play a decisive role. Though in no way smoothing over the contradictions (the ending is an open one in which Jancsó avoids passing even implicit judgment on his characters), *The Confrontation* is basically a simple film, and colour seems to have brought Jancsó back to a more realistic depiction of the world.

Agnus Dei (1970), on the other hand, is his most impenetrable film. It marks Jancsó's return to the life of the plains and the period before he himself

Agnus Dei

was born (the action takes place in 1919). A series of clashes between revolutionary units and the followers of a fanatical religious leader results only in the triumph of the counter-revolution, symbolized in the person of a young violinist. The latter inaugurates a self-destructive ritual for the people and kills the fanatical priest, before departing mysteriously on a train, presumably in search of fresh fields to conquer. Unlike Jancsó's other films, *Agnus Dei* demands a knowledge of Hungarian history: without it the film is virtually impossible to decipher. Much of the meaning is conveyed by symbolic actions and characters who lack a real life of their own, and *Agnus Dei* remains a film of brilliant moments rather than a coherent whole. One recalls the extreme beauty of many of the visuals (the opening of the film for instance), the power with which the rituals used against the people are conveyed, and a few moments of genuine dramatic force (as when the mediaeval account of an agonizing death by torture is read while we look at the naked, undeveloped body of a young girl).

The importance of *Agnus Dei* lies less in what it is than in the manner in which it prepares the way for Jancsó's next film (his twelfth) *Red Psalm*

(1971). In an interview soon after the completion of the latter film, Jancsó explained at length his approach to narrative:

In my opinion, one can imagine a film other than in the form of a story. We must try to widen the limits of expression ... Film, by its nature – people of flesh and blood, landscapes, a combination of real visual elements – is always realistic. But perhaps there are possibilities of making it get beyond this everyday reality, so that it becomes a means of expression with several dimensions. A story, if the film is a good one, carries the spectator away on its wings, it is an evasion. A film like *Agnus Dei* preoccupies him, makes him think – at least he tries his utmost to; already while the film is being projected the spectator racks his brains trying to order the things he is seeing, he sees himself obliged to, he is active. [2]

This concern with creating a new relationship between the film and its audience is very much a modernist concern and emphasizes again the stylistic link binding Jancsó and Robbe-Grillet, despite the latter's total lack of overt political commitment.

Jancsó's working methods are distinctively his own. All his historical films were made after extensive research by his scriptwriter Gyula Hernádi. In the case of *Red Psalm*, they found much to interest them in the studies of the period by the young historian Dezső Nagy, who stresses the importance of music and song (cantatas, psalms and popular folklore) in nineteenth-century insurrections. This recalled to Jancsó the revolutionary excitement of his own youth, and in part *Red Psalm* is a development of themes already sketched out in *The Confrontation*. The film was in fact structured round the music of the period, though the choice of specific songs grew spontaneously out of the interaction of the film-makers and the groups of singers and dancers who were on hand when the shooting was in progress. This attitude of allowing full rein to spontaneity and improvisation round very clearly defined themes also applies to Jancsó's handling of actors. Lajos Balázsovits, who appeared in both *The Confrontation* and *Red Psalm*, has given a clear picture of Jancsó's relationship with his young actors. In *The Confrontation* an atmosphere was created in which actors and director could understand each other without words:

He always went through the motions of every character in each scene, and the most he said was that 'Before this, such and such has happened to you, now this is coming'. He didn't go into any explanation about the character as a whole, such as the portrayal or psychology, or about the meaning of the situations, but he created an atmosphere in which one could move and act completely naturally. With his almost fantastic force and marvellous suggestions he was able to get what he wanted from each actor. [3]

The enormously long five- or six-minute shots took perhaps six hours each to set up, but Jancsó seldom needed more than three takes; sometimes – as with

Red Psalm: the circle closed

the long shot of the massacre in *Red Psalm* – just one was sufficient. While his camera moved and zoomed in among the actors, Jancsó shouted his instructions to actors and crew, capturing in this way the rhythm and pattern of movement he was seeking.

Red Psalm, one of the great works of modern cinema, synthesizes a dozen years of political concern and formal experiment. The setting is again the Hungarian plain, this time in the 1890s, though as usual Jancsó avoids creating any particular period atmosphere. A group of agrarian socialists – young men and women – oppose with their songs and dances, their solidarity and faith, the constrictions placed upon them by the social structure of the time. Basically their movement is a non-violent one, rooted in joy and hope rather than aggression, and in a series of confrontations they successfully oppose the bailiff and the soldiers, the count and the priest. But always, in the background, is the army, and the funeral service they conduct for an old peasant who cannot accept their ideas and commits suicide becomes an anticipation of their own destruction.

The final massacre gives rise to two of the most striking images of the film (which contains only twenty-seven shots in all). The first is a motionless, long-held shot from a nearby hillside of peasants and musicians celebrating round a maypole. Their dances cause the soldiers lined up against them to break ranks and join in the festivity, until a trumpet summons them back to duty – then the circle is closed and the peasants ruthlessly slaughtered. The second image of massacre is the last shot of the film, a prodigious tracking shot unsurpassed even by that virtuoso of the moving camera, Orson Welles. In silence and the gloom of evening, the camera moves to the right along the barrels of the soldiers' rifles, past the pointed bayonets, to the peasants half-hidden behind the ring of guards. We pass men still trying to convert their opponents, men accepting defeat, women comforting each other in face of the ordeal to come. Then the camera continues its movement, passing down the vulnerable naked body of a woman to uncover the corpses of men, women and doves, along to white shirts and shifts, transfixed with daggers and stained with blood. Having moved by a bright orange dress of a kind we have not seen before, the camera rises up the blade of a sword thrust into the ground. At the hilt is a soldier's white-gloved hand holding a glass of wine, and as this moves, the music of a military band bursts in with electrifying effect. Finally, the celebrations of military and nobility are disturbed by the return of a woman clad in orange red – a spirit of vengeance – who mows down the oppressors and reiterates the peasants' marching song, before holding aloft her revolver which, draped with a red ribbon, ends the shot and the film.

Despite the massacres *Red Psalm* is not a story of defeat. In the perspective of history these are merely temporary setbacks which do not affect the ultimate outcome. Jancsó has often affirmed his own sense of purpose in his work (which he shares with his scriptwriter Gyula Hernádi). 'We are revolutionaries and that is why we want to do nothing other than make our contribution, as far as possible, as far as we are allowed, towards changing the world, towards fighting for a more just and simple world.'[4] It is the positive side of the struggle one remembers from *Red Psalm* – the openness of the socialist group (symbolized by the nakedness of the women), their simple faith and humanity, their underlying unity of aim.

Jancsó's formal patterns of images have a beauty which no direct transcription of reality could match, but the groupings of his characters and the movements of his camera are no mere abstractions. Just as Robbe-Grillet's fictional world cannot be analysed in terms of a simple dichotomy of reality and imagination, so too Jancsó's work has no room for Manichean division of the world into good and evil, black and white. There is a great deal of contradiction and disagreement within the socialist camp and their opponents are no mere caricatures of reaction. As always in Jancsó's films there are also figures (here especially the young army cadets) who have an ambiguous relation to the action. Hence there is a real sense of the forces of stability and change meeting, overlapping and conflicting, so that the new society is built out of an impulse to revolution which has been measured against a real social context. Jancsó is in fact one of the few directors able to capture on film the notion of dialectical change. Far from being a formalist excess, his visual style is intimately related to his whole ideological standpoint:

It seems to me that life is a continual movement. In a procession, a demonstration, there's movement all the time, isn't there? It's physical and it's also philosophical: the contradiction is founded on movement, the movement of ideas, the movement of the masses ... A man alone is always surrounded, threatened by oppression: the camera movements I create suggest that too. It is therefore a very realistic technique, though I admit that it may seem a little bit theatrical. [5]

The power of *Red Psalm* comes largely from this total fusion of form and meaning, the way in which the rhythm of the camera translates the flow of life which Jancsó is anxious to uncover. But in the context of Jancsó's dozen years or so as a feature film-maker, *Red Psalm* constitutes a significant advance in another sense too. Throughout his career Jancsó has shown himself to be fascinated by the seizing and maintaining of power, by the way in which repression and authority erode the dignity of man and reduce him to an automaton obeying the rules of a game into which he is denied all insight. The oppressors in Jancsó's films play on their victims' hopes and exploit man's basic need for ritual. In *Red Psalm*, however, the tables are turned. While submitting themselves to the logic of history, the agrarian revolutionaries base their lives on a hope of change which will, ultimately, be proved justified. The sign that theirs is no vain ambition is that the peasant movement has here created, in its songs and dances, a valid ritual expression of its own. The rites of church and state which had enchained the people for so long are transformed from within so as to constitute the true song of revolution.

13. Pier Paolo Pasolini: Myth and Modernity

Pier Paolo Pasolini is a complex and eclectic artist – poet, novelist, dramatist, critic and theoretician as well as film-maker – and his films have a highly ambiguous impact. His range is very apparent in the two films he directed in 1969: *Pigsty* (*Porcile*) and *Medea.* The former contains a virtual anthology of modernist cinematic imagery: naked figures in a windswept Jancsó landscape, Jean-Pierre Léaud and Anne Wiazemsky conducting an interminable Godardian dialogue, static architectural shots and classical music straight from Straub's *Chronik der Anna Magdalena Bach,* and a performance by Pierre Clémenti to remind us of the Buñuel of *Belle de Jour. Medea,* on the other hand, is by no means limited to filmic references and summons up a quite different range of perspectives. Thanks to the appearance of Maria Callas in the title role, it has a Western operatic dimension, but it also contains, at its climax, passages of oriental or Arabic chanting. There is an obvious debt to the Greek tragedy of Euripides in the narrative, but the film adds recollections of mediaeval religious painting in many of its composi-tions, a syncretic style of costume that unites Andalusian jewellery and Mexican masks, and a choice of settings ranging from the tourist attractions of Pisa to a remote Turkish village.

The scope of these allusions is typical of Pasolini, who is by no means an austere modernist carving out a resolutely independent style, but rather an artist whose principal stylistic device is pastiche and whose constant pre-occupation is with creating a metaphoric language of cinema by the use of carefully chosen analogies. Pasolini's films, like those of Jean-Luc Godard, are thus extremely heterogeneous and rely on the force of his personal involvement for their effective coherence. Despite the referential quality of his imagery and music, all Pasolini's films bear the unmistakable stamp of their author, and their inner consistency is emphasized by the reappearance in one film after another of the familiar figures of Franco Citti (who was both *Accattone* and *Oedipus*), the tousle-headed Ninetto Davoli and a host of minor players.

Pasolini's career as a director began with *Accattone* (1961) and *Mamma Roma* (1962). These two films reflect his interest in the proletarian life of the Roman slums which also serves as the basis of the best-known of his novels of the 1950s, one of which, *Una vita violenta*, has been translated into English (as *A Violent Life*). Though Pasolini's style is distinctive, the setting of urban squalor and the evident sympathy for the poor which both these films exhibit make them very much a part of the resurgence of realist cinema that occurred in Italy in the early 1960s with the first films of Ermanno Olmi, Elio Petri, Francesco Rosi and Vittorio De Seta. In 1964, however, with his version of *The Gospel According to St Matthew* (*Il vangelo secondo Matteo*), Pasolini established a radically new style, handling the gospel story in a manner which stripped away the conventional (and now meaningless) pieties which Hollywood has accustomed us to expect in any filming of the bible. This particular style was more fully elaborated in Pasolini's highly personal yet formalized treatment of the Greek legends of *Oedipus Rex* (*Edipo re*, 1967) and *Medea*, and served as a decorative frieze for his zestful and bawdy selections of stories from *The Decameron* (*Il decamerone*, 1971), *The Canterbury Tales* (*I racconti di Canterbury*, 1972) and *The Arabian Nights* (*Il fiore delle mille e una notte*, 1974). Alongside this concern with the primitive past and with religion and superstition, Pasolini has also involved himself in contemporary issues. This interest finds expression in his satiric analysis of Italian left-wing politics, *Uccellacci e uccellini* (1966), in his portrayal of the disintegration of a middle-class family in *Theorem* (*Teorema*, 1968), and in those parts of *Pigsty* which offer some thoughts on post-Nazi Germany.

The basic polarity which gives tension to Pasolini's style can be expressed crudely as an attempt to reconcile Freud and Marx. The implications of this are best seen in *Pigsty*, which contains two episodes, one modern and satiric, the other mythic and orgiastic. The two parts were in fact quite separately conceived, the 'Orgy' half having been originally planned as a companion piece to Buñuel's *Simon of the Desert*, while the 'Pigsty' half was written as one of the half-dozen verse tragedies which Pasolini composed after reading

Pigsty: cannibals

Plato's *Dialogues*. Independently each episode would no doubt have had an impact – the subject matter alone (cannibalism and bestiality) ensures that – but together they take on a unique resonance. Separated by several centuries, the stories of two rebels, one rejecting society in favour of cannibalism and the other his class in favour of pigs, run parallel. The cutting between them creates the kind of tensions which D. W. Griffith was seeking in *Intolerance*, but never offers glib answers to the problems posed. Only at the end, when both heroes are eaten by animals, does the link become explicit, symbolized by the appearance in the final scene of each story of one of Pasolini's favourite actors, Ninetto Davoli (Toto's companion on his wanderings in *Uccellacci e uccellini*).

Pasolini's concern with Marxism has much the same origins as his preoccupation with Freud. In a very real sense it is part of his revolt against the values of his father, who was, by the son's account, both a Fascist and a petit-bourgeois. His first contact with the proletariat was with the peasants of Friuli, and it was only much later in Rome that he came in touch with the urban working class. Like most of the Marxist intellectuals of neo-realism, Pasolini came to Marx indirectly, through the writings of the Italian Communist theoretician (and co-founder of the Party) Antonio Gramsci, who stressed the importance of confronting the problems posed in Southern Italy by the gulf between the great landlords and their labourers employed and paid by the day, and saw the real chance for Italian Communism as being control of the countryside. These ideas are reflected in Pasolini's later works – his view, for instance, of Christ as a rebel marching through country districts and bringing the masses into conflict with the *status quo*. But his first films, like his early novels, show the impact of the Roman slums and their inhabitants upon his sensibilities. A film like *Accattone* self-consciously idealizes the Roman thieves, whores and layabouts, but despite the novelty of its tone, it lacks the originality of Pasolini's mature style. Because of Pasolini's limited technical command the various elements do not blend totally and for much of the time one is confronted with a run-down version of the neo-realist approach. Like Curzio Malaparte in *Il cristo proibito*, made ten years earlier, Pasolini offers an uneasy fusion of realism and religiosity which lacks the precision and attack of the best neo-realist films.

More recently, in *Theorem* and the Jean-Pierre Léaud half of *Pigsty*, Pasolini has confronted the problems of bourgeois society. Here he has evolved a style that is in marked contrast to his studies of Freudian myth. In this urban environment Pasolini presents stories built round elements of irony and parallelism. Unconcerned with mere reportage of social behaviour, he offers startling portraits of bourgeois families which disintegrate under the impact of self-awareness. This detached approach allows Pasolini to indulge in satire. So, in *Pigsty*, the bourgeois parents come to resemble the swine of Georg Grosz's caricatures, and the son, a prisoner of their values, finds his deepest satisfaction in the love of a pig. Pasolini uses literary references here as he uses painterly ones in his historical works. The father is not a direct imitation of Hitler; rather he is a variant on Brecht's transmutation of Hitler as Arturo Ui. In *Medea*, Pasolini's Marxism is applied to the world of myth. Unlike Euripides, who in his tragedy concentrates solely on the final outcome of Medea's jealousy (the murder of her children), Pasolini devotes almost half of his film to an evocation of the primitive culture of Colchis in which Medea was brought up and from which she flees with the Golden Fleece under the influence of her love for Jason. The extraordinary Turkish landscape – a village still inhabited apparently by the people who act as extras in the film – is explicitly contrasted with the more advanced – as it were bourgeois – civilization of Corinth, here represented by Pisa. Hence the tragedy arises not simply from an excess of passion or a conflict of character (Medea and the mediocre Jason), but also from a profoundly observed clash of civilizations.

Pasolini's move from literature to cinema contains in itself a large element of protest. As Luchino Visconti told us in *La terra trema*, Italian is not the

Pigsty: bourgeois father as Hitler caricature

language of the poor. It is a sophisticated construct that is just one of the tools of those who aim to cover up the present divisions, rather than remove the inequalities. The cinema is thus, for Pasolini, a successor to the Friulian dialect which he used – as a conscious act of rebellion – for his earlier poetry. Perhaps because of this use of the cinema for the purpose of social rather than artistic revolt, Pasolini's politically oriented films do not show the kind of stylistic innovation that we find, for instance, in the films of Alain Robbe-Grillet. Pasolini's power comes not from his invention of new structures but from his ability to create novel juxtapositions. On the straightforward realist level the result of this synthesizing approach can be seen in *Accattone*, which is a story of the slums told in a static, reverential style with allusions to the fifteenth-century painter Masaccio and an accompaniment of the music of Bach. It is, however, only in the mythic studies which are his prime contribution to modern cinema that the full force of Pasolini's originality can be seen.

At the root of Pasolini's later style is the notion of analogy. For him the essential difference between cinema and literature is that the language of film

158

lacks metaphor, since it expresses reality with reality. Pasolini has a profound respect for reality itself, but his awareness of the qualities of film as language make him very distrustful of naturalism as a form of artistic expression. He rigorously avoids the mere imitation of life. He likes using, in neo-realist fashion, non-actors chosen for the appropriateness of their faces and figures. But he does not use them naturally: he photographs them in poses taken from Piero della Francesca and dubs them with actors' voices. For Pasolini, the only means which allows the cinema to compensate for the lack of metaphor (and hence, at a certain level, of poetry itself) is analogy. This is the method he adopts in his films of myth. If a film-maker must always use what is real (people, settings, etc.), this can be chosen to represent indirectly the reality with which he is concerned: thus Southern Italy gives us an image of Christ's Palestine and Turkey provides the contours of ancient Colchis. New resonances are set up by this means, and a quite unique effect is created by this remove from naturalism. And it is precisely with resonances of this kind that Pasolini is concerned. Where most of the work of Marxist directors in the Italian cinema is aimed at demystification – at removing the aura of respectability from the exploitation of workers, for example – Pasolini sets out to discover and reveal the mythical aspect of reality. He does not demystify Christ – i.e., show him to be simply a man – he gives us, in *The Gospel According to St Matthew*, Christ *and* two thousand years of Christian legend and art.

In *Medea*, which follows the fortunes of two culturally disparate characters, Jason and Medea, Pasolini achieves a fusion of the epic-religious and the social-critical. Both central characters have a primitive upbringing – Jason at the hands of a centaur (Laurent Terzieff with four legs and a tail!), Medea in the ruling family of Colchis, where human sacrifice is practised with the annual execution of a surrogate king. Each has his own element: Medea the sun (whose granddaughter she is), and Jason the sea, which he conquers with his Argonauts. In their tragic interaction Pasolini sees exemplified his insight into both the working of human relationships and the structure of society. Jason who is sought by Medea while dancing with his male companions, just as Christ was confronted by his mother while surrounded by his disciples, learns the power of a woman's passion. Both he and the King of Corinth discover at fearful cost the price of ignoring the irrational, religious element in man. In this expression of his sense of primitive wonder at life Pasolini is far removed from his neo-realist beginnings, but the evolution he has followed has striking similarities with that of Roberto Rossellini, whose study of St Francis, *Francesco, giullare di Dio*, is perhaps the closest forerunner of this kind of approach to reality.

The Freudian preoccupations of Pasolini are most obvious in his

Landscape and myth: *The Gospel According to St Matthew*

treatments of his own Oedipal situation, the explicit subject of his version of
the Sophoclean tragedy and implicit in many of his other films from *Mamma
Roma* to *The Gospel According to St Matthew*, in which he cast his own
mother as Mary. In one of his interviews Pasolini has made clear his own
obsessive preoccupation with his parents: 'For a time I thought the whole of
my erotic and emotional life was the result of this excessive, almost monstrous love for my mother.'[1] His own personal involvement with the myth he
is narrating adds enormously to the impact of *Oedipus Rex*. The prologue of
the film is wholly autobiographical: the dress of Sylvana Mangano (who plays
the mother and – later in the film – Jocasta) is based on an old photograph of
Pasolini's mother, the father wears a 1930s' officer's uniform, and the scene
in the meadow is one of the film-maker's earliest childhood memories. It was
from his mother that he derived his religion, his deep sense of awe at reality,
which, for an Italian artist, is uniquely free from Catholic influence. Shaped
perhaps also by his contact with Friulian farm labourers in the early 1940s, it
retains a peasant-like primitivism. The same forces are sensed in the ancient
Greece of *Oedipus Rex* and the Colchis of Medea's childhood, as in the
Palestine of *The Gospel* and indeed in the Pan figure, played by Terence

160

Stamp, in *Theorem*. This equation of Christian and pagan, saint and sinner adds to the air of mystery. The prologue of *Oedipus Rex*, which is balanced by a modern epilogue, is one of the most striking aspects of the film. It contains a beautifully lyrical evocation of the enigma of woman – the long-held shot of the mother's blank, mask-like face accompanied by a phrase from Mozart's C major quartet, which recurs as a leitmotif throughout the film. The hostility which the child's presence arouses in his father comes to a climax when the father 'squeezes the child's tiny bare feet as if he wanted to crush them'. And with this Pasolini cuts abruptly but with perfect precision to the empty Moroccan landscape and ancient Japanese flute music which together form the basic elements of his vision of the world of Sophoclean myth.

It is this ability to synthesize the most diverse material which is the key to the richness and ambiguity of Pasolini's imagery. It is most apparent in the evocation of Oedipus's life up to the point at which the tragedy of Sophocles begins. To create a world of prehistoric myth Pasolini draws on elements of Aztec, Sumerian and Black African culture as well as Italian Renaissance painters, and builds up a soundtrack from sources as diverse as Mozart,

Landscape and myth: *Oedipus Rex*

Oedipus Rex: Oedipus and the messenger in a modern Bologna landscape

Japanese flute music and Rumanian folk song. The filmic echoes are, in contrast, rare, though certain compositions (such as some long shots of the queens, Merope and Jocasta, sitting alone in empty landscapes) do recall one of Pasolini's favourite directors, Kenji Mizoguchi, in *Ugetsu Monogatari*. In contrast to the sophistication of the costumes, the presentation of the story through the editing is simple, direct and hence forceful. To evoke the perils of the desert for the infant Oedipus, Pasolini simply cuts in a shot of a snake. The fight between Oedipus and Laius's bodyguards is handled without undue dramatics, so that the actual killing of Laius retains its full impact. In this context too moments like the abrupt cut from the very genuine tenderness of Oedipus and Jocasta alone together in the bedchamber for the first time to a close-up of the mutilated face of a plague victim achieve a great intensity.

The same simplicity is to be found in the characterization. Polybus and Merope welcome the gift of the foundling with childlike joy, and they pass on their uncomplicated approach to life to Oedipus. It is the naïvety of Oedipus, as depicted by Franco Citti, which helps us feel ourselves akin to him despite the monstrous and inexplicable fate which the gods allot to him. He makes his way doggedly and unreflectingly through life. He does not pause to investigate the taunt 'child of fortune' thrown at him by one of the companions he has cheated in a youthful game, and only his dreams (which we do not see) drive him to Delphi, just as chance alone takes him to Thebes. His refusal to look back is what makes him invulnerable to the Sphinx. He ignores the implications of the question put to him about the enigma in his own life and thrusts the Sphinx back into the abyss, despite its explicit warning: 'The abyss you are pushing me into is within yourself.'

It is Pasolini himself, in the role of the high priest, who introduces the section of the film based directly on Sophocles, after a long passage dealing graphically with the plague and its victims. This section is staged basically as a theatrical confrontation, with a frieze of figures along the front of the royal palace and Oedipus as king with the high golden hat and beard inherited from Laius. As he attempts to solve the riddle of the plague and appease the sufferings of his people, Oedipus's eyes go constantly to the barred window from behind which Jocasta watches him. The action moves away from this formal framework only for the moments of high drama, such as the confrontation with Tiresias whose words he refuses to believe. The long conversation with Jocasta in which, by trying to ease his torment, she merely confirms his worst fears, is also shot as a more private scene, the dissolves to black in the midst of what is essentially a single dialogue emphasizing the impact of each new and devastating revelation. Some of Jocasta's actions and gestures (as she runs with her servants or makes love to Oedipus) recall the prologue, but the parallel is never overstressed. The final love-making comes as a gesture of love and defiance after both Jocasta and Oedipus have realized the truth even if they cannot as yet bring themselves to accept it. But Jocasta retains her enigma to the end: she prays, frolics with her maidens, then hangs herself. In Pasolini's personalized version of the theme of *Oedipus at Colonus*, the blinded Oedipus is led out of the world of myth into the present day, to what the director terms his sublimation. The messenger Angelo takes him, a blind flute player like Tiresias whom he had once envied, through the cathedral square of Bologna and the factory-lined streets of Milan. This modern world looks strangely dreamlike after the mythical universe of ancient Greece (an effect emphasized by Pasolini's choice of distorting lenses). Oedipus moves back finally to the world of trees and grass of the prologue, now dark in the evening light, and faint sounds of the military music associated with the father are heard. Oedipus has reached the goal of his wanderings: 'I have come back. Life ends where it begins.'

The mythic stories of man's attempts to come to terms with his own religious sense and complicated sexuality, of which *Oedipus Rex* is such a fine example, have qualities which set them apart from virtually all other modern film-making. Their particular ambiguity arises from the mixture of personal and literary elements, direct involvement and stylized ritual. The relationship between the Oedipus legend and the modern framework in which it is set can be felt emotionally, but becomes distorted as soon as the critic – or Pasolini himself for that matter – tries to define it intellectually. In much the same way, any attempt to break down Pasolini's syncretic style into its constituent parts is unhelpful, since these latter are experienced as a unity when the film is viewed. Ultimately Pasolini's mythic awe and awareness must be accepted or rejected *en bloc*. In the kinds of emphasis he places on such aspects of life, if not in actual content, Pasolini remains remarkably consistent throughout his career (there is already a primitive religious element in his first film, *Accattone*).

One striking aspect of *The Gospel According to St Matthew*, *Oedipus Rex*, *Medea* and the 'Orgy' episode of *Pigsty* is the combination of narrative simplicity and total ambiguity of meaning. The stories follow an uncomplicated linear pattern, but they evoke a very complex response. The films show characters of enormous personal authority, but leave in doubt crucial issues: the divine nature of Christ, the moral implications of Oedipus's or Medea's acts, the impulse behind Pierre Clémenti's savagery in *Pigsty*. This genuine mystery adds to the films' religious quality. As if to compensate for the simplicity and violence of the action, these films include the most striking imagery to be found in Pasolini's work, their visual texture being strongly marked by painterly allusions. The setting is that of a non- or pre-urban society, far removed from the determined ultra-modernity of most contemporary cinema, but such a society is in fact not that remote from us. Pasolini has no difficulty in finding his analogies in the Mediterranean world; and as social anthropologists are constantly reminding us, the beast remains in the most sophisticated of us, as in Medea at Corinth. Pasolini's treatments of myth demonstrate too that the modern predicament is not simply that of coming to terms with an urban environment, but also the mastering of the basic irrational forces within us.

Note: Pasolini was killed in November 1975.

14. Walerian Borowczyk: Space, Style and Fable

One area of modern cinema which is largely ignored in the present study of narrative structure is the animated film. Yet this is an area which allows us to see clearly a great number of the issues involved in modernism, particularly the ambiguous attitude of modern film-makers to past traditions. Walt Disney, of course, reigned supreme in world animation from the advent of sound until the early 1950s. His style of animation set the pattern for cartoonists everywhere, while the distinctive approaches of pioneers such as Emile Cohl and Winsor Macay were forgotten, and the few works that stood aside from Disney's methods (Alexeieff's *Night on a Bare Mountain* or Bartosch's *L'Idée*, for instance) were seen as fringe efforts. While it is possible to attack the sentimentality and false values of most Disney films (as of so much work in Hollywood), no one can deny the sheer skill in animation. As the British animator Richard Williams wrote of *Bambi* in 1970: 'Having ten years of gruelling experience I am in awesome wonder at the achievement. When one knows what is involved in producing work of that calibre one can have no criticism of work of such excellence. One may have one's own ideas, style and approach, and yet be in awe of Disney's achievements.'[1]

All the same, it was only when Disney ceased to reign unchallenged that animation could be regarded as having any real connection with modern painting or graphic art. In the 1950s, when Disney's relentless quest for pseudo-realism was replaced by a new awareness of materials and textures, it became increasingly difficult to generalize about the scope of the animated film, for dozens of artists were pursuing their individual paths. But it was possible for Robert Benayoun in a book published in 1961 to relate certain cartoons to the work of Kandinsky, Miró and Yves Tanguy and to show how individual films exploited the potential of line, sketch or gouache and toyed with blank backgrounds and deliberately crude animation. As a result of such experimentation the way was clear in the 1960s for artists like Walerian Borowczyk, Jan Lenica, Richard Ansorge and John Hubley to present serious and totally individual poetic visions through animation. Borowczyk was the only one of these animators to go on to develop his style to encompass work in the live action feature, and it is with his career that we shall be most concerned here. But another film-maker of an older generation who successfully made the transition from animation to feature film work and who deserves more than a passing mention is the Japanese director Kon Ichikawa. A versatile and eclectic artist, Ichikawa has worked in a variety of styles and genres (among his best-known films are works as divergent as *The Burmese Harp* (1956) and *Tokio Olympiad* (1965)), and most of his output falls outside the category of modern cinema as it has been defined here. But just as Akira Kurosawa's *Rashomon* cannot be overlooked in any consideration of modern narrative structure, so too Ichikawa's *An Actor's Revenge* (1963, also known as *The Revenge of Yukinojo*) has enormous relevance to any discussion of ambiguity in the cinema.

The subject of *An Actor's Revenge* – described by Donald Richie as an 'old tearjerker' and a 'tired melodrama ... old fashioned when it originally appeared back in the 1920s'[2] – is an unlikely source for a film of such striking modernity. But Ichikawa is a director of unusual talents and he has shaped his film (which has a late nineteenth-century setting) so that the ironies and ambiguities are exploited to the full. Everything is built round patterns of opposites. The same actor (Kazue Hasegawa) plays both the immensely masculine thief Yamitaro, a kind of oriental Robin Hood, and the central figure of the film, the actor Yukinojo. In contrast to Yamitaro, Yukinojo is a female impersonator who also lives his life offstage as a woman. The film constantly uses Yokinojo to set up an opposition between stage and reality. Where he, the actor, shrinks from display and hides his real intentions, the criminals in the film openly boast of their thieving and seek fame as much as money. Despite his apparent feminine timidity, Yukinojo is driven by an implacable desire for revenge on the three men responsible for the death of his parents, and his life becomes increasingly filled with paradoxes. To avenge his guiltless parents, he must himself destroy a beautiful and innocent girl. The

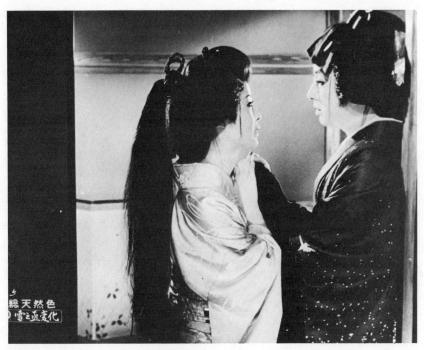

Cross-currents of ambiguity: Ichikawa's *An Actor's Revenge*

ambiguity reaches its height in the film's love scenes, for if it is femininity which attracts the man-hating, tomboyish thief Ohatsu, it is, by contrast, the virility beneath his female garb with which the innocent Lady Namiji falls in love. In the opening sequence on the stage Yukinojo is presented as a tangible and well-defined character, but gradually through his succession of impostures he loses all sense of identity, and the film's ending, in which he is swallowed up by time and the landscape to become a figure of legend, is a fitting one.

As interesting as this narrative complexity is the way in which Ichikawa uses the visual resources of the cinema. He has claimed that the film-maker who influenced him most was Walt Disney and, though it is unlikely that Disney would have found much to admire in the tortuous tale of Yukinojo's love and vengeance, he might well have appreciated the treacly westernized music with which the Japanese director has chosen to accompany his exquisite visuals. Ichikawa's early experience in the animated film is most apparent in his refusal of any kind of realism, as stage and real life clash and blend into one. His inventive use of colour and the wide-screen format and his treatment of the screen as a flat painterly surface is very apparent in compositions in

167

which the attention is focused on one corner of the image while the rest is masked off or blacked out. Tiny figures appear from out of a black background in exaggerated perspective like cartoon characters. During one of the spectacular fight scenes a rope shoots across the screen with almost three-dimensional effect, while at the end of the film, by contrast, the figure of Yukinojo is absorbed into the landscape in a marvellous series of dissolves. This fresh approach to visual style and texture is something we find too in the work of Walerian Borowczyk who, by the 1960s, had established a claim to be considered one of the greatest of all artists to have worked in the field of film animation, and who subsequently directed several strange and haunting feature films, including *Goto Island of Love* (*Goto, L'Ile d'Amour*, 1968), *Blanche* (1971), *Contes Immoraux* (1974) and *La Bête* (1975).

Polish by birth, Borowczyk trained as a graphic artist at the Academy of Fine Arts in Cracow. His early animated films – *Once Upon a Time, Love Requited* and *Dom* (all completed in 1957) were made in collaboration with Jan Lenica, himself an animator of enormous talent. *Dom* uses the situation of a young girl, left alone in the house with her dreams and fears, as the framework for a series of separate scenes, all of them strange and disquieting. These scenes allow Borowczyk and Lenica to explore the whole range of possibilities open to the animator: drawn images, the animation of Muybridge figures and inanimate objects, the film loop endlessly repeating itself, picture postcards as dream images, and an overtly symbolic sequence in which the girl kisses a photogenic dummy which crumbles before her eyes. Of all the half-dozen scenes, the most disturbing is that showing animated objects in which a wig comes to life and moves around a tabletop. It eats pieces of paper, chases and devours an orange, drinks a glass of milk and finally slowly crunches and consumes the glass itself. *Dom* ends with the same menace with which it has begun: a threatening sky and the camera panning down the front of a house to enter a window.

In 1958 Borowczyk went to France, where he has lived and worked ever since, and made first a biting little film on army drill, *L'Ecole* (1958), and then *Les Astronautes* (1959), a science-fiction short using animated photographs, written in collaboration with Chris Marker and showing the latter's customary whimsical humour. For the next ten years Borowczyk explored concurrently a number of the separate possibilities touched on in *Dom*. His interest in drawn animation led to the gently humorous *Le Dictionnaire de Joachim* (1966) and the creation of the ferocious Kabals, who appear in his feature-length cartoon, *Le Théâtre de M et Mme Kabal* (1967). But the climax of Borowczyk's work in this area is the masterly *Jeux des Anges* (1964), a twelve-minute poetic vision of Kafkaesque nightmare and horror.

Renaissance

With this film one can say that the drawn cartoon is vindicated as a totally adult form of expression of the fears and anxieties of our age.

More directly relevant to Borowczyk's feature film work, in which objects often take on an ambiguously charged significance, is *Renaissance*, also completed in 1964. The film begins with an explosion and a shot of a shattered wall. Then the camera pulls back to reveal the twisted mass of debris. Slowly and methodically the objects piece themselves together: a stuffed owl, a tangled trumpet, a picture, a child's doll, a hamper and two books, the penal code and a prayer book. For one glorious moment there is equilibrium and the trumpet celebrates with a cheerful tune. But there remain objects which must still assemble themselves: an alarm clock and a hand-grenade. No sooner are these complete than the explosion recurs and we are back with the shattered room of the opening. Borowczyk includes moments of humour: the prayer book levitating, grapes reappearing on the stalk to the sound of a typewriter. But the general effect is more deeply disturbing, as one recalls the strange stare of the owl or the doll's painful crawl across the floor. Above all there is the poetry which Borowczyk extracts from the paradoxes of destruction and renewal, immobility and animation.

Gavotte: dwarf's eye-view

In the years just before he made his first live-action feature film, Borowczyk experimented with short films using people: *Rosalie* (1966), an adaptation of a Maupassant story with his wife, Ligia Branice (who stars in two of his features), *Diptyque* and *Gavotte* (both made in 1968). In *Diptyque* two quite distinct fragments are put together without comment. In the first half we see an old peasant in his nineties out with his dog in the fields and talking in a broad dialect about his life. In the second, exquisitely framed colour images of flowers in elegant vases and playful kittens are used to accompany a song by Tino Rossi from Bizet's opera *Les Pêcheurs de Perles*. Each half is in itself perfectly realized, but from their juxtaposition comes a still more striking impact: the time-worn peasant set against the frozen beauty of the flowers, realist images with natural sound and in black and white contrasting with the colourful perfection of the flowers and the contrived operatic elegance of the aria. *Gavotte* employs a similar contradiction. While a gavotte by Jean-Philippe Rameau is played on a harpsichord in an elegant eighteenth-century drawing room, we watch the antics of a pair of dwarfs. The first is clearly bored with the music and his attempts to get comfortable are continu-

170

ally thwarted. The fly he captures and imprisons escapes, and his fellow dwarf goes off with a cushion he has purloined. This is too much – after a struggle, he strangles his rival, stuffs him into the ornate wooden bench-seat and, when the music comes to an end, tiptoes off. This tale of malevolence and spite – brilliantly acted by the two dwarfs, Roberto and Ludo – is typical of the director in the unfaltering path it traces from elegance and order to chaos and death. Stylistically the film shows Borowczyk at his most assured. He observes this horrifying corner of the world with an unblinking stare: the camera is planted squarely in front of the action and the slight variations in framing are almost imperceptible. Not only does the height of the image reflect the dwarfs' viewpoint (with the heads of normal human beings cropped off), but the space in which the action occurs is flattened out, so as to become almost a two-dimensional surface. The visual stylization (immobility and foreshortening) complements the highly ornamented music to create a perfect frame for Borowczyk's black vision.

Borowczyk's shorts are exemplary examples of modern cinema in the manner in which they question the whole notion of style in the cinema. Each throws new light on certain basic issues: the nature of the camera's fixity of gaze in *Gavotte*, for example, or our conceptions of sequence and irreversibility in *Renaissance*. Objects are given a new relationship to human beings, and the significance of the way in which they are depicted on the screen is explored. An example is *Rosalie*, which queries our reassuring certainties about the objects we see in a film. In *Jeux des Anges* drawn film images – too long associated exclusively with Walt Disney's sentimentality – are given the kind of impact Picasso achieves in *Guernica*, while *Gavotte* in places uses the conventions of the animated cartoon to give a new view of human behaviour. Seldom has the question of how the juxtaposition of opposites can affect us in the cinema been explored with such concision and rigour as in *Diptyque*, where realism and dream image, banality and ideal are confronted. The range of Borowczyk's investigations is wide and his world is often disorienting at first sight. He offers no explanations (none of his shorts has a commentary), but instead makes us see and feel the power of a vision he presents with unfailing vitality and a rich vein of black humour.

These qualities are carried over into Borowczyk's first feature films, *Goto, l'Ile d'Amour* and *Blanche*. Despite his choice of actors of very dominant personalities (Pierre Brasseur as Goto, Michel Simon as the aged lord in *Blanche*), it is the director's idiosyncratic vision that is communicated. He himself attributes this to the fact that he approaches his films as a craftsman rather than as a virtuoso (though his technical command is never less than outstanding). He once compared his composition of images to the making of a tapestry:

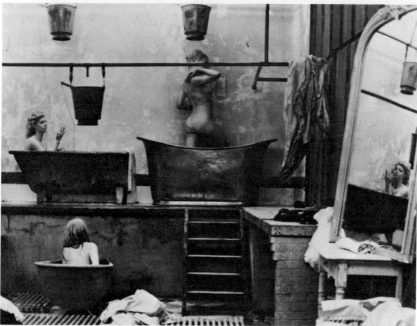

Depth and perspective: *Blanche* and (*below*) *Goto*

What matters is the editing within the frame and the editing together of the frames. Linear composition must be simplified by bringing out the contrasts: light and shade, sharp and soft focus, in two dimensions, breadth and length. That's all that's needed for the purposes of expression. Thus I film a man running from a fixed point. There is a real movement in depth and not an imitation. This play of depth and perspective is sometimes signalled by the movements of characters. In the same way lateral or vertical pans signal the geometry of the frame.[3]

These are attitudes we have already seen in his short film work, and in *Goto* and *Blanche* they are applied to narratives which are in essence fables, the one from an original script by the director, the other adapted from a work by the nineteenth-century Polish Romantic dramatist, Juliusz Slowacki. They are tales of love featuring Borowczyk's beautiful wife, Ligia Branice, but of love destroyed in a world where hate, cruelty and suspicion rule and which, in each case, becomes a prison for the good and innocent. Borowczyk has said that music is one of the things which make him decide on a particular film subject, and Handel is as important to *Goto, l'Ile d'Amour* as the thirteenth-century music is to *Blanche*. In both cases the use of background is equally crucial – the black and white textures of *Goto* and the colour based on mediaeval art in *Blanche*. Thus the two films are formal exercises (in the best sense of the word) rather than purely dramatic structures, and for all their apparent simplicity, they have a great richness and complexity of meaning.

The setting of Borowczyk's first feature – Goto, the ironically named island of love – is a remote imaginary island where progress stopped along with contact with the outside world in 1877 at the time of a great earthquake. The society that has evolved there on the debris of a nineteenth-century civilization under three successive rulers (each named Goto) provides a distorting mirror for our own society. Goto is in one sense a typical fascist state: the governor is revered as a godlike figure (the three Gotos are compared by the schoolmaster to the holy trinity), the regime is militaristic and repressive and the population consists solely of oppressed workers in the quarries, soldiers and whores. Inevitably, when Goto III is overthrown it is by means of a *coup d'état* engineered by a man who had himself once been under sentence of death. Within this society human beings are inevitably degraded. Goto III loves his wife Glossia, but employs her father, Gonor, as his servant (a servant who weeps when he is not patted like a dog by his master), while her mother, Gonasta, works as a whore in the soldiers' brothel. The usurper Grozo starts his climb to power when he is appointed assistant to Gonor, and Borowczyk shows his surrealist inclinations in his choice of the three roles which this trusted servants fulfils: he catches flies, cleans Goto's boots and feeds his dogs. Flies in fact have a quasi-symbolic significance in *Goto, l'Ile d'Amour* and, true to the teachings of Buñuel in *Land Without*

173

Bread, the director includes in his film a short lecture on the fly and its place in the insect kingdom.

Goto is a society in which the only forms of entertainment are, it seems, the whore house and the public executions. It is at one of the latter that we first see Goto III with his beautiful wife: a strange ritual heralded by eerie music performed on improvised instruments, while the participants are winched up from the cages below. On the island of Goto stealing a pair of binoculars or a few windfall apples is a crime on a par with murder, and a pair of criminals undergo a kind of trial by combat to see who will die and who will be pardoned. The beheading of the loser, a still more gruesome spectacle, is equally public and attended by men, women and children alike. No one in the film, not even Glossia, ever raises a protest against such spectacles, or even hints of any alternative. The universe of the film is that of a prison. We never see a shot of Goto's fortress from the outside – only the cells and passages with their dirt, decay and crumbling walls. The image with which the film opens captures the essential quality of the atmosphere: a shot from a motionless, fixed camera of the wall of the riding arena, with horses and riders endlessly circling, dwarfed by the height of the ugly, windowless wall. Their monotonous round seems to underline the futility of all action, dream or endeavour. Occasionally Borowczyk's tale takes us outside the fortress, but the beach is unbelievably bleak and the leaden sea seems to preclude all hope of escape. As always in Borowczyk's work the framing of figures against their backgrounds and the choice of detail is meticulous.

This then is the unlikely setting for a fairytale of love and innocence. While the other characters are dominated by their environment and seem to have less vitality than some of the inanimate objects which the director cuts in enigmatically at various points in the film, Glossia retains her beauty and, for a time at least, her freedom. All her relationships – with her husband Goto, her lover Gono and the treacherous Grozo – are, however, doomed. For Goto, security is all that matters in life and he is at home in his fortress despite its flies and dirt simply because he feels it to be invulnerable. For all his tyranny and his treatment of his parents-in-law (for which Glossia never rebukes him), Goto as portrayed by Pierre Brasseur is not unlikable. His attachment to Glossia is very real and indeed leads to his downfall. The climax of their relationship comes when he takes her to the beach, where they romp together like children. But when he falls into the water and loses his hat, he is suddenly revealed in all his vulnerability. As at the beginning and end of the film, we hear in this scene the soaring music of Handel, which points to a dimension of living denied by the images of the film. But at the same time the camera dwells mercilessly on Goto's face – he is already a defeated man long before Grozo shoots him. Glossia's lover Gono gives her briefly a hope of escape and their love-making together in the stable (when they are spied on by Goto and Grozo) has a real sensuality. But his attempts to arrange their escape are pitifully inadequate and his inability to elude Grozo's scheming comes as no surprise. Grozo himself is the evil genius of the film, envious, deceitful and lustful. With low cunning and a total disregard for his fellow human beings he masters all the hazards of life in Goto and achieves supreme power. But his lust for Glossia can only arouse her revulsion and ultimately he is responsible for her death, though she is the only person in the world he loves.

Goto, l'Ile d'Amour is a strange, haunting work in which Borowczyk succeeds totally in creating a personal vision of a universe in which chance rules, our laws of morality cease to apply and where to see or to love is a source of vulnerability. The stylistic methods he uses are simple: for much of the film he merely holds his shots so that they begin to become oppressive and intercuts actions in such a way as to destroy any chance of a dramatic build-up. In this way he creates an all-pervading sense of the monotony and inhumanity of Goto which he then brilliantly cuts through with tiny enigmatic flashes of life. The film, very much black and white, includes half a dozen quite unexpected bursts of colour. Against the prison greyness of the setting the brief shots of naked bodies – Glossia's in particular – are made to stand out with sensual clarity. In a film which is basically static and detached, the occasional close-ups and camera movements take on (at the end, for instance) an extraordinary sense of life, just as the music of Handel bursts in with overwhelming power thanks to the overall silence of the rest of the film.

As the beauty of love emerges from the background of envy, greed and power, the aptness of Borowczyk's title becomes clear. The continual juxtapositions set up very ambiguous tensions, and fittingly the film ends with a question mark. We see Glossia fall to her death, and her body, as Grozo drags it back to her room, is visually equated with a broken doll. But at the end, as the music of Handel recurs for a final surge of emotion and Grozo weeps inconsolably, Glossia opens her eyes – a sign of life in death that is Borowczyk's last note of affirmation against the black fatalism of the world he has created.

Part Four: Dissolutions

15. The Questioning of Narrative Primacy

There is a broad continuity and definable unity of purpose linking the two groups of film-makers so far considered here. Despite the complexity of structure and ambiguity of meaning which sets them apart from their more traditionally-minded contemporaries such as Visconti and Losey or Chabrol and Anderson, both groups are working within the framework of a narrative cinema. One can draw quite close parallels between specific individual directors from the two age groups: the way in which, for instance, Jancsó uses to new ends techniques developed in the early 1960s by Antonioni, or Robbe-Grillet probes afresh areas of the imagination touched upon by Buñuel. Despite the overlap in time, this is no longer true in quite the same way when we come to consider the films of Jean-Luc Godard and his younger contemporaries. There is a significant change of emphasis away from narrative coherence, as the whole conventional notion of 'making a film' is subjected to a radical re-examination. If the generation born around 1921–3 can be characterized by its desire to fuse together disparate elements to create a unified personal style, Godard and the younger directors are driven more towards fragmentation. The roots of the new approach are less an affirmation than a negation, in the name of increased truth, of everything that has been tried before. This negative approach is reflected in the careers of the film-makers involved. They are frequently rootless, shifting from country to

176

country and trying out (and subsequently rejecting) a diversity of styles, moving first away from and then back towards the mass audience which they are unable to carry with them in their more extreme forays into a 'new' cinema.

The watershed can be seen in retrospect to have been the emergence of Jean-Luc Godard (b. 1930) as a feature film director in 1960. For the following eight years Godard subjected every element of the conventionally financed and distributed feature film to a rigorous analysis, before abandoning commercial production altogether in the aftermath of May 1968, which drove him to rethink his film-making so as to take into account his new political consciousness. Either half of Godard's career – pre- or post-1968 – would have made him a major figure in modern cinema: together they make him without question the most important film-maker of his generation. His influence lies heavily on the work of a variety of directors, both in France and elsewhere; and if his direct impact on such younger contemporaries as Jean-Marie Straub (b. 1933), Bernardo Bertolucci (b. 1941) and Alexander Kluge (b. 1932) varies enormously, all of these can aptly be termed post-Godardian film-makers. The kinds of concern which Godard embodies find their echo too in the Communist states, and these West European directors have been supplemented by a formidable influx from the East, in the persons of a range of brilliant film-makers with a very ambiguous attitude towards Marxism on the one hand and Western material values on the other: Roman Polanski (b. 1933), Miloš Forman (b. 1932), Dusan Makavejev (b. 1932) and Jerzy Skolimowski (b. 1938).

It would be foolish to attempt too rigid a definition of the work of these very diverse film-makers, but at least the context in which they have worked can be described with a fair degree of accuracy. One of the most striking things about this particular generation is the extent to which its culture is primarily a cinematic one. Godard is perhaps the extreme example of a film-maker who for years made films which related in the first instance to other films he had seen and admired and only secondly to the real world; but a wide knowledge of the cinema is common to all these directors. They do not simply follow or learn from the example of the older modernists; they are much influenced by past Hollywood film styles (even if they reject or caricature them) and one can uncover a mass of allusions to and quotations from their favourite directors. Equally, the elements of the urban environment to which they respond most strongly are such things as advertisements, commercials and television images, and in this respect at least there are undeniable similarities to the roughly contemporary phenomenon of pop art.

Counterpointing this involvement with the media environment is the strong influence of the various early 1960s' attempts to redefine the relationship of film and reality, in particular *cinéma-vérité* and the American underground

177

film. On the one hand there is Jean Rouch with his attempt to integrate realist filming methods and fictional, totally improvised story elements, and on the other there is Andy Warhol's conception of the film-maker as voyeur. The effects of these diverse influences were broadly twofold. First, they projected the film-maker into a quite new relationship with the subject of his filming. There was no natural fictional form or narrative event which could simply be filmed unselfconsciously. We find therefore that the modernist film-makers of this generation employ deliberately anti-illusionist techniques and use incidents and actors in such a way that the making of the film becomes a sort of criticism of itself. The second effect was to turn the film-maker very much back on himself, so that his work is personal in quite a new and different manner. Again Godard provides us with the classic and extreme instance of a director whose films are all stages of an extended if confused autobiographical confession, a measure of his own developing consciousness and a sign of his involvement with people and events. The stylistic result, as far as modernism is concerned, is a refusal of conventional narrative approaches in favour of collage and compilation methods. Films are filled with an often discordant mixture of allusion and parody, and self-consciously criticise their own stylistic procedures as well as those of earlier film-makers. Being notebook accumulations of a fairly random variety of styles and ideas rather than straight narratives, these films demand new reactions from their audiences. A juggling with alienation and involvement takes the place of an obsession with illusion and reality as the central feature of films which proclaim endlessly that a film is a film is a film . . .

Of course, not all the important young directors of the 1960s go to these extremes. Indeed the conflicting pressures on this generation of film-makers are very apparent if we look at the careers of three directors who began with very independent styles but have more recently worked on Hollywood-financed productions: Roman Polanski, Bernardo Bertolucci and Miloš Forman. All three are enormously talented *auteurs* whose whole output would repay very detailed study, but their work, like that of Fellini or Truffaut, falls outside the boundaries of modernist cinema as it has been defined here. The strength of the lure of Hollywood is perhaps an indication of the extent to which, despite a veneer of modernity, all three are basically film-makers in a traditional and more reassuring mould.

Roman Polanski's five latest films have indeed been far removed from modernism – a parody vampire movie (*Dance of the Vampires*, 1967), a genuine horror film (*Rosemary's Baby*, 1968), a version of *Macbeth* (1971), an attempt at Felliniesque fantasy (*What?*, 1972) and a fresh look at the 1930s' private detective film (*Chinatown*, 1974). But his earlier work is much more

Polanski's *Repulsion*: Catherine Deneuve

relevant to the subject of this book. Some of his first shorts, notably *The Fat and the Lean* and *Mammals*, are brilliant little parables involving only two or three characters in an empty landscape and calling to mind the dialogues of Samuel Beckett. Some of this quality is retained in Polanski's excellent first feature, the Polish-made *Knife in the Water* (1962), a study of the games of supremacy and sexual dominance played by a trio of people together on a yacht, which ends in a characteristically open manner. But the most fascinating of Polanski's films from the point of view of modern cinema are his two British films of the mid-1960s, the bitter Pinteresque comedy, *Cul-de-Sac* (1966), and, more particularly, *Repulsion* (1965).

There are in *Repulsion* many of the private references so typical of the new cinema – an allusion to *Un Chien Andalou* in the credits, for instance, or the choice of the heroine's name (Ledoux) and place of origin (Brussels) as a homage to the curator of the Cinémathèque Royale de Belgique. In addition, the film has a characteristic modern subject in that it traces the mental disintegration of a young Belgian girl, Carol (played by Catherine Deneuve), who is left alone in her London flat when her sister goes off on holiday with a married man. As in Alain Jessua's *La Vie à l'Envers*, the overall development of the film is unambiguous – there is no doubt ultimately about the reality of the girl's madness – but our response to it is complicated by the extent to which we share her view of events. We see the growing isolation of Carol, as a gulf opens up between her and the activity in the world about her, but we also undergo with her the growing crescendo of horror that leads ultimately to the slaughter of both her boy-friend and her landlord.

Mixing his fantasy sequences with carefully chosen concrete details, Polanski draws us into Carol's own vision of madness. Beginning with the enlarging of a crack in the kitchen wall and with footsteps heard outside her room after dark, the nightmare builds up to embrace fantasies of rape, until the climax comes when the whole fabric of the apartment comes to life, with hands thrusting through the corridor walls to clutch at her. The film's combination of subjective viewpoint and objective observation in the context of a linear plot is less characteristic of modernist cinema than of the traditional approach to thriller structure of which Alfred Hitchcock is the master. But Polanski uses these devices not primarily to manipulate our responses to his story but as ends in themselves. Whereas Hitchcock concludes *Psycho* with an explanation which rationalises and distances the horrors we have experienced, *Repulsion* ends with deliberately ambiguous shots of Carol in the arms of her sister's lover and of the flat into which she had barricaded herself as madness closed in upon her.

Bernardo Bertolucci has also been attracted to a Hollywood style of film-

Bertolucci's *The Spider's Strategy*

making, despite his impeccable modernist origins – poet and amateur film-maker in his teens and assistant on *Accattone* to Pier Paolo Pasolini, who helped him set up his first feature, *La commare secca* (1962), at the age of twenty-one. Bertolucci's text introducing the published script of his second feature, *Prima della rivoluzione* (1964), lists some of his favourite films and film-makers: Mizoguchi, Straub, Ford and Godard; *La Règle du Jeu*, *Viaggio in Italia*, *L'avventura* and *A Bout de Souffle*. He describes his own work as 'an historical film about ambiguity and uncertainty' and states his belief that 'every time you have to rediscover the cinema from scratch. That is the real problem which film-makers must set themselves: what does filming actually mean?'[1]

Prima della rivoluzione itself is a very contemporary set of variations on some themes from Stendhal's *La Chartreuse de Parme*, and it established Bertolucci as a major talent in the Italian cinema. But it is less a work of questioning and doubt than a startlingly mature display of stylistic assurance in the treatment of traditional romantic themes. The ambiguity is rooted in the characters' responses to their situation, rather than in the narrative itself.

181

The Conformist: Jean-Louis Trintignant

Despite the success of the film, it was only after a break of four years that Bertolucci was able to take up his feature film-making career again in the late 1960s, and his work of this period – *Partner* (1968), based on a story by Dostoievsky, and *La strategia del ragno* (1970) – show a more authentic modernism.

The latter film, known in English as *The Spider's Strategy*, is adapted from the Borges story *The Theme of the Traitor and Hero*, which the director has transposed into post-Fascist Italy. It employs a variation on the modernist device of juggling with the interaction of past and present and deals with a young man (played by Giulio Brogi) who sets out to investigate the mysterious death of his father, an anti-Fascist hero apparently killed by Mussolini's supporters. To this end he interviews all those who knew him and, as he uncovers facets of the truth, we see flashbacks to the earlier period, in which the father is also played by Brogi, with little change of make-up. Thus father and son are linked across the years by an uncanny resemblance, and the statue of the father in the town square seems almost a representation of the son as well. The confusion is compounded by the fact that the father's friends and mistress appear in the flashbacks exactly as they are when the son meets them thirty years later. As a result, it becomes impossible always to differentiate between past and present – the effect is rather one of a labyrinth than an historical representation – and the son's inability to tear himself away even when he learns the truth is given added force. The real delight of the film, however, lies not in this narrative ambiguity but in one's response to Bertolucci's beautifully controlled handling of form and colour. The nostalgia for a Fascist period he is too young to have experienced at first hand – which links this film with his masterly adaptation of Moravia's *Il conformista* (*The Conformist*, 1970) – is perhaps a clue as to Bertolucci's real place in contemporary cinema. His flirtation with modernism is akin to Visconti's involvement with neo-realism during the 1940s which, for a time, obscured the fact that his talents, like those of Bertolucci, lie in the evocation of a vanished way of life and a sumptuous romantic exploration of the themes of love and death.

This judgment is confirmed by Bertolucci's immensely successful *Last Tango in Paris* (1972), which starred Marlon Brando and a newcomer, Maria Schneider. Despite the modish touches – the use of Francis Bacon paintings as a background for the credits, the appearance of Jean-Pierre Léaud and some quotations from the French 1930s' cinema of Jean Vigo and Marcel Carné – the narrative structure of *Last Tango* could hardly be further from what we think of as modern cinema. It is characterized by relentless intercutting of parallel action, the compression of the story into tight dramatic scenes, the almost oppressive use of music to underline the emotions, and a dénouement signalled to us by the film's opening shot, a zoom down on to Brando's anguished face. Indeed there are uncanny echoes of the Carné of *Le Jour se lève*: the defeated hero seeking his own doom, the spice of nudity, the opposition between passion and a caricatured everyday life, and a fascination with depicting the flow of time. As Carné shaped *Le Jour se lève* to reflect the movement of night through to dawn, so Bertolucci shows here the three-day birth and death of an apparently timeless passion. Real time is continually dislocated – in the one case by flashbacks and in the other by parallel action – so that the film has a rhythm abstracted from actuality and totally controlled by the director. The limit of Bertolucci's modernity is to transpose the verbal explicitness of Henry Miller's novels and some of the voyeuristic aspects of the underground film into a big United Artists production. This – as far as it goes – works remarkably well. Marlon Brando and his partner together in the flat which is their retreat from the world convey the realities of a sexual relationship with a directness unmatched in the commercial cinema. There is a succession of brilliantly acted and directed encounters in which they make explicit aspects of themselves, both as actors and as real people, which films have customarily ignored.

Last Tango in Paris: Marlon Brando, Maria Schneider

The limitations of *Last Tango in Paris* stem from the way Bertolucci has surrounded Brando and Schneider with his own platitudes, self-indulgences and evasions. Many of one's doubts derive from the appearance of Jean-Pierre Léaud as Maria Schneider's fiancé and the embodiment of conventional values. The idea of the *cinéma-vérité* film which Léaud is making about this particular week in the girl's life is *Last Tango*'s one attempt at a genuinely modern piece of construction, and it might have allowed Bertolucci to give a double view of Schneider, torn between banality and passion and revealing simultaneously two true but contradictory images of herself. But the director has ignored this chance to use Léaud as a kind of *alter ego* for himself and as a means of commenting on the nature of cinematic truth, and has instead reduced the whole role of the reportage to an absurd travesty. Here and in the melodramatic ending which Bertolucci appends to his film, an opportunity is wasted, and for all its moments of genuine observation *Last Tango in Paris* is less a harrowing document than a lyrical piece of conformist reassurance. Its sweeping camerawork and exquisite use of colour (the cool grey landscapes and interiors bathed in a beautiful orange glow) align it with the most traditional sort of contemporary film-making, the kind which – from Claude Lelouch's *Un Homme et une Femme* to Bo Widerberg's *Elvira Madigan* – invites us to shed a sympathetic tear for its tormented heroes, but does not begin to make us question our ways of living and loving.

There is an equal lack of abrasiveness in the work of the Czech director Milos Forman, despite the fact that his satirical approach to authority has caused him some difficulties in his home country. It is less crucial than Bertolucci's evasiveness in *Last Tango in Paris*, however, since Forman works exclusively in the field of comedy. He began his career as a scriptwriter in the 1950s and made a couple of short films before his debut as a feature director in 1963. All his Czech features – *Peter and Pavla* (*Czerny Petr*, 1963), *A Blonde in Love* (*Lasky Jedny Plavovlasky*, 1965) and *The Firemen's Ball* (*Hori, ma Panenko*, 1967) – are marked by wry humour and delicate observation.

A recurring feature of Forman's work since the early short, *Talent Competition*, has been an interest in amateur performers, whether they are singers, brassband musicians or participants in a beauty contest. This interest is carried over into what is perhaps his finest film, *Taking Off*, which he made independently in the United States in 1971. Here the stages of the main narrative – the problems faced by the parents of a fifteen-year-old girl who disappears for a few days – are set against recurring images of young people auditioning for a musical show. It is the marvellously spontaneous quality of Forman's comic inspiration in these audition sequences which is responsible for the film's impact. But there is here none of that questioning of what

Miloš Forman's *Taking Off*: the etiquette of pot smoking

constitutes a film reportage which is so characteristic of modernist cinema – Forman simply uses, immensely skilfully but quite unselfconsciously, the camera's observational power. He has in fact expressed on occasion his dislike of modernist cinema, to which he opposes Italian neo-realism and the early work of François Truffaut (particularly *Les Quatre Cents Coups*), and this defines his position very well.

Taking Off is far from being a Hollywood movie – the story-line is discontinuous and the basic pattern of construction is that of juxtaposition. But this latter is used simply to bring out comic incongruity, in the contrast between the directness of the young and the complicated quirks of the middle-aged, or the very real hesitancy of the girls at the audition and the self-indulgence of the parents playing strip poker. The same quality underlies the success of the 'ode to a screw' (contrasting the outrageous lyrics with the singer's delicacy of tone and phrasing) and the sequence of the dinner organized by the Society for the Parents of Fugitive Children (pot smoking introduced in terms of social etiquette). The various elements are extremely funny in themselves and are put together with an unerring sense of comic rhythm, but the film's impact remains on a single unambiguous level. Forman's methods in *Taking Off* have superficial similarities with those of Makavejev in *W.R. – Mysteries of the Organism*, but his work as a whole lacks totally the questioning of cinema contained in the latter film's multi-layered texture.

The Godardian and post-Godardian cinema with which the following chapters are concerned has been, in many ways, enormously influential, but it has not constituted a total transformation because its wider implications have been largely ignored. One reason for this is that Godardian cinema is not a precisely defined extreme pole of cinematic development, but rather a delicately poised and precarious compromise. It may indeed be best described as the point of tension between conflicting impulses – narrative and fragmentation, reportage and selfconscious manipulation, the wholehearted acceptance of the commercial requisites of film-making for a mass audience (such as we find in Bertolucci) and the absolute rejection of the whole professional structure (which characterizes the underground attitude to cinema). Its limits are tenuous, for, as we have seen, superficial elements of its questioning approach to cinematic reality have been incorporated into the styles of many directors working within the normal production system.

Equally, film-makers who began their careers in the underground milieu have been able to by-pass this area of ambiguity completely when they have set out to acquire a wider audience for their work. Paul Morrissey's association with Andy Warhol and his continued employment of actors and personalities discovered by Warhol cannot disguise the fact that his own films as a director – *Flesh*, *Trash*, *Heat* and his recent parodies of the horror film – are neither underground nor modernist works. Morrissey's reliance on the sour ironies of an unambiguous linear plot and his exploitation of the attractions of bad taste humour relate him more closely to the Hollywood style perfected by Billy Wilder in *Sunset Boulevard* than to the work of Jean-Luc Godard. Even for the film-makers we are most concerned with here – Godard, Straub, Makavejev – the balance has proved difficult to maintain, and their work has encountered an enormous amount of frustration and incomprehension.

16. Jean-Luc Godard: Identity and Communication

The career of Jean-Luc Godard presents the critic with considerable problems. To begin with there is the sheer quantity of his output. Born in 1930, he turned to film criticism in 1950, publishing his first article – on Joseph Mankiewicz – in *La Gazette du Cinéma.* He has remained a prolific critic and his collected critical writings, covering the years up to 1967, occupy some 414 pages. Simultaneously he was working as a film-maker. Between 1954 and 1958 he made five short films, beginning with a documentary, *Opération Béton*, about a dam near Geneva on the construction of which he worked himself. The remaining shorts are light fictional works and in some of them – *Tous les Garçons s'appellent Patrick* and *Charlotte et son Jules*, for instance – a foretaste of his mature style is already apparent. His transition to feature film-making with *A Bout de Souffle* in 1960 began a decade of prodigious activity unequalled by any other major director of the period. In the years between 1960 and 1967 – up to and including *Weekend* – Godard made no less than fifteen features and seven short sketches for episodic films. *Le Gai Savoir*, made for television in 1968, marks the move to a more overtly political style of film-making and was followed by nine further independent films before Godard returned to the commercially financed feature film with *Tout Va Bien* in 1972.

Even within the two major categories – the commercial and the political –

into which his output can be readily divided, the scope of his experimentation is staggering, for no two Godard films are alike and each new work breaks fresh ground. Moreover such has been the influence his work has exerted on young film-makers throughout the world that it is difficult for us now to assess his early work. One's view of even so innovatory a work as *A Bout de Souffle* is inevitably coloured by the existence of dozens of more or less trivial imitations. We are too close in time to cover adequately the whole range of Godard's work and space does not allow each stage of his development to be treated in the detail it demands. I shall therefore concentrate here on the twin themes of identity and communication as they illuminate the early part of his career, when he was still working within the commercial structure of the French film industry. Having looked at the general issues, we shall see how far they are reflected in one of Godard's major films of the period, *Pierrot le Fou* (1965).

Perhaps the first thing which strikes one about a Godard film is the cutting: the jagged fragments put together without an immediately apparent logic, the seeming jumble of images and sounds which sometimes complement and sometimes contradict each other. *Une Femme Mariée* is indeed explicitly subtitled 'Fragments of a film shot in 1964', and *La Chinoise* (1967) 'A film in the process of being made'. Moreover the refusal to follow the then conventional presentational pattern (a general establishing shot, then a medium or two-shot and only finally a close-up) had after all been one of the initially startling aspects of *A Bout de Souffle*. But before one can decide the reasons for these editing patterns, one has to consider what are the characteristic component fragments. First and most obviously, the images of any Godard film are loaded with quotes, references, parodies, allusions and pastiche. The camera dwells constantly on the secondhand imagery which assails us in our everyday urban environment: posters, advertisements, neon signs, photographs, magazine pages, postcards, record sleeves, prints of old masters, book titles, soap-powder packets, and so on.

A place of particular importance is reserved for cinematic references: a one-minute silence in memory of Humphrey Bogart in *A Bout de Souffle* as the camera stops on a still from *The Harder They Fall*, a parody of Lumière in *Les Carabiniers* (1963), clips from Dreyer's *La Passion de Jeanne d'Arc* in *Vivre sa Vie* (1962), from Resnais's *Nuit et Brouillard* in *Une Femme Mariée* and from Godard's own sketch *Le Grand Escroc* (1964) in *Pierrot le Fou*, together with a whole series of incidents handled in conventional genre fashion: car chases, gunfights, confrontations, etc. Godard began as a film critic and is constantly aware of the cinema's variety of styles, masters and movements. A single film, *Une Femme est une Femme* (1961), for instance, contains visual or verbal references to Cyd Charisse, Gene Kelly, Bob Fosse,

Points of reference: Anna Karina in *Vivre sa Vie*

Burt Lancaster, Lubitsch, *Jules et Jim, Moderato Cantabile, Tirez sur le Pianiste, Opéra Mouffe* and Godard's own *A Bout de Souffle*, as well as a personal appearance by Jeanne Moreau. In this way references to film are as natural to him as are literary allusions to James Joyce, and his methods of construction through quotation have analogies with the way in which Joyce used the history of English literature in building up the complex texture of *Ulysses*.

Words in Godard films are also predominantly quotations or allusions of some sort, beginning with the names of characters themselves. *Made in USA* (1967), which is dedicated 'to Nick (Ray) and Samuel (Fuller) who brought me up to respect image and sound', has characters with such names as Donald Siegel, Richard Widmark, Inspector Aldrich and Doris Mizoguchi. In addition real people are frequently interviewed or give spontaneous comment: the director Roger Leenhardt in *Une Femme Mariée*, the philosopher Brice Parain in *Vivre sa Vie*, Fritz Lang in *Le Mépris* (1963), Samuel Fuller in *Pierrot le Fou*. There are lengthy passages from the director's favourite reading: Eluard in *Alphaville* (1965), Racine and Céline in *Une Femme Mariée*, Lorca in *Pierrot le Fou* and an Edgar Allan Poe story in *Vivre sa Vie*.

The same tendency persists in some of Godard's political films, so that Eldridge Cleaver is quoted at length in *One plus One* (1968). Other parts of Godard's work parody a wide range of styles of language: advertisements, political speeches, estate agents' prose, newspaper headlines and so on. Characteristically, Godard's jokes tend to be puns or forms of word play, extreme examples of which appear in *Made in USA*, where a barman and a worker discuss language and make up nonsense sentences: 'The floor is being stubbed out on the cigarette,' or 'There are three bars in the telephone.' The picture of language that emerges from these films is that of a closed system in which the only freedom is to juggle, to quote in a new context, or to fragment. His chosen medium allows Godard to affirm his own identity and individuality only with borrowed words and images and to communicate with no more than a second-hand language.

Just as Godard's films do not record the world directly but become caught up in a mesh of allusion, so too the actors in his films do not play rounded characters in coherent fictions. The illusion is disturbed by the appearance of a surprising number of people as themselves. In addition to those already mentioned, we find the Rolling Stones (in *One plus One*), Brigitte Bardot (*Masculin-Féminin*, 1966), Marianne Faithfull (*Made in USA*), etc. The

'She is Marina Vlady. She is an actress': *Deux ou trois choses que je sais d'elle*

leading players, too, are as much themselves as they are the characters they ostensibly portray, retaining their own gestures and mannerisms. *Vivre sa Vie* is a documentary about Anna Karina (at that time Godard's wife) as well as a story about prostitution. In this connection the way in which we are introduced to the heroine of *Deux ou trois choses que je sais d'elle* (1967) is particularly revealing. As we see shots of the actress, the commentary, spoken by Godard himself, introduces us:

She is Marina Vlady. She is an actress. She is wearing a dark blue sweater with two yellow stripes. She is of Russian extraction. Her hair is dark chestnut or light brown. I don't know exactly.

Now she is turning her head to the left, but that doesn't matter. She is Juliette Janson. She lives here. She is wearing a dark blue sweater with two yellow stripes. Her hair is dark chestnut or light brown. I don't know exactly. She is of Russian extraction.

Godard's usual method of working without a tightly fixed script also has the effect of blurring the distinction between acting and being. Faced with a text improvised by the director just before shooting, the actors react with equal spontaneity and their response becomes part of the film. Occasionally, as with Marina Vlady in *Deux ou trois choses*, Godard talks to, questions and provokes the actress by means of a tiny hidden microphone during the shooting, so that she as actress talks to him as director, though in the context of the completed film we assume we are seeing one fictional character addressing another. The direct statement to camera is a recurring stylistic feature, but it is often impossible to distinguish real interviews from fake ones.

In *Pierrot le Fou*, for instance, three people successively introduce themselves to us in big close-up. While the second and third seem to be real people giving their true identities, the first is clearly the actor Laszlo Szabo, though he claims to be Laszlo Kovacs (one of Jean-Paul Belmondo's aliases in *A Bout de Souffle*), a political refugee from Santo Domingo. Stylistically, however, there is absolutely no distinction between the three shots. Characters in Godard films of the mid-1960s may speak each other's lines or describe each other's thoughts, one may read long quotations at another or both may speak at once. But seldom do we get any sense of true dialogue or of a real interchange of ideas and feelings between characters. The situation in *Le Mépris*, in which the main characters – two French, one American, one German – converse through an Italian interpreter, is a perfect example of the communication process in a Godard film. The selfconscious manipulation of actors and the combination of fictional narrative events with undigested chunks of reality give his work its particular tone. There is neither pure reality nor pure illusion, but rather a constant questioning of the boundaries of acting and life and of the nature of communication through the processes of illusion. The actors and actresses are trapped in a closed circle of non-communication, in that they can neither be themselves nor lose their identity in an acted role.

The environment in which Godard's characters live is a place affording equally little hope. Urban society is depicted as a prison and the picture is consistently bleak, whether it is the world of political assassination of *Le Petit Soldat* (1960), the drab suburbs of *Bande à Part* (1964), or the Paris of adolescent protest and aspiration in *Masculin-Féminin*. Even when he looks to the future in *Alphaville* Godard sees no way out, merely the same weight of authoritarianism and pointless killing. The social system forces two roles on the individual, that of submission or revolt. Both of these, interestingly enough, are close approximations to conventional roles in the American gangster movies which influenced Godard so strongly, and this allows him to express his social concerns within a largely parodied genre context. For the submissive role Godard chooses the image of the prostitute. This is used literally in *Vivre sa Vie*, where the heroine, Nana, becomes a whore, and *Deux ou trois choses que je sais d'elle*, in which Juliette Janson participates in casual prostitution to pay the rent. The same elements persist in Godard's vision of the future: in *Alphaville*, where Anna Karina appears as a 'Seductress, Third Class', and in the sketch *Anticipation* (1967), which echoes the mood of the earlier feature by showing prostitution in the year 2000, a time when the functions of verbal and physical love have become so totally separated that no whore is capable of dealing with both simultaneously. Allied notions are to be found in *Une Femme est une Femme*, where the heroine is a stripper, and in *Le Mépris*, in which a scriptwriter virtually sells his wife to his producer in exchange for a contract. Indeed the idea of prostitution may be expanded to embrace the whole experience of living in society. In so far as we are dominated by society, we prostitute ourselves, if not with our bodies then with our minds.

If, on the other hand, we react positively to confront the violence exercised on us by society, we are akin to the gangsters of so many Hollywood 'B' pictures. At first the gangster figures in Godard's work are lone individuals: the petty crook turned killer in *A Bout de Souffle*, the political assassin of *Le Petit Soldat*, the crooks who control Nana in *Vivre sa Vie*. But gradually the focus widens to take in the soldiers of *Les Carabiniers* and the reporter–revenger figure of Lemmy Caution in *Alphaville*, and eventually we begin to find a political flavour – the pair of killers in *Made in USA* are called Nixon and MacNamara, and the Seine et Oise Liberation Front flourishes in *Weekend*. Thus over the course of seven years of film-making, the United States remains in the forefront of Godard's consciousness, but its role shifts from that of being a source of inspiration for a certain kind of individualist enterprise (Humphrey Bogart) to that of constituting the prime example of indefensible collective violence (Vietnam). Again, as with language and the idea of acting, we have an inability on the part of the individual to define an identity freely. Society is a third closed system offering no scope for reciprocal interaction of the individual and his environment, and constituting a system in which he is annihilated or at best stunted.

This fundamentally pessimistic view of man, language and society underlies all Godard's work. His style is fragmented and his films seem disjointed because they reflect the fact that he can find none of the links that might allow the individual to come to terms with himself, to make contact with his fellows or to live and work creatively in society. Godard has sought in two main ways to break out of this system of defeat – through love and political action – but in both areas his reactions are so contradictory that the notion of defeat persists. This is borne out by *Pierrot le Fou*, a film which Godard himself described as the story of the last romantic couple. It tells of Ferdinand Griffon (Jean-Paul Belmondo) who decides in the course of a fashionable party to give up his marriage to a rich Italian and go off with Marianne (Anna Karina), an enigmatic girl whom he had known and loved years before. There is an enormous zest in their actions as they head South, glorying in their freedom and irresponsibility, but their idyll by the sea soon turns sour. Ferdinand is drawn more and more into the world of violence inhabited by Marianne and her 'brother' until, deceived and humiliated, he kills first the girl and then himself. His death is one of the most remarkable scenes in Godard's work. Ferdinand paints his face blue, ties several sticks of dynamite around his head and lights the fuse. He seems to change his mind, but it is too late and the film cuts to a long shot of the explosion. As the smoke billows up, the camera pans slowly away to take in the sea in all its beauty.

The dream of love – that non-verbal understanding which will transcend the difficulties of language and create a defence against the intrusions of society – is very real, but doomed from the start. All Godard's early films after *A Bout de Souffle* are strongly marked by his response to the beauty of Anna Karina, whom he married in 1961. She appeared briefly but memorably in *Le Petit Soldat* and Godard painted full-length portraits of her in *Une Femme est une Femme*, *Vivre sa Vie* and *Bande à Part*. But Godard's personal dream failed and *Pierrot le Fou* was made under the impact of the break-up of their marriage. The basic incompatibility of Ferdinand and Marianne, despite their great intimacy, is summed up in the brief dialogue when each defines what love means. For Karina it is 'flowers . . . animals . . . the blue of the sky', but for Belmondo it is 'ambition . . . hope . . . the movement of things'. Or again when Marianne explains her present unhappiness: 'You talk to me with words and I look at you with feelings.' Instead of giving Ferdinand a true sense of identity, Marianne denies him even his

Pierrot le Fou: the romantic impulse

name, persisting throughout in calling him Pierrot despite all his protests. Love is explored in Godard's films of the early 1960s as the one possible way out of the dilemmas of communication, but from the very first Godard displays a view of women as enigmatic and perfidious. The actions of Marianne here are not markedly different from those of Patricia in *A Bout de Souffle* (betraying her lover to the police) or Angéla in *Une Femme est une Femme* (sleeping with both her husband and their best friend to get the baby she desperately wants).

Pierrot le Fou is a key work in Godard's development in that it is not only the last of his films to focus primarily on the personal problems of the couple, but also the first in which the political awareness which dominates his late 1960s' work begins to become apparent. Political issues are, it is true, touched on directly only in the clip from a Vietnam newsreel (which bores Ferdinand) and in the performance – 'Uncle Sam's nephew versus Uncle Ho's niece' – put on by Belmondo and Karina to entertain the tourists. Yet this is the beginning of a concern which is continued in the subsequent films – the Ben Barka affair in *Made in USA*, more thoughts on Vietnam in Godard's contribution to *Loin du Vietnam* (1967), and Mao and the students in *La Chinoise* – before becoming the exclusive theme of his post-1968 work. In *Pierrot le Fou* we can see clearly the basic contradictions in Godard as a political film-maker. First there is the ambiguity of his love–hate relationship with America. He expressed this predicament very well in one of his articles: 'How can I hate John Wayne upholding Goldwater and love him tenderly when abruptly he takes Natalie Wood into his arms in the next-to-last reel of *The Searchers*'.[1] Again we find in *Pierrot le Fou* all the romantic nostalgia for escape, the impulse to seek out a private refuge, which persists as an undercurrent in the later work. Above all there is the contradiction of Godard's ideological simplicity (witnessed by his definition, in *Made in USA*, of a political film as 'Walt Disney plus blood') and the complexities of a style based on such sophisticated manipulation of image and sound that it is bound to cut him off from a mass audience.

Godard is a very selfconscious film-maker and his dissatisfaction with the idea that the camera can ever reveal the true meaning of objects, let alone of people, is explicit in several parts of *Pierrot le Fou*. Early in the film Marianne tells of the fascination photographs have for her because of their ambiguity: 'You see a still photograph of some man or other, with a caption underneath. He was a coward perhaps, or pretty smart. But at that precise instant when the photograph was taken, no one can say what he actually is, and what he was thinking exactly . . . about his wife maybe, or his mistress, his past, his future, or basketball . . . One never knows!' Later Ferdinand talks directly to the camera about his own feelings for Marianne: 'We have entered the age of the Double-Man. One no longer needs a mirror to speak to oneself. When Marianne says "It is a fine day" what is she really thinking? I have only this image of her, saying "It is a fine day." Nothing else?' The clip from his own short film *Le Grand Escroc* included in *Pierrot le Fou* is about a *cinéma-vérité* film-maker called Patricia Leacock (after the character Jean Seberg also plays in *A Bout de Souffle* and as a little homage to the American documentarist). She is attempting to uncover the truth about a mysterious forger with her 16mm camera, seeking the moment when a person sheds a fictitious character and reveals his real one, but her search is fruitless. Godard's own concern in *Pierrot le Fou* is not to transcribe reality in this way but to capture, as it were, the spaces in between. The long passage quoted by Belmondo at the beginning of the film from a book by Elie Faure states the theme. After the age of fifty, Velasquez, we are told, 'no longer painted anything concrete and precise . . . His only experience of the world was those mysterious copulations which united the forms and tones with a secret but inevitable movement.' While imitating the voice of the actor Michel Simon, Ferdinand expresses the same idea: 'I've found an idea for a novel. No longer to write about people's lives

... but only about life, life itself. What goes on between people, in space ... like sound and colours.'

The ambiguity of *Pierrot le Fou* lies in the relationship between the narrative form Godard chooses and the use he makes of it to explore these gaps and discontinuities of experience. He learned his film-making from the American cinema of Preminger and Ray, and here he tries to follow the definition of cinema offered by Samuel Fuller in the early party sequence: 'Film is like a battleground. Love, hate, action, violence, death. In one word ... emotion.' He takes the tight, explicit form of the thriller and includes the obligatory chases, acts of violence and bloody deaths. But at the same time he explodes the narrative framework from within, because his real interest is not in the action, but the inaction, not with Marianne's presumed connection with gun-runners, but with the moment when she walks along the sea shore shouting 'What am I to do? I don't know what to do!' over and over again.

The truths Godard is seeking can only be captured obliquely, so that the aside is more important than the big moment of decision. He conveys the hollowness of Ferdinand's marriage not with dramatic confrontations but by means of the party sequences with their non-naturalistic lighting effects and their dialogue echoing the trite and meaningless phrases of advertisements for cars or hair spray. The portrait of Marianne is built up similarly with colour and light, the songs she sings and the dresses she wears, the sense of spontaneous movement, the sunlight, the sea. Godard does not eliminate the irrelevances, smooth out the gaps in the continuity or fuse everything into a coherent flow of incident. Instead the spectator of *Pierrot le Fou* is left to make his own selection, to build up his own picture of people and events, to piece together the fragments in his own mind. But however one juggles with the constituent elements of the film, the contradictions of identity and ambiguities of communication remain.

17. Dusan Makavejev: Collage and Compilation

The film-making of this third generation of modernists – Jean-Luc Godard, Dusan Makavejev, Jean-Marie Straub – is much influenced by the new relationships between the film-maker, his subject matter and his audience which were created initially in the various forms of documentary film-making during the early 1960s. One of their prime concerns might indeed be defined as that of blurring the boundaries of the factual and the invented by applying the new documentary styles and techniques to fictional material. Godard, for example, has been deeply influenced by the *cinéma-vérité* approach, as can be seen by his choice of cameramen for some of his films. Though Raoul Coutard has been his principal collaborator throughout his feature career, Godard worked with Pierre Lhomme (Chris Marker's photographer and co-author for *Le Joli Mai* in 1962) on the sketch *Anticipation*, and even earlier he had used the American *cinéma-vérité* film-maker Albert Maysles as cameraman for the short *Montparnasse-Levallois*. This sketch for the collective film *Paris vu par* ... (1964) was particularly interesting in that Godard limited himself to directing the action and left Maysles to film it as if it were a real event.

One of Godard's fellow contributors to *Paris vu par* ... was Jean Rouch, whose experiments in mixing documentary filming methods and improvised acting techniques undoubtedly opened the way for some of Godard's work. *Gare du Nord*, for example, Rouch's contribution to the collective film, was a prescripted sketch with a fairly conventional plot: a woman quarrels with her husband, runs out of their flat and meets a man contemplating suicide who promptly offers her everything she has ever dreamed of. She goes back to her husband, however, and he kills himself. Rouch filmed this in just two ten-minute shots, with direct sound and a single take. There was no editing, and as a result we get a real sense of the look and sound of Paris as well as a complete equation of real time and film time. The techniques which Rouch brought to such experiments from his documentary origins in the ethno-graphic film − the handheld camera, use of natural light and real locations, synchronous sound recorded with directional or neck microphones, the mix-ing of observation, genuine interviews and improvised acted sequences − all find their echo in Godard's work in the period up to 1968.

Despite this there is still an enormous gulf between Godard and a true *cinéma-vérité* approach, as became very clear early in 1969, when Godard went to the United States to make a political film for the *cinéma-vérité* unit Leacock-Pennebaker Inc. Work on *One A.M.* (*One American Movie*) began in an atmosphere of mutual respect, with Rip Torn as the film's central figure and appearances by Eldridge Cleaver, Tom Hayden, LeRoi Jones and the Jefferson Airplane. Richard Leacock and Donn Alan Pennebaker had agreed to act as Godard's cameramen, but as soon as the shooting got under way they found themselves in an awkward situation. The key element in any *cinéma-vérité* approach is the cameraman's sensitivity to events, his im-mediate response to what he actually sees. It soon transpired, however, that Godard was not interested in any of the unexpected discoveries his two cameramen might make during the shooting, since he himself had set out with a very clear set of preconceptions which he wanted his cameramen to realize. Neither Leacock nor Pennebaker was temperamentally suited to take on this role of mere director of photography, since this kind of hierarchical division of responsibility runs contrary to all the principles of *cinéma-vérité* filming. Moreover they became increasingly frustrated because they really had no idea what was going on in Godard's head. As Leacock put it: 'You're sitting there thinking, instead of saying to yourself "Wow! Look!" You're thinking, what does the man want? Does he want this, does he want that, and what am I supposed to do?'[1]

All the same Pennebaker found the situation as a whole very intriguing and began shooting footage of his own:

I got more interested in the effect he had on people, in his machinations, and started to shoot ... kind of notes ... His relationship with people, the way he manoeuvred them, the way it didn't work finally, and his attempt to come to grips with what he considered to be the American Revolution, which I don't think he had the foggiest notion about.[2]

Leacock's own conclusions about the whole experience were that the gulf between Godard's methods and their own was total: 'He's not the least bit interested, as I can see, in observing. To me he's essentially theatrical.'[3] Not surprisingly Godard lost interest in the project and abandoned the film before it was edited. As a salvage job, Pennebaker assembled the rushes, trying not to edit them too much, but putting them in his own order and with additional material – the film notes he himself had shot of Godard at work. The resulting ninety-minute film, *One P.M.* (*One Parallel Movie*), is a confused but immensely revealing picture of the clash of two styles of film-making.

The films of Straub and Makavejev also seek to relate film and reality in fresh ways, and show clear parallels with other forms of non-fiction film-making, though again the techniques acquire quite a different meaning in their new context. Straub's methods of counterpointing images and sounds, for example, are to some extent anticipated in the work of French documentary film-makers of the 1950s, particularly Georges Franju and Alain Resnais. In *Le Sang des Bêtes* Franju achieves great impact from the contrast of observational shots of slaughterhouse activity with carefully posed, deliberately lyrical shots taken around the banks of the Seine. In *Hôtel des Invalides* he sets up new interactions between image and music by such devices as printing the words of a popular war song, so that we actually understand the meaning contained in the familiar phrases. Equally, the enormous power of Resnais's *Nuit et Brouillard* derives partly from the film-maker's total commitment to his subject (the Nazi concentration camps) and partly from the complex tensions set up between colour and black and white, music and image, movement and immobility, the banal emptiness of the landscape and the knowledge of six million deaths. In a similar way – and again the parallel should not be overstressed – the work of Dusan Makavejev, and in particular the use he makes of film archive material, can be related to the resurgence of the compilation film in the early 1960s, with such works as Erwin Leiser's *Mein Kampf* (1960), Paul Rotha's *The Life of Adolf Hitler* (1962) and Frédéric Rossif's *Mourir à Madrid* (1962).

Makavejev, who was born in Belgrade in 1932, graduated in philosophy before becoming a film student. He wrote some critical articles, made a few experimental amateur films, then worked as a documentary film-maker on some thirteen shorts between 1958 and 1964. His first feature film, *Man is not a Bird* (*Covek Nije Tijka*), which appeared in 1966, is his most conventional one, with a simpler, more coherent narrative line than he employs in his subsequent work. But already many of his later concerns are apparent in embryo – in the wryly humorous tone of the film and its combination of analysis of Marxist society as it exists in Yugoslavia with comment on the

The Switchboard Operator: telephonist and rat exterminator

sexual nature of man. The beginnings of the characteristic Makavejev interest in contradiction and juxtaposition can also be detected, particularly in the film's most celebrated sequence, which intercuts a performance of Beethoven's Ninth Symphony with the heroine making love in a lorry, the music and the lovers reaching a simultaneous climax.

The Switchboard Operator (*Ljubavni Slucaj*, 1967) has a very simple plot tracing the affair between Isabella, a very sexually aware young telephonist, and an older, more serious man, Ahmed, a party member who works as a rat exterminator. They meet, fall in love, and for a time live happily together. But while he is away, she allows herself to be seduced by a younger man. When he finds out, they quarrel and he gets drunk. Struggling to hold him back from a suicide attempt, she falls to her death and he is arrested for murder. This banal story is brought to life partly by the naturalness and vitality of the girl (played by the Hungarian actress Eva Ras) and partly by the way in which Makavejev relates it to the other strands of the film. For example, the time scheme is juggled with so as to give a series of transitions which are audacious and disturbing. The recovery of Isabella's body follows immediately after her first meeting with Ahmed (before we even suspect that she will die), and the film cuts from the couple naked together in bed to a detailed discussion of the findings at the post mortem. As a result our reaction to even the most banal moments of the couple's life together is extremely complex.

Equally striking is the way Makavejev illuminates his central themes with a whole range of factual and archive material which might seem to have very little to do with the couple but in fact fuses perfectly with their story to create a picture of human activity in all its contradictions. Isabella's seduction of Ahmed is intercut with television images from Dziga Vertov's *Enthusiasm* depicting the dismantling of some very phallic-looking church spires in the name of the Russian revolution. The combination of sexual desire and revolutionary fervour makes an odd and ironic comment on the attitudes of the two people involved. Later there is an equally startling cut away from the very erotic scene of Isabella's own seduction to some chastely posed and very dated nude tableaux uncovered by Makavejev in the Yugoslav film archives. In addition the director builds into the structure of his film several talks by a learned sexologist, a lecture on modern methods of detection by a criminologist, a short documentary on rat extermination and a descriptive sequence on cooking. The fusion emphasizes the ambiguity – the sexologist's theories are engaging but seem irrelevant to the very real sexual relationship we see developing, and the much vaunted police methods do not prevent the police from arresting Ahmed for a murder he did not commit.

The film's impact derives not from any pornographic content or intent, but from the great sensuality of Makavejev's images, as in the series of shots moving from Isabella lying naked on her bed with a cat, to a close-up of eggs being broken, and then to the cooking sequence, all to the accompaniment of operatic music. The result is a sense of the randomness and complexity of life; and though Makavejev has clearly learned from Godard's techniques of fragmentation, he shows none of the clinical approach to sex which the French director displays in *Une Femme Mariée*. The life-enhancing quality of Makavejev's work is very apparent in the film's ending. After the death of Isabella and the arrest of Ahmed, he cuts back to a shot of the couple arm-in-arm at their moment of supreme happiness, accompanied by a stirring revolutionary song by Mayakovsky and Hanns Eisler. Having fused fact and fiction in unlikely ways throughout the film, Makavejev now offers a very human triumph over death.

The collage method employed in *The Switchboard Operator*, and brought to its highest point subsequently in *W.R. – Mysteries of the Organism* and *Sweet Movie* (1974), is given a new twist in Makavejev's third feature, *Innocence Unprotected* (*Nevinost Bez Zastite*, 1968). This, as a prefatory note announces, is 'a new edition of a good old film', namely the first Serbian feature, made in 1942 by the professional strongman, Dragoljub Aleksic, whom the young Makavejev had seen perform. A naïve and ponderous piece of melodrama, Aleksic's *Innocence Unprotected* tells of a girl who loves the strongman but is almost forced to marry an ugly old man by her wicked stepmother. It is also a primitive example of the kind of collage mixture of fact and fiction that Makavejev himself favours, in that the action is broken up by the inclusion of clips from film records, shot between 1929 and 1940, of Aleksic's more spectacular exploits. It extols virtue and strength in unambiguous terms and, when first shown during the Occupation, it was very popular with local audiences, who preferred its simple heroics to the insidious subtleties of the German propaganda film.

Makavejev has taken over the main outlines of this 1942 film, re-edited it, tinted some of the sequences by hand and interspersed it with fresh material assembled by himself. A double focus is provided by the interviews, twenty-five years on, with the survivors of the original cast and crew: a group of rather plain middle-aged people, who sit picnicking at the grave of the now dead villain of the film and reminisce about the problems of shooting clandestinely, the curious financing of the film (by the sale of plywood sandals designed by the intrepid Aleksic), and the irony of the subsequent accusation of collaboration levelled at the film's makers. Makavejev cuts tellingly from Aleksic in the original film to colour shots of the older, plumper Aleksic of today, still willing to show off some of his feats of strength and to pose for the cameras in his swimming trunks. Most strikingly of all, Makavejev mixes German newsreel material of the 1940s into the action of the original *Innocence Unprotected* – cutting away from the villain's attempts to rape the heroine to maps depicting the progress of Hitler's armies, for example, and moving from scenes of domestic drama to the realities of hunger and bombing in 1942.

The director maintains throughout his respect and affection for the simple film-makers, whom he never patronizes or mocks, however naïve their words or behaviour. But through the multiple perspective he creates, he is able to use the original *Innocence Unprotected* to probe both the ironies of history and the paradoxes of film. Which is the real 1942 – the film's heroics or the newsreel horror? What do we mean by innocence? Which is truer, Aleksic's vision of virtue triumphant or the Nazi propaganda film's declaration of Serbo-German friendship? Again Makavejev finds the perfect ending for his film, with the camera tracking slowly up the torso of the unselfconscious strongman, while a hymn in praise of his feats is sung – a touching farewell to an engaging and disarming personality.

Makavejev's most complex film and his masterpiece to date is *W.R.–Mysteries of the Organism* (*W.R.– Misterije Organizma*, 1971). All pretence of a single unifying narrative structure is gone and the film functions on a great number of levels simultaneously, thanks to its splendidly vivid collage of some of the

203

Collage: the American segment of *W.R. – Mysteries of the Organism*

implications of the thought and teachings of Wilhelm Reich, a subject which
had preoccupied Makavejev since he had first read Reich's *Dialectical
Materialism and Psychoanalysis* in English as a student in 1950. The film's
opening moments set the tone for what is to follow. Tuli Kupferberg (founder
of the Revolting Theatre) stalks the streets of New York in a tattered army
uniform, brandishing a machine-gun and demanding to know who will judge
our judges. Milena Dravic and her friends sensuously pass an egg yolk from
hand to hand to the sound of a vigorous folk tune. Kaleidoscopic images from
erotic films ('Filme der Sexpol') show couples fucking happily, while a song
extols the glories of the Communist Party. Then and only then does the film
move on to its ostensible subject, with passages of documentary on Reich.

Makavejev's material falls into two broad categories. First, there is the
16mm footage which he shot in the United States in 1970 with his cameraman Aleksandar Petkovic: interviews with people who knew Reich, his wife
and son, and doctors who follow his teachings, together with scenes of therapy
sessions with patients writhing and screaming as they release their pent-up
feelings. In addition Makavejev filmed a number of sequences showing underground figures who represent the sexually liberated side of contemporary

Milena Dravic in the Yugoslav part of *W.R.*

American society. As well as Tuli Kupferberg prowling among the shoppers, chanting his song 'Kill for Peace', and masturbating his machine-gun, there is Betty Dodson describing how good it is for people to be painted by her while they masturbate, Jackie Curtis eating ice-cream while listening to radio commercials and talking about the difficulties of love for a transvestite, and Nancy Godfrey, a rather nice and business-like young lady, giving Jim Buckley, editor of *Screw*, an erection so that she can make a plaster cast of it.

The second half of the film, shot in 35mm, is organized round a fictional story set in present-day Yugoslavia and featuring Milena Dravic as a young Marxist preaching Reichian liberation. While she harangues the crowds, her friend and an enthusiastic soldier put her ideas into practice, screwing ecstatically all round the room, on top of and underneath the furniture. Milena is less fortunate. She falls for a handsome Russian ice-skater who turns out to be totally repressed sexually, so that when she does finally arouse him with some very unambiguous gestures, he loses control and chops off her head with one of his skates. The final sequences show him singing a Russian lament begging God for forgiveness (in fact, an *Ode to François Villon* by the Soviet underground poet Bulat Okudjava, whose voice is the one we actually hear), while Milena's decapitated head keeps up its harangue. Like the American sequences, these Yugoslav scenes are intercut with a variety of other material – what is alleged to be a Russian skating show ('Bolshoi on ice'), shots of a Peking rally, and excerpts from Chiaureli's film *The Vow* (with Mikhail Gelovani as Stalin) and from a Nazi film advocating euthanasia.

W.R. – Mysteries of the Organism is a film worthy of its subject, a man who set himself the task of reconciling Freud and Marx and, as a result, was expelled from the German Communist Party in 1933 and from the International Psychoanalytic Association the following year. Makavejev's commitment to both causes is equally unquestionable; and, as Reich found his books banned and burned in the United States, so *W.R.* has been refused a showing in Yugoslavia. Makavejev makes his films by bringing together a mass of material and arranging it so that established form, tone, style and rhythm are continually disrupted. A great many young film-makers of the post-Godardian generation work in this way, but Makavejev is unique in his use of humour and the extent to which he is able to fuse together the most disparate material and bridge the most startling juxtapositions. A favourite device in all his films is to set up an emotional charge in one scene and then, by well-timed cutting, carry this emotion over into the following sequence to which the spectator, left to his own devices, might well have responded very differently. In *W.R.* the opening sequence of images serves to put the spectator into just the frame of mind which Makavejev needs to carry him along through the subsequent ninety minutes. Perhaps the most outrageous linking in the whole film is when Makavejev moves in quick succession from the pink wax cast of Jim Buckley's penis to the figure of Stalin in the embalmed world of Chiaureli's film, and, before the audience has recovered, on to the torment of victims in the Nazi euthanasia film.

Clearly a succession of images of this kind, or the linking of image and sound which Makavejev uses equally audaciously (Sexpol film plus hymn to Communism), sets up a very complex response; particularly as the director, true to his philosophy of guerrilla film-making, is prepared to use any material at hand, even that taken from the enemy. Makavejev respects his audience's intelligence and our ability to make up our own minds, yet at the same time he thrusts images and juxtapositions at us with great zest and wit. A state of doubt and self-questioning is an inevitable response to *W.R.* What connections are we to see between the many masturbatory scenes in the film and what have they to do with sexual liberation? Is there a link between the writhings of Reichians undergoing therapy and mental patients suffering electric shock treatment? Yugoslavia is a society in many ways curiously balanced between the American and the Soviet ways of life, and Makavejev, as a true Yugoslav, deals with paradoxes – those of liberation (New York) and repression (Stalinist Russia); of theory (Milena) and practice (her friend Jagoda); of fact (the tortured Nazi victims) and fiction (the talking head of the dead Milena); of observation (the 16mm sequences) and *mise en scène* (those shot in 35mm). While Tuli Kupferberg sums up the US ideology in the phrase 'Kill for Peace', the Yugoslavs watch socialist art in Tsarist costumes. The United States offered Reich a refuge but burned his books; it is the home of the totally liberated and also of the repressed seekers of therapy. The U.S.S.R. is Stalin, but also the truths of Lenin, just as Communism is both *The Vow* and the rally to greet Chairman Mao. Milena proclaims that politics is for those whose orgasm is incomplete, but she, like Makavejev, is passionately concerned with such ideas. Communism without free love is a cemetery, shouts Milena, but *W.R.* is a film full of people whose sexual drives are thwarted or turned in on themselves.

Here then is a form of cinema in which the film-maker does not provide answers but questions – directed at himself and at us. Makavejev has compared his own attitude to that of Buñuel, who likewise often mocks and blasphemes but whose work shows a deep reverence for life. Wishing to avoid the conformism of the right and the doctrinaire didacticism of the left, Makavejev is inevitably forced to follow a path of ambiguity; but his affection and concern, his sense of humour and his true involvement with questions of sex and politics, are always apparent. The last image of the film sums up the mood of *W.R.* Here, at the end, the face of the dead Milena catches the particular smile of Wilhelm Reich, under whose understanding gaze the whole film has unfolded.

18. Jean-Marie Straub: Strict Counterpoint

One of the most significant contributions of modern cinema is its redefinition of the cinema's own past. Such a rediscovery of the origins of film is one of the more immediately apparent aspects of the work of Jean-Marie Straub, who in just five films completed between 1963 and 1969 already asserted a claim to be considered as one of the most distinctive and uncompromising of contemporary directors. Straub exhibits the fundamental rootlessness so typical of the post-Godardian generation. Though French by birth, he has lived for ten years in Germany and his one film with French dialogue was made, characteristically, in Rome. Of his five films of the 1960s, only one, *Chronik der Anna Magdalena Bach* (*Chronicle of Anna Magdalena Bach*, 1968), falls within the category of 35mm feature-length films with which we are primarily concerned here. The others are two shorts – *Machorka-Muff* (1963) and *Der Bräutigam, die Komödiantin und der Zuhälter* (*The Bridegroom, the Comedienne and the Pimp*, 1968) – a medium-length adaptation of a novel, *Nicht Versöhnt* (*Not Reconciled*, 1965), and the feature-length colour film in 16mm, *Othon* (1969).* All of them, however, share certain qualities which set them apart from virtually all other contemporary film-making.

We have already mentioned possible links between Straub's work and the French documentary style, but there are other connections which are equally

---

* Straub's films of the early 1970s – *A History Lesson* (1972) and *Moses and Aaron* (1974) – are equally remote from the concerns of the ninety-minute narrative feature.

if not more significant. Richard Roud in his sympathetic monograph on Straub points out the director's roots in the French cinema of the 1940s and his debt above all to Jean Grémillon, a great but neglected film-maker who was also an accomplished musician, and to Robert Bresson, whose second film, *Les Dames du Bois de Boulogne* (1943), was indeed the film which revealed his vocation to Straub when he was still a student. Bresson, with his extreme austerity and his literary preoccupations, is the director whose work most clearly prefigures that of Straub, who likewise uses non-professional players for their inexpressiveness and avoids direct confrontation with the problems of the immediate present.

But Straub's conception of narrative differs sharply from Bresson's, and for parallels to the visual style Straub adopts in *Chronicle of Anna Magdalena Bach* one must look to film-making of a much earlier period. He himself has admitted being very much influenced by D. W. Griffith, three of whose films he saw just before he began his own shooting. Indeed three apparently irrelevant exterior shots in *Chronicle of Anna Magdalena Bach* seem to have been included as a kind of homage to Griffith and an answer to his statement that 'what the modern movie lacks is beauty, beauty from the moving wind in the trees'.[1] In fact one can trace the roots of Straub's style back even further than Griffith and see it very literally as a rediscovery of the cinema from its origins. At a retrospective showing some years ago I sat through two and a half hours of Louis Lumière films: totally static shots, all of the same length and taken from the same angle, shot by a camera planted at the roadside, on a railway platform or before an imposing building. Then suddenly came a shot that had quite a new impact and it took a moment or so to realize what was happening: the camera had been placed on a tram and the image itself was moving. I felt that I was witnessing the true birth of the cinema – the very art of movement – for the first time.

It is this effect which Straub recaptures in *Chronicle of Anna Magdalena Bach*, where it is not until ten minutes before the end that the camera loses its stolidity and pans slowly across the rococo ornamentation of an opera-house ceiling. Elsewhere the ponderousness of Straub's film is total. As if in imitation of Lumière, the director plants his camera in front of his musicians and refuses to cut until a particular passage of music is at an end. Occasionally he tracks in to frame a couple of figures out of the mass of musicians, or draws back to reveal more of the setting. But he never does more than this, and after a short while one hardly needs to look at the screen any more. The first glance at a shot will suffice to tell one whether or not there will be movement and, if so, in which direction this will occur (there are no dazzling manoeuvres to achieve movement from seemingly impossible positions). Paradoxically, therefore, *Chronicle of Anna Magdalena Bach*, which sets out to be about music

The angle of vision: *Nicht versöhnt*; *Der Bräutigam, die Komödiantin und der Zuhälter*; and (*opposite*) *Chronicle of Anna Magdalena Bach*

in a way that few other films ever have been, is a film explicitly based on the techniques of the early silent cinema. Straub looks back at this era much as a painter might seek inspiration in primitive art or children's drawings – he himself described *Chronicle* as a film for cavemen, while his wife and collaborator, Danièle Huillet, called it a work for children. But whereas in the case of a painter like Paul Klee what is borrowed is totally transformed by irony and humour, Straub views his subject with monolithic dourness.

Straub's return to the sources of cinema throws up some very interesting contradictions. In a sense he becomes trapped by the weight of pre-cinematic traditions, for it was only when Griffith succeeded in building up a complex film syntax in works like *Birth of a Nation* and *Intolerance* that the cinema freed itself from a purely illustrative role and began to function autonomously. As a general rule it is true to say that nothing is more derivative than 'pure' cinema, and it is surely not by chance that all of Straub's films have their roots in other art forms. *Chronicle of Anna Magdalena Bach*, in which music is given such an important role, is in fact the only one of his films which does not have a literary source. The very titles of some of his works point to Straub's extremely literary frame of mind. Heinrich Böll's novel, *Billiards at Half Past Nine*, becomes *Nicht Versöhnt, oder Es hilft nur*

211

Gewalt, wo Gewalt herrscht (*Not Reconciled, or Only Violence Helps When Violence Reigns*), while the full title of his adaptation of Corneille's play *Othon* is *Les Yeux ne veulent pas en tout temps se fermer ou Peut-être qu'un jour Rome se permettra de choisir à son tour* (*Eyes do not want to close at all times, or Perhaps one day Rome will permit herself to choose in her turn*).

In his treatment of such source material Straub shows a characteristically idiosyncratic approach. As his visuals look back to the origins of cinema, so his handling of sound recalls that of the early talkies, which for him remains 'the best that has ever been done'.[1] Among films that impressed him deeply were Robert Flaherty's *Man of Aran* and the early Jean Renoir films *Toni* and *La Chienne.* He refuses to post-synchronize his own films, insisting on the importance and unique quality of direct sound. Yet despite this stress on the aural aspect of cinema, Straub's films contain a great deal of deliberate obscurity, as in *Othon*, where the whole of the fourth act is performed beside a fountain which renders much of the dialogue inaudible.

In Straub a passion for accuracy of detail goes hand in hand with an unshakeable conviction that the film-maker is totally free to reinterpret and reshape his material. In *Chronicle of Anna Magdalena Bach*, Straub insists on accuracy of costume and setting, shows genuine musicians performing and records his sound direct. Yet the diary of Anna Magdalena, around which the film is ostensibly built, is a pure fabrication by Straub and his wife, who pieced it together from fragments of letters by Bach himself and from secondary sources. The novel by Heinrich Böll which forms the basis of *Nicht Versöhnt* has been transformed from a fairly conventionally told story to a complex elliptical narrative which needs several viewings before it can be properly unravelled. Straub has been even more cavalier in his treatment of the Ferdinand Bruckner play, *Krankheit der Jugend*, which was the starting point for *Der Bräutigam, die Komödiantin und der Zuhälter.* The two-hour original has been condensed to eight and a half minutes (filmed in a continuous take from a single camera position) and sandwiched between a long tracking shot along the Landsbergerstrasse in Munich and a piece of contemporary fictional melodrama incorporating in its dialogue fragments of poetry by St John of the Cross. But perhaps the clearest example of the multi-layered structure of Straub's work is to be found in *Othon*, which is superficially a simple record of an amateur production. Here he films Corneille's play in its entirety, but in the open air; the actors wear vaguely Roman dress, but the landscape is that of modern urban Rome, with cars and motorcycles clearly visible in the background (and audible on the soundtrack); the dialogue is composed of formally elegant seventeenth-century French Alexandrines, but it is spoken by non-actors, all but two of them foreigners speaking with a noticeable accent; the play is filmed complete, act by act, but there are frequent visual discontinuities between individual shots. It is paradoxes of this kind which reflect Straub's originality as a director.

Chronicle of Anna Magdalena Bach raises questions about the way in which modern cinema is developing, about the relation of image and sound and about film's connection with the world of everyday reality. The narrative content is minimal. The film contents itself with tracing, in pseudo-documentary detail, the sequence of musical and domestic events leading to Bach's death. The real tensions arise, however, not from such biographical incidents but from the interplay of image, music and voice. It is in his visual style that Straub shows the greatest austerity. At times he dispenses with people altogether and substitutes long-held shots of manuscripts and the title-pages of Bach's published compositions, together with occasional letters and engravings. The film was shot on twenty-five different locations throughout Germany, but the same imagery occurs again and again. The camera shows us the angle of a room with only a trace of decoration or ornament. In one corner white light streams through a window and, grouped around Johann Sebastian, we see the musicians and singers, all in period dress and resplendent wigs. We are never aware of an audience or of life going on around these musical groups. This pattern is only rarely broken. There are the brief exterior shots already referred to: one shot of tree-tops against the sky (when Bach is separated from his sick wife) and two brief images of waves breaking on a rocky shore (each prefacing a dramatized scene, Bach's quarrel with the authorities and the suicide of his superior). Otherwise the flow of static interiors is unrelenting. Such tiny potentially dramatic incidents as do occur are recorded flatly, with all the drama drained out of them. Gustav Leonhardt simply *presents* Bach without aiming at an impersonation or building up a character. The moment of his death is a typical instance of Straub's approach: while the commentary speaks of Bach's trouble with his eyes and the manner of his death, we see Leonhardt looking blankly out of the window.

Set against these images are the music of Bach and the comments of his wife. Though Straub uses long takes and direct sound, there is no attempt to record an extended piece of Bach's music in its entirety. We simply have extracts, often overlaid with words or faded out before a climax is reached. Though the arrangement is basically chronological, there is no sense either of any growth or development in Bach's musical style. Indeed the whole handling of the music is perhaps the best illustration of the subtlety with which Straub avoids his ostensible subject. Far from bringing the music to the fore, the extreme visual simplicity of the film in fact constantly undermines it. It is so simple as to be obtrusive, yet at the same time it leaves the eye unengaged and the mind free to wander. When combined with the fragmentary nature of the film's musical offering the effect is that – paradoxically in a film containing

213

so much music – one actually listens to very little. Instead one ponders on the style of performance and the nature of the film itself. Pinned down by the weight of Straub's visuals and diminished as an emotional experience by the banality of the commentary, the music is never allowed to be more than one further element in a three-fold pattern of juxtaposition. It is not for nothing that the film is called *Chronicle of Anna Magdalena Bach*, for Bach's music fails to impose its inherent nobility on the film in the face of Anna Magdalena's gabbling about the family's domestic problems (the careers of the elder children and the deaths of so many of the younger ones) and about the material worries of an eighteenth-century musician's life. It is as if one were to write a biography of Beethoven in which his laundry lists were given the same weight as his later quartets. Perhaps the most striking example of the tensions created by this method is when a glorious 'Kyrie' (the text of which we see) is joined to a simultaneous account of the composer's financial uncertainties. The very unmusical rhythms of Anna Magdalena's commentary affirm the conception of life as a treadmill as forcefully as Bach's music soars to an acclamation of higher truths.

Like so much modern film-making, *Chronicle of Anna Magdalena Bach* derives a great part of its impact from its distinctive blend of realism and artifice. Though, on one level at least, a documentary picture of Bach's life, it is far removed from naturalism. The costumes were made with great concern for accuracy, the actors photographed without make-up, the interiors rendered as true to the period as Straub could make them, and the instrumental playing aims to reflect that of the time. Yet in a very real sense the immaculately clad and richly bewigged characters assembled to play or sing could hardly be more artificial, and by concentrating on the playing of the music to the exclusion of all else, Straub continually reminds us that what we are seeing are performances. Straub toured Germany looking for examples of the churches and interiors of Bach's time, but he uses these buildings as no more than settings for the music, never as entities in their own right. The sense of removal from ordinary reality is enhanced by the lighting of the film. In the quest for accuracy that led him to devote so much time to showing documents of the period, Straub was also concerned to avoid anachronistic stained-glass windows. Scene after scene shows white light streaming through plain glass, yet the players themselves are illuminated from quite different sources. The shadows make us very much aware that we are not eavesdropping on reality but watching a scene composed and lit for the film camera. Far from trying to breathe life into his documents, or to use the conventional resources of the cinema to bring a scene alive, Straub enhances its embalmed quality. Gustav Leonhardt moves through the film with the impassivity of a figure from Madame Tussaud's, never ageing and never expressing direct emotion, while the settings look like the corners of a museum display (which in some cases they are).

214

A projected transparency: *Chronicle of Anna Magdalena Bach*

In this way the film takes on a visual texture unknown in the cinema since the pre-1920 days, but found, for example, in the serials of Louis Feuillade. There one sits through seemingly hours of identical settings and camera set-ups, to be rewarded ultimately by fascinating moments of pure and unequalled lunacy or surreal poetry. Straub has maintained that film is only valid and only moves people deeply if it is based on fascination. Certainly in *Chronicle of Anna Magdalena Bach* he achieves at times an impact akin to that of a Feuillade serial, so that the rigours of watching the film are as nothing when weighed against these moments of total surreality. One example occurs when we see the figure of Bach conducting at night against a background of a castle exterior which, even if real, is lit so as to have the air of a projected transparency. The lighting of Bach's face and of the score in front of him is quite unrelated to the torch flickering behind his shoulder and visually dominating the left-hand half of the screen. Bach is quite clearly suspended in a void, gesticulating to a non-existent orchestra which, however, miraculously gives forth the noble tones of his music. It is the unique resonance of such a moment which is the essence of Straub's contribution to modern cinema.

215

19. May 1968: Towards a Political Cinema

Jean-Marie Straub once described *Chronicle of Anna Magdalena Bach*, no doubt with a deliberately provocative intent, as a contribution to the South Vietnamese struggle against American imperialism. Such political meaning – like that claimed by Marguerite Duras for her own first feature, *Détruire Dit-Elle* – may remain merely on the level of intention, but the need for a film director to assert the political relevance of films which are principally experiments with new stylistic patterns, is very much a sign of the times. The late 1960s and early 1970s have seen the spread of directly political film-making of a kind previously almost unknown in Western Europe.

The French tradition, for example, has been apolitical and serious examinations of political issues are largely non-existent before 1968. Even in Italy, which has a tradition of committed film-making, the concerns have been predominantly social. The fortunes of the neo-realist movement during the postwar years were directly linked to those of the left-wing political parties. It was born in 1942 with the first timid examples of political opposition to Mussolini, and its extinction coincided with the resurrection of the neo-Fascist party in the early 1950s. But the Marxist directors involved in the movement offered few examples of political analysis, concentrating instead on attacking bureaucratic indifference in social terms or offering picturesque studies of agrarian problems in the South. More recently, however, there has

Pontecorvo's *Battle of Algiers*

been a resurgence of political film-making in both Italy and France, though it would still be fair to say that this is an area in which greater advances have been made outside Europe – in the work of the young and committed film-makers of the Third World, for example.

Even within the cinema that calls itself political it is important to distin-guish between works which are made along traditional lines within the industry and designed for a mass audience, and the newer, more radical kind of political cinema which exists quite independently of the industry but is very closely linked to political groups and working-class or student organizations. The first of these categories demands no more than a brief discussion here, since the sole novelty of these films lies in their subject matter. In Italy the most striking works of this kind are those of Gillo Pontecorvo (b. 1919), an ex-journalist whose first features had been honest films of social commitment. *Battle of Algiers* (*La battaglia di Algeri*, 1966) and *Queimada!* (1970), however, revealed an enormous advance in force and assurance. Vividly shot in black and white with a simulated newsreel style, *Battle of Algiers* keeps close to the events of the 1950s but personalizes the conflict in terms of the clash of two individuals – the French paratroop leader and counterrevolutionary expert, Colonel Mathieu, and the last remaining FLN leader, Ali la Pointe. The brutalities of both paratroops and guerrillas are vividly shown, but both sides are allowed to present the justifications for their actions. Pontecorvo's objectivity does not prevent him from coming down on the side of the Algerians (even Mathieu has a distaste for the settlers he is there to protect), but basically French and Algerians are both depicted as prisoners of circumstances from which it is impossible to break free. The same determinism is to be found in *Queimada!*, a richer and more complex work, shot in colour and with Marlon Brando in the lead. It is a nineteenth-century tale of colonialism, combining an adventure story texture with a demonstration of political action and reaction conducted with exemplary logic. In both films Pontecorvo shows great skill in manoeuvring the masses of people who form almost as crucial a focal point as the central protagonists themselves, and his sense of atmosphere and of the ambiguity of human action is always apparent.

Pontecorvo's somewhat less subtle counterpart in France is the Greek-born director Costa-Gavras (b. 1933), who began his career with two features in a conventional thriller format. *Z* (1969), the first of his political works, contains many echoes of Alain Resnais's *La Guerre est finie* – the same writer (Jorge Semprun), the same star (Yves Montand) and even many of the same supporting players – but with Costa-Gavras's own vigorous and more extrovert style revealed in the choice of Raoul Coutard as photographer. *Z* and *L'Aveu* (made by the same team the following year) have much in common. Both are examinations of political oppression – the one dealing with the Greek dictatorship of the 1960s, and the other with Stalinism in Czechoslovakia in the 1950s – and are securely based on real events. They unfold with all the intricacy of a good detective story but, being entertainments first and political analyses only second, they are marred by occasional moments of facility and melodramatics. The link with Pontecorvo is typified by the fact that the third of Costa-Gavras's political studies, *Etat de Siège* (1972) was scripted by Pontecorvo's usual collaborator, Franco Solinas. Dealing with the role of an American 'adviser' tried and executed by the Tupamaros guerrillas, it generates the same forceful emotional impact as Costa-Gavras's earlier work, but contains too the same manipulation of political events to achieve dramatic effect.

While Costa-Gavras has been working with his all-star casts and big budgets, there has also been political film-making of a very different kind in France. The forerunner of this new 'alternative' cinema was the film *Loin du Vietnam* (1967), organized by a group among whom Chris Marker was prominent. Some 150 technicians contributed their services free to the film, which

Loin du Vietnam

contained sections or episodes by a number of important film-makers. Indeed *Lion du Vietnam* constitutes a kind of anthology of styles and approaches to political film-making. Alain Resnais offers a fictional episode, a long, self-analytical monologue scripted by Jacques Sternberg (author of *Je t'aime, je t'aime*) and acted by Bernard Fresson, who played the German lover in *Hiroshima Mon Amour*. Jean-Luc Godard talks directly to camera about his personal doubts and confusions, while Agnès Varda offers a television style report. Joris Ivens, the Dutch-born documentarist, sends back footage of Hanoi under siege from American bombers, and Claude Lelouch, in Saigon for the filming of his feature *Vivre pour Vivre*, contributes shots of the American war machine preparing for action. There is a report on New York demonstrations against the war by William Klein, material shot in Vietnam by the journalist Michèle Ray, and a compilation section tracing the history of the war. *Loin du Vietnam* offers few conclusions, but it is an honest and revealing record of the confused French attitudes to a war that began as France's own colonialist struggle to hold on to her possessions in Indo-China.

Loin du Vietnam might have remained an isolated experience but for the events of May 1968, which brought film-makers together with students and workers and provoked a number of them, such as Chris Marker and Jean-Luc Godard, to undertake a fundamental reassessment of their role. The immediate results were the production of a great many anonymous *Cinétracts* (brief slogans and statements reflecting the mood of revolution), the setting up of the Etats Généraux du Cinéma in an attempt to reshape the whole French film industry and, when this failed, the creation of a number of film collectives. These were designed to offer an alternative production and distribution system with an emphasis on 16mm work and on direct political engagement. SLON, the company founded to produce *Loin du Vietnam*, was revived to serve as distributor for such films as *A Bientôt, J'Espère*, made in 1967 by Marker and Mario Marret about a strike at the Rhodiacéta factory in Besançon. The showing of this film to workers there led to the formation of a collective, the Medvedkin group, in which workers and film-makers worked together on such films as *Classe de Lutte*, a reply to the Marker–Marret film by Besançon militants, and a series of short films grouped under the title *Nouvelle Société*.

SLON also undertook to distribute Alexander Medvedkin's 1934 Soviet silent film, *Happiness*, for which Marker produced a preface, *Le Train en Marche*, a thirty-minute interview with the seventy-one-year-old director in which he talks about the making of *Happiness* and about his work as director of the Soviet film propaganda trains in 1932. Furthermore the group looked abroad and began to distribute independent films made in Greece, Cuba, Brazil and elsewhere, under the general title *On Vous Parle*. Marker, who had previously made *La Sixième Face du Pentagon* with François Reichenbach about the march on the Pentagon in October 1967, and *Jour de Tournage*, an eleven-minute account of the shooting of Costa-Gavras's *L'Aveu*, now went to Cuba where, with Valérie Mayoux, he made *La Bataille des Dix Millions* (1970), dealing with the sugar crisis in Cuba and Castro's historic response.

Other collectives formed out of the impetus of May 1968 include Dynadia, a group affiliated to the French Communist party and concerned with directly propagandist works, and C.R.P. (Cinéastes Révolutionnaires Prolétariens), which has made studies of strike action in France as well as a film on the Palestinian situation, *Palestine Vaincra*. But the most interesting group, and the one which allows us best to assess the implications of this political film activity for modern cinema as a whole, is the Dziga-Vertov collective, founded by Jean-Luc Godard and the young militant who has collaborated on all his post-1968 work, Jean-Pierre Gorin. Strictly speaking, this period of Godard's work falls outside the scope of this study, since it involves the use of images and sounds for political ends, not for the creation of narrative structures. But it is worth tracing Godard's progress from the individualist despair of *Weekend* to the anonymity of the Dziga-Vertov collective, since this work represents a determined attempt to destroy that basic ambiguity of film which he, like all the other film-makers dealt with here, had earlier been concerned to exploit.

It becomes clear, if we look at the four films he made in 1968 prior to his ill-fated visit to the United States to shoot *One A.M.*, that Godard's film-making had reached a crisis point even before the student upheavals of May. *Le Gai Savoir*, completed early in 1968 for French television, was his most negative film to date. A totally plotless film, it intercuts the night-time meetings in a black void of two symbolically named characters (Emile Rousseau and Patricia Lumumba) with a variety of magazine clippings, handwritten slogans, tape recordings of political speeches and comments by the author. The tendency for sound to predominate over image, already apparent in the later feature films, is taken a stage further, culminating in a long passage consisting solely of voices over a totally blank screen. Moreover the two characters indulge in a questioning of the whole nature of communication, of truth and lies, and set themselves a programme of analysis, only to conclude that *Le Gai Savoir* is 'not the film that has to be made'. Godard's immediate response to May 1968 was to participate in the making of some of the *Cinétracts* and the completion of a virtually unseen film, *Un Film Comme les Autres*. In this context, *One plus One*, begun in England in June 1968, was clearly a further digression from what were now his real concerns. The plot originally envisaged was a variation on an old idea of his – that of a woman (Eve Democracy, played by Godard's second wife, Anne Wiazemsky) caught up with two men of divergent political views, a Fascist and a black militant. But the narrative links are never made in the film; and, instead of a Makavejev-style collage, we find only isolated pieces of political attitudinising interspersed with unconnected shots of the Rolling Stones rehearsing the number which gives the film its alternative title, *Sympathy for the Devil.*

If both *Le Gai Savoir* and *One plus One* are basically negative works, *British Sounds*, commissioned incongruously enough by London Weekend Television, marks a fresh beginning, the attempt to create a positive political film. In his published notes on the film, Godard starts with a quotation from Marx, 'The bourgeoisie creates a world in its own image,' and continues: 'Good. Comrades, let us begin by destroying that image.'[1] Scenes in the film include the British Motor Corporation production line confronted with quotations from the Communist Manifesto; shots of a naked woman wandering aimlessly about her house overlaid with the voice of a woman militant discussing the oppression of her sex; discussions among Dagenham militants about their role, and among students of Essex University about how to

Re-definition: Godard's *Le Gai Savoir* (Jean-Pierre Léaud, Juliet Berto)

politicize a Beatles song. The whole film is linked by voices teaching a child to repeat key dates in the class struggle, and ends with the image of a blood-stained hand raising the red flag to the music of revolutionary songs. The problems of political film-making are apparent in the ambiguity of one's response to this last image – the way one cannot avoid a sensuous response to the sight of the hand making its way, snakelike, across the mud, and by the contradictions set up by the contrast between the red paint used as blood here and the documentary imagery of the rest of the film.

British Sounds looks forward to Godard's subsequent work in the way it sets 'true' words against 'false' images (as in the B.M.C. sequence) and in the simplicity of its structure. This structure is deliberately designed so as to allow audiences to criticize it and, in doing so, to define their own position in bourgeois or proletarian terms. But Godard came to feel that making political films of this kind expresses an idealistic and metaphysical conception of the world and must therefore be opposed by making films politically, i.e., in accordance with a Marxist and dialectical conception of the world. In his January 1970 manifesto, 'What is to be done?', Godard sets out his new position. The important thing is not to make descriptions of situations but to make concrete analysis of a concrete situation:

To carry out 1 is to give a complete view of events in the name of truth in itself.
To carry out 2 is not to fabricate over-complete images of the world in the name of relative truth.
To carry out 1 is to say how things are real.
To carry out 2 is to say how things really are. [2]

This new and more radical position is reflected in the work of the Dziga-Vertov collective during the years 1969–70: *Vent d'Est* and *Lotte in Italia,* both made in Italy in 1969; *Pravda*, a study of Czechoslovakia shot in June 1969; *Vladimir et Rosa*, made for German television; and *Jusqu'à la Victoire*, which was shot in Palestine. Both *Pravda* and *Vent d'Est* contain discussions of film method as well as debate about revisionism and revolution. Just as Godard's earlier fictional films had examined the nature of illusion and identification, so too his political films all contain explicit analyses of film as a tool in the revolutionary struggle. *Pravda*, for example, looks at Czechoslovakia firstly in terms of tourist snapshots offering simple, fragmentary descriptions. Then the same images are re-edited and analysed by a man's voice which picks out the signs of revisionism (Skodas on hire from Hertz and Avis at Prague airport, a socialist film industry turning out films in Hollywood fashion, etc.). Intellectuals preaching the false gods of individualism, egotism and sexuality are blamed for revisionism and its distortion of language (the turning of socialism into social imperialism). Then,

The opening shot of *Vent d'Est*

as a third stage, 'true' sounds are added to the same 'false' images, as a woman's voice offers Marxist–Leninist exhortations about the army, the peasants and the intellectuals. The film-makers, dissatisfied with this too, proclaim the need to think about the class struggle, the struggle for production and scientific experimentation, and the film ends with a slogan – 'Long live Mao Tse Tung's thought' – and the image of a red flag and the sound of the 'Internationale'.

Vent d'Est, a 16mm colour film starring Gian-Maria Volonté and Anne Wiazemsky, runs for over ninety minutes and is far more complex. The images are deliberately banal and uninvolving and contain a much interrupted series of shots, taken in a loose, home movie style, of figures in conventional film costume (a woman in a pretty dress, a cavalryman, an Indian, a union delegate, etc.). Usually without any obvious connection, the soundtrack offers an analysis of the stages of political action and the ensuing alternatives, pouring out facts and opinions and constantly urging the audience to think in Marxist–Leninist terms. In addition, there is a short history of revolutionary cinema: victory on 19 July 1920 with a speech by Dziga-Vertov, defeat on 18

225

November 1924 with the making of *Potemkin*; a false victory on 29 August 1962 when the African states decide to rely on the Western film industry, and real victory on 2 February 1956 when a leader by Comrade Tian-Tsin in *Red Flag* marks the birth of the materialist feature film.

Bourgeois cinema and Stalinist cinema are equated in their concern with representation: 'If you're not working for Brezhnev Studios-Mosfilm, you are working for Nixon-Paramount. It means that ultimately you are always doing the same thing ...' Both are rejected, along with underground cinema ('A drug cinema. A sex cinema ... A cinema without taboos, except against the class struggle'). Progressive cinema is defined as one which 'has naturally understood that a film is the relationship between images• and sounds', but few positive examples are cited. The Brazilian director Glauber Rocha is asked by a pregnant woman, 'Which is the way to the political film?' Standing at a crossroads he offers a choice: 'That way is the unknown cinema, the cinema of adventure ... That way is the Third World cinema, a dangerous cinema – divine, marvellous.' The first of these is the path Godard himself has followed since his first feature in 1960, but here in *Vent d'Est* he seems lost and uncertain. Though the film itself ends with the customary rhetorical affirmation, which is here more than ever out of keeping with the rest of the film ('The revolutionary forces have achieved an overwhelming superiority over the imperialist forces'), the last thoughts on the cinema are more modest: 'What is to be done? You've made a film, you've criticized it. You've made mistakes, you corrected some of them. Because of this you know a little more about making images and sounds. Perhaps now you know better how this production can be transformed. For whom and against whom? Perhaps you have learned something very simple.'

The enormous contradictions in Godard's current position – his search not for new forms but for new relationships linked to social conditions – are very apparent in *Tout Va Bien*, the commercial feature film co-directed by Godard and Gorin in 1972. Despite the years of self-criticism and analysis, this film hardly constitutes an advance either ideologically or artistically. Made in colour, with the collaboration of the stars, Yves Montand and Jane Fonda, and with a budget of a quarter of a million dollars, it has a curiously muted impact. All the narrative logic Godard rejected in his pre-1968 work is back, and the subject – the reactions of the boss, the workers and intellectuals working in the communications media to a factory strike – is treated with neither the rigour nor the fervour one might have expected. The boss is a totally farcical caricature, complete with a broad Italian accent; the workers, despite their brave refusal to be betrayed by their union representatives, look and act like characters from a 1930s' René Clair comedy; and the intellectual

Tout Va Bien

couple merely indulge in impotent, self-pitying monologues about the impossibility of communication.

Far from liberating him, Godard's political commitment has clearly plunged him into fresh difficulties (he has commented that it is more difficult for him to express himself than it is for a Palestinian or a Negro from the Southern states of America). Marxist involvement has in fact forced him to work in a void, since by rejecting all traditional patterns of filmic communication in favour of esoteric investigations into image and sound, he has cut himself off from any hope of reaching the audience his films are made for – it is as if Karl Marx had structured *Das Kapital* on the model of *Tristram Shandy*. There is a fatal narrowing down of perspective and denial of intellectual subtlety, as fiction is equated with lies and representation with bourgeois mystification. Film history is distorted in the name of dogma, so that Eisenstein, whose *Battleship Potemkin* was a genuinely revolutionary work which influenced a worldwide audience, is branded a 'bourgeois carried along by the revolution' and the 'first revisionist film-maker'.

Godard and Gorin have tried to create a cinema which is simple, explicit and unambiguous. In Gorin's words, 'For four years we decided to cool

227

down, slow down, to make only stationary shots, to make flat films and try to work out the white screen as a blackboard.' As a result, they have made films they can explain: 'We know perfectly well why we use the tracking shot at this particular point. We can speak about our films and explain in very simple terms how they are made, why we used that image, why we framed it that way, why we used that form after that form and for what purpose.'[3] The final paradox, however, as they found on their tour of the United States to promote *Tout Va Bien*, is that there is no one outside their own tiny group who is really interested in posing the questions.

Part Five: Conclusion

20. Modern Cinema and Contemporary Culture

One of Jorge Luis Borges's fictions, *Tlön, Uqbar, Orbis Tertius*,[1] tells of the gradual uncovering of an alien world of the imagination. First comes the discovery, in a pirated encyclopedia, of a description of a non-existent country, then a whole volume is uncovered of the history of an imaginary planet, Tlön, whose inhabitants see the world not as a 'concourse of objects in space' but as a 'heterogeneous series of independent acts'. Here idealism is the only reality, with the result, for example, that objects which have been lost on the planet have the power to duplicate and reduplicate themselves as secondary objects or *hrönir*. Gradually, after a full forty-volume encyclopedia of Tlön has come to light, and objects from the imaginary planet have begun to intrude mysteriously into the world of human reality, the lore and language of Tlön displace the real history of our universe.

Is a progression of this kind one which is likely to be followed by modernism in the cinema, which is equally concerned with the permeation of reality by the powers of the imagination? The answer would seem to be no. Modernist cinema will never become the only cinema, for there will continue to be a need for film to fulfil other functions, even if the mode of distribution of the work produced is the television tube instead of the cinema screen. Since interest in the narrative – whether in the form of thriller or Western, domestic comedy or romance – shows no sign of diminishing, film will have a role as a purveyor of stories. Equally inexhaustible is the desire for factual information, and it seems certain that the camera will still be used for documentary explorations of the world in which we live. In addition, given the current technological developments leading towards the provision of simple and extremely flexible equipment for the individual film-maker, the underground seems likely to expand, with forms of cinema in which the emphasis is not on the showing of films to a paying audience, but on a personal investigation of the equipment, materials and processes of film.

In this context, modernism is merely one of a series of ongoing possibilities; but already it has established itself as a major development of film history, rather than as simply a movement restricted in place and time, so that in retrospect 1959 can be seen as constituting as great a watershed in the cinema as 1929. Where such influential movements as German expressionism and Italian neo-realism lasted no more than five or six years, modernism has already been in existence for over twice that period; and from *Hiroshima Mon Amour* (1959) to *W.R. – Mysteries of the Organism* (1971), from *L'avventura* (1960) to *Red Psalm* (1972), the inspiration offered to filmmakers by modernist narrative structures shows no sign of flagging. The time span of a dozen years or so is sufficient for themes and preoccupations to be traced from one film-maker to another and for some tentative connections to be made between the cinema and the broader cultural context. The old arguments about whether or not the cinema can be considered an art form have lost their validity in face of the achievements of film-makers like Antonioni and Bergman. Now an investigation of the relationship of film and literature would not need to concern itself primarily with the problem of adaptation (comparing, say, film versions of Dickens with the originals), but could take examples of work by Pasolini, Duras and Robbe-Grillet which show decisively that for a modern artist novel and film are both to be considered valid and fruitful modes of expression. Comparisons with other art forms can now be made from a basic assumption of equality, and there is no incongruity in considering the cinema as a vital and at times even dominant part of contemporary culture.

If we relate the modernist art of the 1950s and 1960s to its origins in the period around the First World War, the links with contemporary developments in the cinema are very apparent. It is clear that modernism's tendency to turn in on itself during recent years has been reflected in a change in the major preoccupations of the movement. If one had to pick out one central characteristic of modernism in the 1910s and 1920s it would be the opening up of new areas of experience and in particular the investigation of the unconscious. This forms a link connecting Joyce's *Ulysses* and the novels of Virginia Woolf, expressionist distortion and surrealist exploration of dreams, the music of Schoenberg (*Erwartung*) and of Stravinsky (*Le Sacre du Printemps*), the painting of Klee and Kandinsky.

Over the same period the cinema was concerning itself primarily with a very different task, namely that of developing narrative film styles which would allow reality to be rendered satisfactorily either by direct transcription (Flaherty or the Stroheim of *Greed*) or by the creation of facsimile worlds (the Hollywood studios). In the 1950s and 1960s, however, both the cinema and the arts share a common focus, with the imagination taking over as the pivotal point of modernism. That is to say, a modernist work in any medium is now most likely to deal in some way with the interaction of real and imaginary, fact and fiction, or with the contradictions of art and life. Borges's imaginary objects and Claes Oldenburg's six-foot hamburgers occupy the same ground, the disturbing area of our mental life where the impossible assumes concrete shape and form. One effect of this has been to bring the visual arts nearer to the cinema, for new techniques and technologies become necessary as canvas gives way to collage, the three-dimensional painting becomes a free-standing object, and art in motion develops into an all-embracing environment.

The location of the centre of interest has also often changed. With the advent of abstract expressionism, New York took over from Paris as the focal point of new developments in painting, and in a similar way the true heirs of Joyce and Kafka are the practitioners of the New Novel in France. Something of the same is true of the cinema, with Europe asserting a new importance *vis-à-vis* Hollywood. Partly this derives from the breakdown of the studio system which, combined with political pressure, drove many Hollywood film-makers and stars abroad in the 1950s (the careers of Joseph Losey and Jules Dassin are instructive examples of the effect this kind of change may have on an established film-maker). Another factor has been the change in audience habits and expectations brought about by the arrival of television on a large scale, for the absorption by the new medium of those spectators accustomed to indiscriminate twice-weekly visits to the cinema rendered many of the basic assumptions of Hollywood outdated.

But the movement has not all been in one direction. Just as in America abstract expressionism drew on the European surrealist heritage, so too film-making in Europe in the 1950s and 1960s derives much from the Hollywood past. For individual film-makers of the younger generation a total change of tradition is impossible, for it denies the tension of interplay which is one of the most fruitful aspects of the connection of Europe and Hollywood: Arthur Penn's European style movie *Mickey One* is as as questionable as Jacques Demy's film in Hollywood, *The Model Shop*. The films of Penn, as Robin Wood has observed, show that he is always very much aware of the European

231

Europe in Hollywood: Jacques Demy's *Model Shop*

cinema, the cinema of intellectual ideas, but he continues to do his finest work within the American tradition (*The Left-Handed Gun* or *Bonnie and Clyde*, for instance). In a similar way, Jacques Demy's best films are very much a Europeanization of the Hollywood musical, and as such akin to Jean-Pierre Melville's French gangster films and Sergio Leone's Westerns. The comparison with Melville is particularly instructive since the latter too took his mythology of America to the United States and made a film in New York. But the resulting work, *Deux Hommes dans Manhattan*, had none of the impact of the later, more detached films he made in France (particularly *Le Samourai*) in which the gangster elements from Hollywood movies were totally digested and consciously manipulated.

While Hollywood itself has vanished as a physical entity – the stars dead or departed, the studio lots sold to real estate developers and even the props and costumes auctioned off – nostalgia for the Hollywood past is growing. In the pre-1914 period artists were likely to be excited by the space-time potential of the film medium as a whole, but now it is specific films which are important, and an awareness of Hollywood is assumed as a part of general

232

Hollywood in Europe: Jean-Pierre Melville's *Le Samourai*

literacy. In this vein one might cite the opening of Edward Albee's play, *Who's Afraid of Virginia Woolf?* ('It's from some goddam Bette Davis picture . . . some goddam Warner Brothers epic . . .'), or the erudite allusions of Gore Vidal in *Myra Breckinridge* (' "Mr Loner", I began in a carefully low-pitched voice, modelled on that of the late Ann Sheridan (fifth reel of *Doughgirls*)'). In the visual arts, Andy Warhol makes his spoof Western, *Lonesome Cowboys,* and Richard Hamilton paints *My Marilyn* and *Portrait of Hugh Gaitskell as a Famous Monster of Film-land.* As a result the whole of the Hollywood past is now in need of revaluation so as to take into account the influence certain film-makers exercise on the contemporary scene. As the music of Pierre Boulez forces us to a re-examination of Webern's position in modern music, so the films of Truffaut and Chabrol make us look again at Alfred Hitchcock. Moreover, as Christopher Finch points out in *Image as Language,* it is now not the film's power to open up fresh areas of reality but the sheer skill in presentation of the classic Hollywood movie which is, for many artists, the greatest achievement of the cinema as a medium. This change too finds its reflection in film criticism. For many years – in the

233

New forms of narrative: Resnais's *Muriel*

writings of André Bazin and Siegfried Kracauer, for example – much of the most important analysis of film, like much of the thinking about a movement such as cubism, was concerned with the relationship of art to reality. In terms of the cinema this meant seeing the documentary tradition stemming from Robert Flaherty and the Soviet film-makers as central. The current trend, as represented by Peter Wollen in *Signs and Meaning in the Cinema*, for example, is much more concerned with the way a film communicates its meaning. In this new perspective Hollywood assumes its natural place of importance, for it is in the American cinema that the communicational aspects of film – among them the conventionalized genres and the elaboration of a film rhetoric – are to be explored.

This study has been primarily concerned with the ambiguity of form and narrative in modernist cinema, and as such has emphasized the extreme complexity of the individual works considered. But modernism is important too for the way in which it has turned to the basic characteristics of film as the source of its style. The refusal of ambiguity and narrative which we find in

234

Jean-Luc Godard's political cinema may represent an impoverishment compared to the style he had developed before 1968, but his clear desire to return
to the fundamentals of image and sound is a logical extension of his earlier
questioning of the essentials of fictional feature film-making. If we wish to
survey a dozen or so years of modernist achievement in the cinema, we can in
fact do this in terms of an exploration of some of the most simple and basic
aspects of the film experience. For example, the film image merely presents
objects, settings, people – it does not offer explanations. The close-up of a
blank face is an instance of total filmic ambiguity and can be experienced as
conveying virtually any emotion the film-maker wishes, depending upon the
dramatic context into which it is put. Much of the very best film acting
reflects the same awareness, in that it involves an underplaying of the role, a
simple presentation of actions without dramatic emphasis.

The film grammar developed by academically-minded film directors like
David Lean on the basis of silent film techniques has traditionally used
variations of such things as the tilting of the camera to indicate response (awe,
superiority) in a rather simplistic fashion as a way of avoiding this ambiguity.
But the basic neutrality remains, and it is to overcome this that film drama
has customarily been structured as melodrama, using a musical score to
shape and guide the audience's emotional response to the action contained in
the images. Modern cinema has discarded much of the grammar and most of
the melodrama, and instead of attempting to diminish this area of ambiguity
many modernist film-makers play on it very consciously. Obvious examples
which have been considered at length are Buñuel in *Nazarin,* Melville in *Léon
Morin, Prêtre* and *Le Samourai* or Ferreri in *Dillinger e morto.* In addition,
part of Bresson's avoidance of what he considers theatrical falsity involves a
refusal of all psychological explanation of his characters' actions, which are
presented without comment; while Antonioni builds *Blow-Up* around the
indecipherability of an image, which here becomes a symbol for the hero's
inability to make contact with a reality just out of reach. Similar preoccupations can also be traced in Godard's *Pierrot le Fou.* The result is a form of
cinema which presents behaviour with a certain detachment, a cool elegance
which, in the case of Jancsó or Ichikawa, moves towards abstraction.

A corollary of the camera's neutrality is its transparency, the way in which
it can function as a mechanical recording device, so that while the boundaries
of what is seen are defined by the director's hand and eye, and the images
themselves are not mediated through a human consciousness. In the past, it is
this transparency which has been used by some critics as the keystone for a
rather oversimplified justification of realist and documentary film-making and
an equally unjustified denigration of expressionist and theatrical styles. The
studio tradition is in one sense an attempt to thwart the camera's objectivity

Reality in the mind: Antonioni's *Deserto rosso*

by making it possible to control precisely the lighting of characters and settings and in this way to shape the film image. Modernism as a whole rejects studio techniques and adopts a less restrictive approach to styles which in the past were regarded as mutually incompatible. Some of the contradictions of realist film styles are uncovered and explored. The work of Tati and Antonioni can, as we have seen, be closely related to earlier developments during the neo-realist period in Italy, while Rosi in *Salvatore Giuliano*, Resnais in *Muriel*, Godard in *Une Femme Mariée* and Makavejev in *W.R. – Mysteries of the Organism*, all explore new forms of film narrative which try to avoid the constrictions of a totally preconceived structure and so remain truer to the experience narrated. Just as the visual arts have shown an increasing interest in all forms of collage techniques, so too has film modernism. Pasolini creates a highly personal visual style by bringing together ancient myth and modern landscape and synthesizing elements taken from a variety of cultures. In their very different ways Godard, Makavejev and Forman have followed the example of Jean Rouch to break down the barriers separating the real and the fictional. They incorporate documentary and observational elements into their fictional narratives and in doing so demonstrate conclusively the falsity of labelling one set of techniques 'realistic' and another 'theatrical'.

Perhaps more striking still is the way that modern cinema has handled the notion of time. Basically the film image shows actions as they unfold in time. Conceiving this as a limitation, film-makers of the past evolved a whole complex grammar, using flashbacks introduced by slow dissolves or written captions to convey to the audience past happenings. Modernism in the cinema may be said to begin with a re-examination of a structure based on flashbacks in order to bring out the ambiguity inherent in the construction of a narrative out of images derived from different points in time or from differing personal viewpoints. It is here that the originality of such films as *Citizen Kane* and *Rashomon* lies. Instead of evolving a new set of formal conventions, modernism has accepted the fact that the cinema presents all experience – past, present and future – as a single uninterrupted flow. In this way we find films showing the past flowing into the present (Bergman's *Wild Strawberries*), past and present fusing to become an indissoluble one (Resnais's *Hiroshima Mon Amour*) and a present destroyed by an unseen past (the same director's *Muriel*). Equally, the possibilities of journeying through time and space have begun to be examined in Marker's short *La Jetée*, Godard's *Alphaville* and Resnais's *Je t'aime, je t'aime*. Simultaneity is a constant feature of post-cubist art and in exploring its implications for the cinema, these film-makers bring film into a closer contact with other twentieth-century art forms and at the same time explore fully the too often neglected basic nature of the cinema's presentation of time and duration.

Parallel to this recognition that film has no tenses is the investigation of what is implied by the fact that the cinema presents the real and the imaginary without differentiation. Emotional involvement in dramatic situations has traditionally been increased by a judicious mixture of objective observation and subjective viewpoint, within a framework of rationality which gives a spurious sense of reality to the experience. Modern cinema has removed the framework and shown how the unreal world of a personal myth can be made tangible (in Cocteau's *Orphée*), or how inner developments and outward experiences can be fused to form a single continuum (in Buñuel's *Belle de Jour* or Antonioni's *Deserto rosso*). Resnais and Robbe-Grillet have explored the mental world of their characters in *Last Year at Marienbad* and *L'Immortelle*, and Robbe-Grillet himself has gone on to investigate the way a film can create itself as it proceeds – as a story unfolds with all its initial inconsistencies (*Trans-Europ-Express*), as a man creates himself a past and a character with his own words (*L'Homme qui ment*), or as sets of images generate their own interconnections (*L'Eden et Après*). The result is a fresh

Last Year at Marienbad

awareness of the complex mixture of truth and lies which goes to make up a fictional narrative in the cinema.

This study of the cinema of the past two decades has been couched largely in terms of stylistic analysis, because it is precisely in its creation of forms that the novelty of modernist cinema lies. This should not, however, be taken as implying in any way that, in pursuing these formal aims, modernists have turned their backs on the important issues of our age. Albert Camus, in a speech delivered at the outset of the period with which we have been concerned here, defined very clearly the problematic nature of mid-twentieth-century art: 'If it adapts itself to what the majority of our society wants, art will be a meaningless recreation. If it blindly rejects that society, if the artist makes up his mind to take refuge in his dream, art will express nothing but a negation.'[2] The first of these dangers has clearly been avoided – no one could accuse modernist cinema, from *Last Year at Marienbad* to *Red Psalm*, of pandering to its audiences. I hope that the analysis undertaken here will also have shown that modernists, demanding though their films may be, remain deeply concerned with communicating their meanings. The difficulty of

Red Psalm

modern art arises not from wilful obscurity but from the nature of the questions the artist puts to himself and to us. Feature film-making, even of the independent, comparatively low-budget kind with which we have dealt here, can never be an occupation for those in search of an ivory tower existence, since any film implies an act of communication with a wide audience.

It is clear that modern film-makers, perhaps because of the medium's uniquely close connection with reality, have confronted directly many of the problems that face us in our personal, social and political relationships. Nevertheless their work is based on a recognition that the truths of the twentieth century cannot be fully expressed in forms obeying the rules of nineteenth-century narrative. Modern cinema has that positive, creative aspect so important to Camus, because it acknowledges that new styles are needed to embody new perceptions. Modernism shows a great awareness of the discordances of life – the difficulties, discontinuities and inconsistencies – but at the same time the works produced are so rewarding an experience, because the struggle for coherent, albeit complex, expression of this awareness is based on a genuine faith in art and life.

239

Notes

1. The Context of Modern Cinema

1. Abel Gance: *Le Temps de l'image est venu* in *L'Art Cinématographique* (Alcan, Paris, 1926).
2. José Ortega y Gasset: *The Dehumanisation of Art* (Princeton University Press, 1968), p. 5.
3. Pauline Kael: *I Lost It At the Movies* (Jonathan Cape, London, 1966), p. 186.
4. Pauline Kael: *Kiss Kiss Bang Bang* (Calder and Boyars, London, 1970), p. 133.
5. Pauline Kael: *Going Steady* (Temple Smith, London, 1970), p. 216.
6. Pauline Kael: *I Lost It At the Movies*, p. 181.
7. Robin Wood: *Arthur Penn* (Studio Vista, London, 1967), p. 44.
8. Sheldon Renan: *An Introduction to the American Underground Film* (E. P. Dutton, New York, 1967), p. 246.
9. *Monthly Film Bulletin* (March 1962), p. 30.
10. John Ward: *Alain Resnais or the Theme of Time* (Secker and Warburg, London, 1968), p. 39.
11. Herbert Read: *Art Now* (Faber and Faber, London, 1948), p. 138.
12. Marshall McLuhan: *Understanding Media* (Routledge and Kegan Paul, London, 1964).
13. Bernard Bergonzi: *The Situation of the Novel* (Macmillan, London, 1970), p. 17.
14. Alberto Moravia: *Man As An End* (Secker and Warburg, London, 1965), p. 184.
15. José Ortega y Gasset: *op. cit.*, p. 9.
16. Edward Lucie-Smith: *Movements in Art Since 1945* (Thames and Hudson, London, 1969), p. 7.
17. *ibid.*, p. 11.
18. Quoted in Harold Rosenberg: *The Anxious Object* (Thames and Hudson, London, 1965), p. 52.
19. Joseph Gelmis: *The Film Director as Superstar* (Secker and Warburg, London, 1971).
20. Harold Rosenberg: *op. cit.*, p. 21.

21. Christopher Finch: *Image as Language* (Penguin Books, Harmondsworth, 1969), pp. 12–13.
22. Herbert Kohl: *The Age of Complexity* (New American Library, New York, 1965), p. 15.
23. Alain Robbe-Grillet: *Snapshots and Towards a New Novel* (Calder and Boyars, London, 1965), p. 73.

2. The Link with the Past
1. José Ortega y Gasset: *op. cit.*, p. 15.
2. Charles Higham: *The Films of Orson Welles* (University of California Press, Berkeley, 1970), p. 46.
3. Donald Richie: *The Films of Akira Kurosawa* (University of California Press, Berkeley, 1965), p. 75.
4. Alain Robbe-Grillet: interview translated in *Films and Filming* (March 1962).
5. Jean Cocteau: preface to *Orphée* (André Bonne, Paris, 1950).

5. Michelangelo Antonioni: Figures in a Mental Landscape
1. Michelangelo Antonioni: *Screenplays* (Orion Press, New York, 1963), p. viii.
2. Robin Wood: *Hitchcock's Films* (A. Zwemmer, London, 1965), p. 119.
3. Michelangelo Antonioni: *Reality and Cinéma-Vérité*, reprinted as part of introduction to script of *Blow-Up* (Lorrimer, London, 1971), pp. 1–3.
4. Michelangelo Antonioni: *Antonioni – English Style* in *op. cit.*, pp. 14–17.

6. Jacques Tati: The Open Window of Comedy
1. All quotations in this chapter taken from an interview given by Jacques Tati in *Cahiers du Cinéma*, no. 199 (March 1968).

8. Ingmar Bergman: The Disintegrated Artist
1. Pauline Kael: *Raising Kane* in *The Citizen Kane Book* (Secker and Warburg, London, 1971).
2. Michelangelo Antonioni: interview with Pierre Billard in *op. cit.*, p. 5.

3. Ingmar Bergman: two articles, *I am a Conjurer* and *Dreams and Shadows*, in *Films and Filming* (September and October 1956).
4. Ingmar Bergman: *The Snakeskin* in *Persona and Shame* (Calder and Boyars, London, 1972), pp. 11–15.
5. Robin Wood: *Ingmar Bergman* (Studio Vista, London, 1969), p. 147.
6. Peter Cowie: *Sweden 2* (A. Zwemmer, London, 1970), p. 184.
7. Susan Sontag: *Styles of Radical Will* (Dell, New York, 1969), p. 131.
8. George Steiner: *Language and Silence* (Penguin Books, Harmondsworth, 1969), p. 13.

10. Alain Resnais: The Simultaneous Experience
1. John Berger: *Success and Failure of Picasso* (Penguin Books, Harmondsworth, 1965), p. 70.
2. Arnold Hauser: *The Social History of Art* (Routledge and Kegan Paul, London, 1962), vol. iv, pp. 230–1.
3. *ibid.*, p. 228.
4. Siegfried Giedion: *Space, Time and Architecture* (Oxford University Press, London, 1959).
5. Wylie Sypher: *Rococo to Cubism in Art and Literature* (Alfred Knopf, New York, 1960), pp. 177–9.
6. Jacques Sternberg: in preface to script of *Je t'aime, je t'aime* (L'Avant-Scène no. 91, April 1969).
7. André Breton: *First Surrealist Manifesto*, reprinted in Patrick Waldberg: *Surrealism* (Thames and Hudson, London, 1965).

11. Alain Robbe-Grillet: The Reality of Imagination
1. Alain Robbe-Grillet: *The Erasers* (Calder and Boyars, London, 1966), p. 174.
2. Alain Robbe-Grillet: *Snapshots and Towards a New Novel*, pp. 58–74.
3. *ibid*, p. 147.
4. *ibid*, p. 148.

5. Alain Robbe-Grillet: *The Erasers*, p. 3.
6. Jorge Luis Borges: *Labyrinths* (New Directions, New York, 1964), p. 26.
7. Alain Robbe-Grillet: *Snapshots and Towards a New Novel*, pp. 149–50.
8. Alain Robbe-Grillet: interview with Roger Régent in *Art et Essai* no. 6.
9. Alain Robbe-Grillet: interview with Pierre Demeron in *Lui* no. 28.
10. Alain Robbe-Grillet: *The House of Assignation* (Calder and Boyars, London, 1970), p. 9.
11. Alain Robbe-Grillet: *Snapshots and Towards a New Novel*, p. 102.
12. *ibid*, p. 151.
13. Pierre Boulez: programme note for BBC Symphony Orchestra Concert in the Royal Festival Hall on 21 October 1970.

12. Miklós Jancsó: Dialectic and Ritual
1. Miklós Jancsó: interview with Istvan Zsugan in *Hungarofilm Bulletin* 1966 no. 3.
2. Miklós Jancsó: interview with Istvan Zsugan translated in *Cinéma 72* no. 165 (April 1972).
3. Lajos Balazsovits: interview with Istvan Zsugan in *Hungarofilm Bulletin* 1969 no. 1.
4. Miklós Jancsó: quoted in *Ecran 72* no. 10 (December 1972).
5. Miklós Jancsó: interview with Claude Beylie and Marcel Martin in *Ecran 72* no. 10.

13. Pier Paolo Pasolini: Myth and Modernity
1. Pier Paolo Pasolini: in Oswald Stack (ed): *Pasolini on Pasolini* (Thames and Hudson, London, 1969), p. 13.

14. Walerian Borowczyk: Space, Style and Fable
1. Richard Williams: article in the 1970 Oxford Animation Festival programme.
2. Donald Ritchie: *Japanese Cinema* (Secker and Warburg, London, 1972), pp. 190–1.

3. Walerian Borowczyk: interview with Emile Verdi in *Cinéma 72* no. 164 (March 1972).

15. The Questioning of Narrative Primacy
1. Bernardo Bertolucci: preface to script of *Prima della rivoluzione* (*L'Avant-Scène* no. 82, June 1968).

16. Jean-Luc Godard: Identity and Communication
1. Jean-Luc Godard: in Tom Milne (ed): *Godard on Godard* (Secker and Warburg, London, 1973).

17. Dusan Makavejev: Collage and Compilation
1. Richard Leacock: in G. Roy Levin: *Documentary Explorations* (Doubleday, New York, 1971), p. 204.
2. Donn Alan Pennebaker: in *op. cit.*, p. 245.
3. Richard Leacock: in *op. cit.*, p. 202.

18. Jean-Marie Straub: Strict Counterpoint
1. Jean-Marie Straub: interview with Andi Engel in *Cinemantics* no. 1 (January 1970).

19. May 1968: Towards a Political Cinema
1. Jean-Luc Godard: *British Sounds* in *Afterimage* no. 1 (April 1970).
2. Jean-Luc Godard: *What is to be Done* in *op. cit.*
3. Jean-Pierre Gorin: quoted by Robert Philip Kolker: *Angle of Reality – Godard and Gorin in America* in *Sight and Sound* vol. 42 no. 3 (Summer 1973).

20. Modern Cinema and Contemporary Culture
1. Jorge Luis Borges: *Ficciones* (Weidenfeld and Nicolson, London, 1962), pp. 17–35.
2. Albert Camus: *Create Dangerously* in *Resistance, Rebellion and Death* (Hamish Hamilton, London, 1961), p. 178.

Bibliography

I. General Studies

ADAMS SITNEY, P: *Visionary Film* (Oxford University Press, New York, 1974).

ARMES, Roy: *French Cinema Since 1946* (A. Zwemmer, London, and A. S. Barnes, New York, 1966, 1970).

ARMES, Roy: *Film and Reality* (Penguin Books, Harmondsworth and New York, 1974).

BENAYOUN, Robert: *Le Dessin Animé Après Walt Disney* (Jean-Jacques Pauvert, Paris, 1961).

BROOK, Peter: *The Empty Space* (McGibbon and Kee, London, 1968).

CAMERON, Ian (ed): *Second Wave* (Studio Vista, London and Praeger, New York, 1970).

CLOUZOT, Claire: *Le Cinéma Français Depuis La Nouvelle Vague* (Fernand Nathan–Alliance Française, Paris, 1972).

COVI, Antonio: *Dibatti di film* (Gagoriana Editrice, Padova, 1971).

COWIE, Peter: *Sweden 2* (A. Zwemmer, London, and A. S. Barnes, New York, 1970).

CURTIS, David: *Experimental Cinema* (Studio Vista, London, and Universe Books, New York, 1971).

FINCH, Christopher: *Image as Language* (Penguin Books, Harmondsworth, 1969).

FLETCHER, John: *New Directions in Literature* (Calder and Boyars, London, 1968).

GELMIS, Joseph: *The Film Director as Superstar* (Doubleday, New York, 1970; Secker and Warburg, London, 1971).

GREGOR, Ulrich: *Wie Sie Filmen – Fünfzehn Gespräche mit Regisseure der Gegenwart* (Sigbert Mohn Verlag, Gütersloh, 1966).

243

GREGOR, Ulrich & PATALAS, Enno: *Geschichte des Modernen Films* (Sigbert Mohn Verlag, Gütersloh, 1965).

HARCOURT, Peter: *Six European Directors* (Penguin Books, Harmondsworth and New York, 1974).

JACOB, Gilles: *Le Cinéma Moderne* (Serdoc, Lyon, 1964).

KOHL, Herbert: *The Age of Complexity* (New American Library, New York, 1965).

KOVACS, Yves: *Surréalisme et Cinéma* (Les Lettres Modernes, Paris, 1965).

LEVIN, G. Roy: *Documentary Explorations* (Doubleday, New York, 1971).

LUCIE-SMITH, Edward: *Movements in Art Since 1945* (Thames and Hudson, London, 1969).

MAMBER, Stephen: *Cinéma-Vérité in America* (MIT Press, Cambridge (Mass), 1974).

MANVELL, Roger: *New Cinema in Europe* (Studio Vista, London, and E. P. Dutton, New York, 1966).

MARJOLAIS, Gilles: *L'Aventure du Cinéma Direct* (Seghers, Paris, 1974).

MATTHEWS, J. H.: *Surrealism and Film* (University of Michigan Press, Ann Arbor, 1971).

MELLEN, Joan: *Women and their Sexuality in the New Film* (Horizon Press, New York, 1973).

METZ, Christian: *Film Language* (Oxford University Press, New York, 1974).

MITCHELL, Donald: *The Language of Modern Music* (Faber and Faber, London, 1963).

NEMESKURTY, Istvan: *Word and Image – History of the Hungarian Cinema* (Corvina Press, Budapest, 1968).

RENAN, Sheldon: *An Introduction to the American Underground Film* (E. P. Dutton, New York, 1967). As *The Underground Film* (Studio Vista, London, 1968).

ROBBE-GRILLET, Alain: *Snapshots and Towards a New Novel* (Calder and Boyars, London, 1965).

ROSENBERG, Harold: *The Tradition of the New* (Thames and Hudson, London, 1962).

SARRIS, Andrew: *Interviews with Film Directors* (Bobbs-Merrill, New York, 1967; Avon Books, New York, 1969).

SONTAG, Susan: *Against Interpretation* (Dell, New York, and Eyre & Spottiswoode, London, 1967).

SONTAG, Susan: *Styles of Radical Will* (Farrar, Straus and Giroux, New York, 1969).

SPENDER, Stephen: *The Struggle of the Modern* (Hamish Hamilton, London, 1963).

STEINER, George: *Language and Silence* (Penguin Books, Harmondsworth, 1969).

STEPHENSON, Ralph: *Animation in the Cinema* (A. Zwemmer, London, and A. S. Barnes, New York, 1967). Revised as *The Animated Film* (same publishers, 1973).

TAYLOR, John Russell: *Cinema Eye, Cinema Ear* (Methuen, London, and Hill & Wang, New York, 1964).

TYLER, Parker: *Underground Film – A Critical History* (Grove Press, New York, 1969; Secker and Warburg, London, 1971).

VOGEL, Amos: *Film as a Subversive Art* (Weidenfeld and Nicolson, London, 1974).

WHYTE, Alistair: *New Cinema in Eastern Europe* (Studio Vista, London, and E. P. Dutton, New York, 1971).

II. Individual Studies and Scripts

Antonioni

CAMERON, Ian and WOOD, Robin: *Antonioni* (Studio Vista, London, 1968; Praeger, New York, 1969).

CARLO, Carlo Di: *Michelangelo Antonioni* (Bianco e nero, Rome, 1964).

ESTEVE, Michel (ed): *Michelangelo Antonioni – L'Homme et l'Objet* (Les Lettres Modernes, Paris, 1964).

HUSS, Roy: *Focus on Blow-Up* (Prentice-Hall, Englewood Cliffs, 1972).

LEPROHON, Pierre: *Michelangelo Antonioni* (Seghers, Paris, 1961). Translated: (Simon and Schuster, New York, 1963).

TAILLEUR, Roger and THIRARD, Paul-Louis: *Antonioni* (Editions Universitaires, Paris, 1963).

THIRARD, Paul-Louis: *Michelangelo Antonioni* (Serdoc, Lyon, 1960).

Scripts in Italian:

Sei film (*Le amiche, L'avventura, Il grido, La notte, L'eclisse, Il deserto rosso*); *Blow-Up; Chung Kuo, Cina* (*Einaudi, Turin*).

Il grido; L'avventura; L'eclisse; Il deserto rosso; Zabriskie Point (Cappelli, Bologna).

Scripts in French:

Le Désert Rouge (L'Avant-Scène, Paris).
L'avventura; La notte (Buchet-Chastel, Paris).

Scripts in English:

Screenplays (*L'avventura, Il grido, La notte, L'eclisse*) (*Orion Press, New York*).
Blow-Up (Lorrimer, London).

Bergman

BERANGER, Jean: *Ingmar Bergman et ses Films* (Terrain Vague, Paris, 1959).

BJORKMAN, Stig, MANNS, Torsten and SIMA, Jonas: *Bergman om Bergman* (Norstedt and Soners, Stockholm, 1970). Translated as *Bergman on Bergman* (Secker and Warburg, London, 1973).

DONNER, Jörn: *Djävulens ansikte: Ingmar Bergmans filmer* (Aldus-Bonniers, Stockholm, 1962). Translated as *The Personal Vision of Ingmar Bergman* (Indiana University Press, Bloomington, 1964).

ESTEVE, Michel: *Ingmar Bergman – La Trilogie* (Les Lettres Modernes, Paris, 1966).

GIBSON, Arthur: *The Silence of God – Creative Response to the Films of Ingmar Bergman* (Harper and Row, New York, 1969).

GUYON, Francis and BERANGER, Jean: *Ingmar Bergman* (Serdoc, Lyon, 1964).

SICLIER, Jacques: *Ingmar Bergman* (Editions Universitaires, Paris, 1960).

SIMON, John: *Ingmar Bergman Directs* (Harcourt Brace Jovanovitch, New York, 1972; Davis-Poynter, London, 1973).

STEENE, Birgitta: *Ingmar Bergman* (Twayne, New York, 1968).

245

WOOD, Robin: *Ingmar Bergman* (Studio Vista, London, and Praeger, New York, 1969).

YOUNG, Vincent: *Cinema Borealis* (D. Lewis, New York, 1971).

Scripts in French:

Oeuvres (six screenplays); *Une Trilogie* (Robert Laffont, Paris).

Le Silence; Persona; Une Passion; Cris et Chuchotements (L'Avant-Scène, Paris).

Scripts in English:

Four Screenplays (*Smiles of a Summer Night, The Seventh Seal, Wild Strawberries* and *The Magician*) (Secker and Warburg, London, and Simon and Schuster, New York).

The Seventh Seal; Wild Strawberries (Lorrimer, London).

A Film Trilogy (*Through a Glass Darkly, The Communicants* and *The Silence*); *Two Screenplays* (*Persona* and *Shame*); *Scenes from a Marriage* (Calder and Boyars, London, and Orion Press, New York).

The Virgin Spring (Ballantine Books, New York).

Borowczyk

STRICK, Philip: *The Theatre of Walerian Borowczyk* in *Sight and Sound* vol. 34 no. 4 (Autumn 1969).

BOROWCZYK, Walerian: interview with Michel Delahaye, Sylvie Pierre and Jacques Rivette, followed by two articles, in *Cahiers du Cinéma* no. 209 (February 1969).

Bresson

BRESSON, Robert: *Notes sur le Cinématographe* (Gallimard, Paris, 1975).

BRIOT, René: *Robert Bresson* (Edition du Cerf, Paris, 1957).

CAMERON, Ian (ed): *The Films of Robert Bresson* (Studio Vista, London, 1969; Praeger, New York, 1970).

ESTEVE, Michel: *Robert Bresson* (Seghers, Paris, 1962).

SEMOLUE, Jean: *Bresson* (Editions Universitaires, Paris, 1959).

Scripts in French:

Mouchette (L'Avant-Scène, Paris).

Le Procès de Jeanne d'Arc (Julliard, Paris).

Buñuel

ARANDA, Francisco: *Luis Buñuel: A Critical Biography* (Secker and Warburg, London, 1975).

BUACHE, Freddy: *Luis Buñuel* (La Cité, Lausanne, 1970). Translated as *The Cinema of Luis Buñuel* (Tantivy Press, London, and A. S. Barnes, New York, 1973).

DURGNAT, Raymond: *Luis Buñuel* (Studio Vista, London, 1967; University of California Press, Berkeley, 1968).

ESTEVE, Michel (ed): *Luis Buñuel* (Les Lettres Modernes, Paris, 1962).

KYROU, Ado: *Luis Buñuel* (Seghers, Paris, 1962). Translated as *Luis Buñuel – An Introduction* (Simon and Schuster, New York, 1963).

Scripts in French:

Un Chien Andalou, L'Age d'Or and L'Ange Exterminateur; Le Journal d'une Femme de Chambre and Las Hurdes; Nazarin; La Voie Lactée and Simon du Désert; Tristana; Le Charme Discret de la Bourgeoisie; Los Olvidados; Le Fantôme de la Liberté (L'Avant-Scène, Paris).

Scripts in English:

Three Screenplays (*Viridiana, The Exterminating Angel* and *Simon of the Desert*) (Orion Press, New York).

L'Age d'Or and *Un Chien Andalou; Tristana; Belle de jour; The Exterminating Angel, Nazarin* and *Los Olvidados* (Lorrimer, London, and Simon and Schuster, New York).

Godard

BROWN, Royal S.: *Focus on Godard* (Prentice-Hall, Englewood Cliffs, 1972).

CAMERON, Ian (ed): *The Films of Jean-Luc Godard* (Studio Vista, London, 1967; Praeger, New York, 1969).

COLLET, Jean: *Jean-Luc Godard* (Seghers, Paris, 1963).

ESTEVE, Michel (ed): *Jean-Luc Godard – Au Delà du Récit* (Les Lettres Modernes, Paris, 1967).

GODARD, Jean-Luc: *Jean-Luc Godard par Jean-Luc Godard* (Pierre Belfont, Paris, 1968). Translated as *Godard on Godard* (Secker and Warburg, London, and Viking Press, New York, 1972).

MUSSMAN, Toby (ed): *Jean-Luc Godard – A Critical Anthology* (E. P. Dutton, New York, 1968).

ROUD, Richard: *Jean-Luc Godard* (Secker and Warburg, London, 1967; Doubleday, New York, 1968).

VIANEY, Michel: *En Attendant Godard* (Bernard Grasset, Paris, 1966).

Scripts in French:

A Bout de Souffle; La Chinoise; Deux ou Trois Choses que je Sais d'Elle; Une Femme Mariée; Vivre sa Vie. (L'Avant-Scène, Paris) *Le Gai Savoir* (Union des Ecrivains, Paris).

Scripts in English:

Le Petit Soldat; Pierrot le Fou; Alphaville; Made in USA; Weekend and *Wind From the East; A Woman is a Woman, A Married Woman* and *Two or Three Things I Know About Her* (Lorrimer, London, and Simon and Schuster, New York).

Masculine Feminine (Grove Press, New York).

Jancsó

ESTEVE, Michel (ed): *Le Nouveau Cinéma Hongrois* (Les Lettres Modernes, Paris, 1969).

247

LEVENSON, Claude B.: *Jeune Cinéma Hongrois* (Serdoc, Lyon, 1966).

OUDART, Jean-Pierre and others: articles under the general title *Jancsó Miklós: Hier, Aujourd'hui* in *Cahiers du Cinéma* no. 219 (April 1970).

ZSUGAN, Istvan: *Five Hungarian Artists of the Cinema* (Hungarofilm, Budapest, 1967).

Makavejev

MAKAVEJEV, Dusan: interview with Christian Braad Thomsen in *Cinéaste* vol. 6 no. 2 (1972–3).

ROBINSON, David: *Joie de Vivre at the Barricades* in *Sight and Sound* vol. 40 no. 4 (Autumn 1971).

WOOD, Robin: *Dusan Makavejev* in Ian Cameron (ed): *Second Wave* (Studio Vista, London, and Praeger, New York, 1970).

VOGEL, Amos: *Makavejev – Towards the Edge of the Real ... and Over* in *Film Comment* vol. 9 no. 6 (November–December 1973).

Scripts in English:

W.R. – Mysteries of the Organism (Avon Books, New York).

Melville

NOGUEIRA, Rui: *Melville on Melville* (Secker and Warburg, London, and Viking Press, New York, 1971). Translated as *Le Cinéma selon Melville* (Seghers, Paris, 1974).

VIALLE, Gabriel: *Jean-Pierre Melville* (Anthologie du Cinéma, Paris, 1974).

WAGNER, Jean: *Jean-Pierre Melville* (Seghers, Paris, 1963).

Scripts in French:

Léon Morin, Prêtre; Le Doulos (L'Avant-Scène, Paris).

Pasolini

ANZOINI, Tommaso: *Pier Paolo Pasolini* (La Nuova Italia, Florence, 1974).

DUFLOT, Jean: *Entretiens avec Pier Paolo Pasolini* (Pierre Belfont, Paris, 1970).

GERVAIS, Marc: *Pier Paolo Pasolini* (Seghers, Paris, 1973).

STACK, Oswald (ed): *Pasolini on Pasolini* (Thames and Hudson, London, 1969; Indiana University Press, Bloomington, 1970).

Scripts in Italian:

La commare secca (Zibetti, Milan).

Accatone; Il vangelo secondo Matteo; Uccellacci e uccellini; Edipo re; Teorema; Medea; Ostia (Garzanti, Rome).

Mamma Roma (Rizzoli, Rome).

Script in French:

Oedipe roi (L'Avant-Scène, Paris).

Script in English:

Oedipus Rex (Lorrimer, London, and Simon and Schuster, New York).

Resnais

ARMES, Roy: *The Cinema of Alain Resnais* (A. Zwemmer, London, and A. S. Barnes, New York, 1968).
BOUNOURE, Gaston: *Alain Resnais* (Seghers, Paris, 1962, 1974).
ESTEVE, Michel (ed): *Alain Resnais et Alain Robbe-Grillet – Evolution d'une Ecriture* (Les Lettres Modernes, Paris, 1974).
PINGAUD, Bernard (ed): *Alain Resnais* (Serdoc, Lyon, 1961).
PINGAUD, Bernard (ed): *Alain Resnais ou la Création au Cinéma* (L'Arc no. 31, Aix-en-Provence, 1967).
PREDAL, René: *Alain Resnais* (Les Lettres Modernes, Paris, 1968).
RESNAIS, Alain and SEMPRUN Jorge: *Répérages* (Chêne, Paris, 1974).
WARD, John: *Alain Resnais or The Theme of Time* (Secker and Warburg, London, 1967; Doubleday, New York, 1968).

Scripts in French:

Hiroshima Mon Amour; Je t'aime, je t'aime (L'Avant-Scène, Paris).
Hiroshima Mon Amour; La Guerre est Finie; Le Stavisky d'Alain Resnais (Gallimard, Paris).
L'Année Dernière à Marienbad (Les Editions de Minuit, Paris).
Muriel (Editions du Seuil, Paris).
Je t'aime, je t'aime (Eric Losfeld, Paris).

Scripts in English:

Hiroshima Mon Amour (with *Une Aussi Longue Absence*); *Last Year at Marienbad* (Calder and Boyars, London, and Grove Press, New York).

Robbe-Grillet

ESTEVE, Michel (ed): *Alain Resnais et Alain Robbe-Grillet – Evolution d'une Ecriture* (Les Lettres Modernes, Paris, 1974).
GARDIES, André: *Alain Robbe-Grillet* (Seghers, Paris, 1972).
ROBBE-GRILLET, Alain: *Pour un Nouveau Roman* (Les Editions de Minuit, Paris, 1963). Translated in *Snapshots and Towards a New Novel* (Calder and Boyars, London, 1965) and as *For a New Novel* (Grove Press, New York, 1965).

Scripts in French:

L'Année Dernière à Marienbad; L'Immortelle; Glissements Progressifs du Plaisir (Les Editions de Minuit, Paris).

Scripts in English:

Last Year at Marienbad; The Immortal One (Calder and Boyars, London, and Grove Press, New York).

Straub

ROUD, Richard: *Jean-Marie Straub* (Secker and Warburg, London, and Viking Press, New York, 1972).

Tati

AGEL, Geneviève: *Hulot Parmi Nous* (Editions du Cerf, 1955).

CAULIEZ, Armand J.: *Jacques Tati* (Seghers, Paris, 1962).

TATI, Jacques: interview with Jean-André Fieschi and Jean Narboni, followed by five articles, in *Cahiers du Cinéma* no. 199 (March 1968).

Index

Index

253

Index

Acknowledgments

My first debt of gratitude is to James Price who gave initial encouragement to this book many years ago. I also extend my thanks to those editors – particularly Alan Ross of *London Magazine* – who have published the articles and reviews in which many of the ideas brought together here were first expressed.

For illustrations I am indebted to Hungarofilm, Unifrance, Unitalia, the National Film Archive, distributors: British Academy/Connoisseur, Columbia, Contemporary, Eagle, Gala, Hunter, Miracle, M-G-M, The Other Cinema, Polit Kino, Rank, RKO, Svensk Filmindustri, United Artists and *Sight and Sound*.